PAVAROTTI
My Own Story

PAVAROTTI

MY OWN STORY

WITH WILLIAM WRIGHT

DOUBLEDAY & COMPANY, INC.

GARDEN CITY, NEW YORK

1981

Designed by LAURENCE ALEXANDER

Library of Congress Cataloging in Publication Data
Pavarotti, Luciano.
Pavarotti, an autobiography: My own story.

Discography: p. 291.
Includes index.
1. Pavarotti, Luciano.   2. Singers—Biography.
I. Wright, William, 1930–
ML420.P35A3   782.1'092'4   [B]
ISBN: 0-385-15340-6
Library of Congress Catalog Card Number 80–1990

CONTENTS

CONTENTS

CONTENTS

PREFACE

William Wright

When negotiations for this book were about to be concluded and a collaboration agreement signed between Pavarotti and myself, he suddenly startled all concerned parties by saying he was against the book being authored by him; he preferred instead to cooperate fully in a third-person book authored by me. The suggestion flummoxed the editor and agents who had spent a year assembling the project.

My first reaction was the vain one you would expect from a writer: no shared by-line. Instead I would get a solo one. More cogent considerations quickly overruled the vainglory. Pavarotti's many admirers wanted *his* version of his own story, not filtered through another consciousness. Autobiographies have an authority that can't be equaled by even the most assiduous and scrupulous researcher. Also, and most alarming, Pavarotti was proposing a very different book from the one Doubleday was commissioning.

The assembled mustered their confusion into a chorus: "Why?"

"Well," Pavarotti said thoughtfully, "I feel that a biography should tell both the positive and the negative. If *I* tell it, it will only be the negative."

Aside from the manifest charm, the anecdote is revealing about Pavarotti. He is modest, quick to self-deprecate, and rarely satisfied with himself. At the same time, he is proud of his accomplishments and grateful to be given such a rare talent. He wanted to avoid a book that minimized his achievement or magnified his failings through some overexercised sense of seemliness.

Pavarotti knows what he wants, and he knows his own foibles that might hinder getting it.

As soon as Pavarotti saw the consternation that his suggestion was causing the rest of us, he agreed to let matters stand as they were. The resulting book, with his narrative interspersed with other voices, is the compromise we evolved. At the time, I assured him that, as his collaborator, I wouldn't let him paint a totally negative portrait.

After a year working together, I realize the negative book would have been a slim one indeed.

The basic outline of his history is overwhelmingly positive. He rose from inauspicious origins to become one of the great artists of the century. He worked slavishly for many years to perfect his instrument, many more years to establish his career. He achieved the pinnacle of his profession while maintaining the love and respect of both his colleagues and a burgeoning following. He excelled in an exceedingly demanding and specialized field while retaining a broad range of nonmusical enthusiasms: painting, tennis, driving, cooking, to name a few. And he presides over a large and close-knit family that he is determined to keep large and close-knit.

Where was the dark side of all this? To a commercially minded collaborator, this landslide of good news suggested the opposite problem of too little negativism. How do you fashion an engrossing book from a forty-year succession of happy victories? "Where's the conflict?" as they say around swimming pools in Beverly Hills.

As bad luck would have it, Pavarotti's life has had its share of adversity. But more to the point, I quickly learned that hard times are not essential to a story when you are fortunate enough to have as your subject an intelligent, feet-on-the-ground author-guide with whom to tour not just the rococo world of contemporary opera but the many worlds his forty-year odyssey has brought him through.

That this author-guide happened to be one of the top practitioners in opera only adds authority to the Pavarotti wit, insight, sensitivity and, more than anything else, his remarkable perspective on both his esoteric profession and his own unique place in it.

Putting his worst foot forward was not the only danger

Pavarotti foresaw in doing this kind of book. He did not want his biography to be, as are the books of many opera stars, a catalogue of artistic triumphs. Such formats are so frequent, he pointed out, it is as though the great singers were hoping, by inscribing every success on paper, to can and preserve their ovations. It would, Pavarotti and I agreed, be like asking readers to listen to the applause without hearing the performance.

Besides, there were too many interesting things to write about to dwell overmuch on frenzied receptions and delirious critics. We agreed that the book should have enough of his personal and career history to satisfy his most fervent admirers. It should also throw light on a number of related subjects: the tenor phenomenon, Pavarotti's theories on singing, insights into his artistry, the present-day opera world, its personalities, and a glimpse of the big-talent industry in the second half of the twentieth century.

More than anything else, the book had to present, I was convinced, the remarkable personality of Luciano Pavarotti. Of course this should be an aim of any biography, but with Pavarotti I felt that the personality, more than the incredible voice, was the key to the entire phenomenon.

Looking back over the great singers of this century, it is remarkable how many possessors of monumentally great voices have left cold a general public which, while not impassioned for operatic singing, were still rapacious for heroes and giants. Some of these singers, like Kirsten Flagstad, Beniamino Gigli, Lauritz Melchior, Zinka Milanov, Helen Traubel, while unarguably vocal talents of the first magnitude, evoked little response from the *broad* public.

This, of course, says much about the public and little about the talent of these great artists. It does, I feel sure, say *something* about them, especially when held up against the great singers who have made the breakthrough beyond voice enthusiasts and found a warm welcome with millions who are not opera fans. Singers in this category would include Caruso, John McCormack, Marian Anderson, and Maria Callas, and—to an astounding degree—Luciano Pavarotti.

The lack of impact on the public at large enjoyed by the first group of great artists suggests that exceptional voice by itself succeeds as a communicating instrument only to devotees of *bel canto* singing and lyric opera. The unbounded celebrity of the second group suggests that the public—even a public that prefers the vocal equipment of a Bob Dylan or a Janis Joplin—is not against large *bel canto* voices, they only seem to require something more to accompany the beautiful sounds.

It is my belief that this something is an admirable, recognizable personality. I also began to suspect that the more magnificent and impressive the vocal talent, the greater the hunger in some listeners for something to be communicated through the communicating instrument besides the composer's artistic intention. More than the soulless but flawless voice perhaps being unmoving to large numbers of people, there is something downright off-putting about the magnificent talent of a great voice emanating from an enigma, an unapproachable marvel performing superhuman feats in a nonhuman way.

There is a deeper level to this, a mechanism that strikes at the core of major vocal artistry. In writing about Enrico Caruso in his book *The Great Singers*, Henry Pleasants says:

"The secret of [his voice's] beauty lay not in the voice alone, nor even in this singer's extraordinary, probably intuitive, sense of form in the shaping of every phrase and of every song and aria, but rather in the fact that there were most marvelously united in Enrico Caruso a beautiful voice and a beautiful nature."

Could it be that the general public is better at perceiving an essential to great artistry than the people who know or follow voice?

Part of the mystique of the singer is the glorious self-sufficiency of the talent, without benefit of sounding boards, cat gut, metal wire, empty canvases, chunks of marble. The singer can stand alone on a mountaintop and put true beauty into the world, perhaps history-making beauty. As with Superman's ability to fly, no equipment or special set of circumstances is necessary. Whenever it is needed or wanted, the talent is available.

Here again, a unique facet of the vocal talent would seem to heighten the need for an engaging personality in the person possessing it. With such a rare and expressive means of communicating the listener becomes more concerned about not only what is being communicated—the song, of course—but who.

If the importance of personality to the vocal artist is granted, it is remarkable that today's outstanding voices are such a faceless, earthbound group. This is a reversal from the situation among singers in earlier times. Opera lore overflows with personality, ranging from the warm-hearted hijinks of a Caruso (pressing a warm sausage into his soprano's hand during a duet) and Leo Slezak ("What time does the next swan leave?") to the galloping eccentricity of a Luigi Ravelli who could cancel a performance if his dog, Niagara, growled during the warm-up vocalizing.

Today's voices are, for the most part, hardworking professionals, sober and decorous. There is very little backstage vase-throwing and minimal on-stage pranking. Even the star-type demands are approaching the within-sight unreasonableness of top performers in other fields.

Several developments may have caused this flattening out of the operatic personality. Standards and competition are at an all-time high, necessitating an obsessive discipline. The business side of today's opera stardom is complex and unnerving, requiring many support activities and many support individuals—managers, publicists, coaches, secretaries, throat doctors, faith healers, and astrologers. Arranging and subsidizing all of this can take the fun from the most ebullient spirit.

Probably the biggest difference in being an opera star today from livelier past days is the constant travel imposed on the voices by the jet plane. The stars of past years would sing a well-spaced season of a few weeks or a few months in one place, then board a ship for an enforced vacation before settling in for a modest performance schedule somewhere else. Today a car is often waiting at the stage door to rush the precious voices to the airport so they can arrive in yet another city—they often forget which—with too few rehearsal days left before the performance. Maybe today's opera singers aren't dull, merely in shock.

Even those contemporary stars who possess lively personalities often go to pains to hide them. They seem to fear that revealing their human side might diminish their stature as artists. Interviews with them often emerge as from the disembodied Spirit of Art rather than from a human bristling with the same appetites and disgusts that propel the rest of us.

Against such a lineup of august effigies, Pavarotti's irrepressible humanity blows like a welcome whirlwind, with a force sufficient to escape the opera house and refresh the public at large. No one who has heard him sing could miss that the personality is there in abundance. So is the beautiful nature.

Then why worry about a book with too many negatives or positives? This would not be the problem. Neither would the illumination of areas attendant to his epoch-making career; that would come inevitably. The book must, above all else, present in generous quantity and make clearer this extraordinary personality, a personality that may be inseparable from his art, but that is beyond question cheering the second half of the twentieth century as much as his voice is beautifying it.

ACKNOWLEDGMENTS

Recovering forty-four years of a life is, in itself, a difficult undertaking. With Luciano Pavarotti the difficulties multiply. Not only is he in the midst of one of the century's most phenomenal and demanding careers, he is a man who, by nature, lives intensely in the moment. The rations of energy and attention that can be diverted from his immediate action—a performance, an interview, a painting—are needed for the complicated and thorny decisions concerning his future.

As collaborator on his book I realized early on that to resurrect the past, Pavarotti would need more help than mine alone. To reduce the demands on his memory, I spoke with as many as possible of the people who have touched his life. I contacted his family, friends, and professional colleagues, and quickly found myself the beneficiary of large accumulations of love and esteem that for years had been building in the Pavarotti account.

It is further tribute to the man that many of those closest to him were not hesitant to mix a few grumbles and grievances with the outpouring of affection. Performers of Pavarotti's immense popularity are in danger of finding themselves surrounded with sychophantic hooray-sayers. Happily for this book—and for Pavarotti—this was not the case.

Foremost among the many to whom I feel gratitude is Pavarotti's extraordinary wife, Adua, whose role as family archivist I taxed shamelessly and who never responded to my many requests with anything but good-humored efficiency. My deep gratitude is offered as well to his parents, Adele and Fer-

ACKNOWLEDGMENTS

nando Pavarotti, his sister, Gabriella Pavarotti, and his three daughters, Lorenza, Cristina, and Giuliana. They all exceeded the renowned Italian tradition of warmth and hospitality toward a stranger thrust into their midst. They also showed a saintly patience with my improbable Italian.

Here follows a partial list of the many people whom I wish to thank. The degree of their assistance varies widely, but they all demonstrated an equal enthusiasm for the subject and an eagerness to help that was a biographer's dream.

Edwin Bacher, Kathryn Bayer, Mariarosa Bettelli, Umberto Boeri, Richard Bonynge, Hans Boon, Stanley A. Bowker, Herbert Breslin, Kirk Browning, Mario and Sonia Buzzolini, Antonio Cagliarini, Bob and Joan Cahen, Moran Caplat, Cesare Castellani, Michele Cestone, George Christie, Robert Connolly, John Copland, Julia Cornwall-Legh, William and Allison de Frise, Mrs. Arturo di Filippi, Gildo di Nunzio, Max de Schauensee, Giuseppe di Stefano, Judy Drucker, Mirella Freni, John Goberman, Kathleen Hargreaves, Robert Herman, Merle Hubbard, John Hurd, Joan Ingpen, Robert Jacobson, Nathan Kroll, Richard Manichello, Stephen Marcus, Walter Palevoda, Arrigo Pola, Judith Raskin, Madelyn Renee, the late Francis Robinson, Richard Rollefson, Susanne Stevens, Alan Stone, Susannah Susman, Dame Joan Sutherland, Annamarie Verde, Peter Weinberg, and John Wustman.

I would like to give special thanks to my editor, Louise Gault, for the patience and wisdom with which she confronted the extraordinary problems that invariably plague projects of this nature.

PAVAROTTI

My Own Story

LUCIANO PAVAROTTI

Growing Up in Modena

My childhood was ideal. Our family had very little, but I could not imagine having any more. We lived in an apartment building on the outskirts of Modena, a medium-sized city in the region of Emilia in north-central Italy. In front of our building was nothing but fields and trees, a wonderful place for children to grow up. Sixteen other families lived in our building; all were either friends or relatives.

Our apartment was on the first floor—just two rooms for my mother, my father, and me. My sister, Gabriella, didn't come along until I was five. When she joined us, she slept in the bedroom with my parents. I slept in the kitchen on an iron bed, the kind that serves as furniture in the daytime but at night pulls out to make a bed. If I could find that iron bed now, I would pay its weight in gold; it would bring back so much.

The apartment building had several entryways with apartments opening from the stairs. In our entryway also lived two of my aunts plus my grandmother, so I was surrounded by adoring relatives. From my earliest recollection I was engulfed with love and attention. Of all the people who cared about me, my grandmother Giulia was the central figure. She was a wonderful woman. I adored her. She had just lost her daughter Lucia, my mother's sister, shortly before I was born; I was named after this aunt who died. I think it was my coming into the world just when this beloved daughter left it that explained my grandmother's special feeling for me.

She was a strong woman; everyone respected her and listened to her, and they also loved her. Her husband, my grandfather, was a charming man but a little too fun-loving and irresponsible. My grandmother Giulia had the final word on most family matters. I was her favorite and she was the most important person in my life. She probably would have been in any case because of her strong personality, but my mother and father both worked in those days and my grandmother Giulia was left in charge of me. She rarely restrained or disciplined me but

3

treated me like a little wild animal, a precious animal, one with a soul.

My grandmother was not an educated woman, but she was intelligent and philosophical. She was a very Italian family woman—just the house, her children and grandchildren—that was her life. She never cared what her husband did—and he did everything—but it wouldn't have made any difference if she had cared. She never asked him to stay home at night. He was a big Romeo, I think.

The women's liberation people would consider my grandmother very stupid. But she kept her family together and in her way she was happy—a lot happier, I think, than many liberated women. My grandmother made me feel fantastic. She understood me and was always protecting me.

It wasn't just my grandmother or parents and my aunts who made my childhood such a happy one. When I was born on October 12, 1935, I was the first boy born in that building in ten years. That alone made me a tiny superstar. The Italians' fondness for children is well known; there were at least one hundred children in the neighborhood. I was the youngest and the only boy in our immediate area. Everybody looked after me; they were on my side in any problem that came up. They let me do as I pleased.

I guess it was because they all liked me and fussed over me that I became outgoing. I certainly had no reason to be shy and unfriendly. I enjoyed their liking me and I worked to keep it that way. Even as a small boy I told jokes, made little surprises, anything to liven up things, but always in fun. I think I added something to that building because the other families were always asking me to eat with them. My mother and father would complain, "We haven't had Luciano at dinner for four days now," they would say, "it's time for him to come home to eat."

My mother worked long hours in a cigar factory, so it was useful sometimes to have people feed me. Even when she was not at home, my grandmother would sometimes make me turn down invitations to the others and eat with her. I can still hear the shouts in that stairway, "*Luciano! Vieni mangiare con noi.*"

Mother is a small woman and quite emotional. She loves music—too much, as she says, because it affects her so strongly. For that reason, she will not come to hear me sing in opera houses today. The music, by itself, affects her so much, she fears that the added nervousness and excitement at seeing her son singing would overwhelm her.

Mother likes telling people that when I was born and lying screaming beside her, the doctor said, "*Mama mia, che acuti!*" ("What high notes!"). Mothers everywhere have anecdotes to pull out when life makes the prophecies in the stories true, especially Italian mothers. Now mother says that I got the voice from my father, and from her, the heart and romance in my music.

My father's name is Fernando. He was a baker. I never thought of ourselves as rich or poor. We always had enough. We never had an automobile and we didn't have a radio until long after most people had them. My father's little motorbike was the family transportation. I never thought about what we didn't have; I am still that way. All around me I see people making themselves unhappy by such thoughts.

I didn't think about the future either. What child does? I just lived every day as it came, and the days were beautiful.

My biggest memory of my childhood was my playing all the time. No child ever played as long and as hard as I did. There were so many other children in the neighborhood and so much open space. Every moment we weren't in school, we were outside playing—soccer mostly—but we played every game you can imagine. I was crazy for sports and still am.

My parents never bothered me about this. I would be out playing soccer all afternoon. They would yell for me to come eat my supper. I would say, "I'll be right there. Start without me. I'll be along." Then I would rush up the stairs, eat in about three minutes, and rush back to the game.

I had no special friends as a child—no one I would have been willing to die for and he for me. With such a large group of kids, everyone is your friend, and everyone is a potential enemy. I was very nice with them but I was tough. When you are the youngest among many, many kids, you must be ready to fight with your mouth or your fists. You never know when someone is going to attack you. You must be ready to stand up to it. At that age, we fought a lot. Since I was smaller, I was a little afraid of the others, but I knew how to deal with them, to avoid trouble with them.

With the people in my building I was very clever. As far as their adult matters were concerned, they made much effort to keep them from me; I was too little. I kept my eyes and ears open and learned *everything* that was going on. I knew which girl was going with which boy. They talked openly in front of me, because they never thought I took it in, but I usually did.

Sometimes I would hear something I didn't understand. I remember when I was only about five, I heard the word "abortion." From the way the word was used I knew it was something important, something very, very grown-up. I was crazy to know what it meant, but in a small community like ours, you must be very careful. I had no one to ask. If you ask the wrong person, he screams, "Listen to this everybody! This moron Pavarotti doesn't know what 'abortion' means!"

Every incident becomes public in seconds. Finally, when I was about twelve, I looked it up in the dictionary. But for years I wondered about it, afraid to ask.

My world was a small one. The main highway was only a few blocks from our building, but we rarely went out there. It was full of cars and horses and mostly strange faces. As a child I was very shy with people I didn't know. Maybe that was the result of being so happy and comfortable in my little world. That world was perhaps a five-hundred-meter radius from my house.

One project I had as a child was to build an airplane. A neighbor worked in a factory that made airplane parts. He told me he would bring me the parts from which I could assemble a plane, a real plane that would fly. Until I was about eight or nine, I believed this completely and worked very hard on the project. I don't know where I wanted to fly to. It was just the idea.

Nowadays, if you ask my daughters about building an airplane, from the age of five they will know all about it, how impossible it is. But I was back a generation. I wasn't more stupid, just more naïve, more trusting. I think I am still that way.

Another thing we used to love to do as children was hunt lizards and frogs. We would spend hours doing that in the woods around our building. Frogs don't sing in Italy the way they do in America. And that is strange because in Italy everybody sings.

I was only about five or six when I discovered I had a voice. It was a fine alto voice but nothing sensational. Even though my voice was only average, I used to love to sing. My father had a very fine tenor voice—he still does—and thought of attempting a career himself. He decided against it, mainly because he didn't feel his nerves were strong enough for the professional life. Even today when he sings a solo for the church, he is a nervous wreck a week ahead of time.

Vocal music was the most important thing in the world to my father. He would bring home records of all the great tenors of the day—Gigli, Martinelli, Schipa, Caruso—and would play them over and over. Hearing those great voices all the time, it was inevitable that I would try to sing like that too. It was almost as though I was forced to become a tenor.

I used to go into my room and close the door and, at the

top of my lungs, sing *"La donna è mobile"*—in a child's voice, of course. Of the sixteen families in the building, fourteen of them would yell at me to shut up.

That's funny because when I was very small—about five—I had a toy mandolin. I would take it into the courtyard behind our building where there was a fountain. I would carry a little child's chair and set it up by the fountain and serenade all the apartments. The neighbors used to love these concerts—maybe I didn't scream so much—and would toss candies and nuts to me. Does this mean I became a professional at five?

When I tried singing opera a few years later, they all went crazy and wanted to kill me. Not all. One man, I remember, told me I would be a singer. He knew, he said, because I had the right breathing. Everyone in Italy is an expert on singing—everyone—my barber, my father, my grandfather. They all have opinions about how to sing, what voices sound right, which are being incorrectly produced, and on and on. One neighbor, at least, heard in my child's voice the potential of a singer.

In those early years, however, serious thoughts of singing were very far away. My childhood was too full of loving relatives and sports-loving friends to think of anything in the future. Even the nightmare of World War II took awhile to penetrate my idyllic world.

The dominant event of my childhood was World War II, but at first I was only dimly aware of it. I was too young and the war was not very intense near us. Then, when the Americans and British started bombing Modena, I became brutally aware of it and it was terrible. Modena had a lot of industry and it was an important target. The bombings got so bad we had to leave the city. I was there, however, the first time the planes struck Modena. It was dreadful. An hour before the actual bombing, planes flew over the city and dropped smoke bombs. This was the signal that a real bomb was on its way. We had an hour to get out of the buildings. I remember being terribly frightened. That was the first time. The second time there was no warning; we heard the noise of the planes and the noise of the bombs at the same time.

When the bombings became regular, my father decided we should leave the city. The Pavarotti family joined the *sfolla-mento*, the name given the masses of Italians who were leaving the cities to take refuge in the country. Near the town of Carpi, my father found us a room with a farmer. He was not a relative, just a farmer who rented us a room. To be more exact, the farm was outside a tiny village called Gargallo. This was in 1943 when I was eight years old.

The real war was far away in the south, but our area, even out so far in the country, was full of partisans. Every night they conducted their private war with the local Fascists and the Germans. I would go to sleep each night with the sound of their gunfire. Rat-a-tat-tat. If I have a good sense of rhythm, it's from having that beat of the automatic weapons drilled into my head as a child.

Aside from the danger, the war was a catastrophe for most Italians. Food was scarce and very expensive. We were more fortunate than most families in this regard because my father was a baker. He could always bring us something, so we never were hungry as so many were in those days. We had bread and salt, the two most important items. Salt was terribly scarce. If you had salt, you could get anything. One half kilo could get you a liter of olive oil or two kilos of sugar. It was because of my father's being a baker that he was excused from military service by the Fascists.

My grandfather worked in the Accademia Militaria which was also a great advantage to the rest of us. He would bring home what the soldiers didn't eat. Most important of all, my father was making bread for the Germans as well as the local people. That made him important to them, so we didn't feel quite so

9

threatened as some of the other people who were useless to the Germans.

One night, even this small edge of security was shattered. Riding his bike back home from his work in Modena, my father was stopped by the Germans. His papers said "Baker" so they always let him pass. But for some reason, on this night they didn't believe him. They took him to jail.

When he didn't come home that night, my mother almost died. We were all frantic. Then we learned from a friend that he had been taken prisoner by the Germans. The partisans had killed a number of Germans and the Germans were taking in victims for reprisals. The closer to the end of the war we came, the worse it became between the Germans and the Italian partisans. The hatred on both sides rose to an incredible degree. We were driven crazy with fear for my father's safety.

Some time earlier, my grandfather had taken into his house a refugee from the south of Italy, someone he knew from earlier years. After settling near Modena, this man went on to become an important Fascist in the area. He remained grateful to my grandfather. When it came to executing Italians, the Germans often left the selection of victims in the hands of the local Fascists. I suppose they assumed the Italian Fascists knew better who were the most useful, who were the most anti-Fascist.

The Fascist official who knew my grandfather was involved in the selection of reprisal victims. As soon as he saw my father, he let him go. It was only the day after he had been arrested, but that one night had to be, for all my family, the worst time of the war.

The war years had one good aspect for me. Young as I was, I was put to work in the farmer's fields. How I loved that work! It was so free, so healthy. At the age of nine, I became a dedicated farmer. I couldn't imagine doing anything else. Back in Modena, even living in an apartment, we were at the edge of the city. There were farms all around us and I grew up among farmers doing their work. I already had a feeling for that life; to be thrown into a working farm at such an impressionable age was a great thrill for me.

My friends from Modena were scattered in every direction. I had no idea where most of them were. The farmer who rented us the room had four sons and another nearby farm had four boys and two girls. I made friends easily. I hope I still do.

Another aspect of that time on the farm I liked enormously was the contact I had with animals. By the time I was nine I had seen all the animals make love. All of them—cows, chickens, pigs, rabbits, horses—I can tell you how they all make love. For a young kid that was fascinating. Nowadays, they teach all about sex in kindergarten, I think, and nine would seem old to first learn about such things. I may have had a late education but it was a very natural one, with no accompanying moral message.

I think that entire experience on the farm at such a formative age explains much about my character today. I have an undeniably earthy side; no matter how much I delve into the nuances of Rossini's half-tone scales or Verdi's characterizations, or how much I mix with the most cultivated, refined people around the world, that side always stays with me. It is a basic approach to life with all the layers of civilization stripped away. I hope I always have the civilization, but I hope I always have these other qualities that I acquired during the war, in Carpi.

I have recently bought and done over a large house on the outskirts of Modena; surrounding it are about five acres of farmland. I greatly look forward to working the piece of land myself—sometime in the future when I am not too busy making high C's—when I can no longer reach them—then I will console myself with something I adore: farming.

The wartime days in the country were surprisingly peaceful, but the nights allowed us no doubt that a war was raging around us. It wasn't only the gunfire; partisans frequently came to our house for food and support. As soon as we had helped them and they'd gone on their way, the Germans would arrive asking if we'd seen any partisans. They were not nice about it. The game was nerve-racking and frightening.

As the end of the war approached, the more confused the situation became in Northern Italy, the worse things became for all of us. By August 1944, the Allied Armies had fought their way as far north as Florence, but those ten months remaining before the Nazis finally collapsed were the worst months for those of us still living under the Germans.

The partisans were getting stronger and more active. Some areas were completely under their control. But those under the Germans were treated with greater and greater harshness. The worst reprisals of the war occurred in our province only twenty-five miles from Modena in the town of Marzabotto. In that tragic town, 1,830 civilians were rounded up and shot at one time.

I never witnessed anything that horrible, but I wasn't spared seeing people I knew killed—no one close to me, I am grateful to say, but neighbors; faces I knew well. I once came on a neighbor I knew very well lying dead in the street. I saw many others hanging by the road. These were very bad things for a nine-year-old to see.

If a child is very young, he does not really understand death. He plays with his toy gun, "Bang, bang, you're dead," but he doesn't know what he is saying. As a child grows older, he may start to understand what it means, but still his view of death is different from an adult's. In some ways I think the child is more philosophical than the adult; he looks at death and the other big catastrophes of life less emotionally. He can accept other people's death as part of fate. Maybe this is because the child's world, the world he really cares about, is a small world made up of elements that seem to be permanent and indestructible. Death has no meaning for him until it is a parent's death or that of one of those fixed elements close to him. In this way, seeing death on the large scale of wartime may not be as hard on a child as on an adult.

I did understand death when I saw those people killed in front of me in Modena. I was nine or ten years old and perhaps at an age when I was beginning to comprehend things from a broader point of view. For me it was a terrible sight and made me feel sick inside. I became an adult right away. Seeing that impressed on me how easily life can be destroyed, how quickly it can end. It has given me, I think, my terrific enthusiasm for life.

This was the most important effect the war had on me. Twice during my life I have come very close to death myself. These two experiences—one, an illness when I was twelve, the other, a plane accident just a few years ago—reinforced my reverence for life, my feeling of how precious it is. But this outlook was started in me by those terrible days during the last months of World War II.

In the final days of the war, with the collapse of the Fascists, the partisans grew stronger and eventually took control. There were tremendous vendettas of the partisans against the Fascists. An ugly, murderous mood threatened to do as much harm as the war itself. That was why the whole city of Modena was so relieved when the Americans arrived.

I remember that day vividly. When the Americans rolled into our streets in their tanks and armored cars, the whole city went crazy. I had never seen anything so festive. We were delirious not only to be liberated from the Germans, but from each other.

Even before the Americans arrived, the partisans had the city functioning remarkably well as far as the basics of life were concerned. Of course there were severe shortages and other hardships and they lasted for some time after the coming of the Americans, but since everyone was so elated to have the war finished, we thought little about such minor matters.

I was still nine years old when the north of Italy was liberated, so I still had an amount of childhood left to go. I wasted no time getting down to my postwar activities—mainly playing soccer on the neighborhood lots.

Throughout my youth, school gave me few problems and I did well with a minimum of work. I would listen very carefully in class, then study at home a few minutes—maximum one hour —and that was all I needed to earn good grades. Later on, when I got to high school, I kept to this same work schedule—nonwork schedule, rather—and I had trouble. But elementary school was a party for me.

I began singing in our church choir. My father sang with them too. He and I would go in the evening to sing vespers— music of different composers—Vivaldi, Palestrina, and others. My voice was pretty good, but I wasn't the soloist; another boy was. I like to think that was because I was an alto and he was a soprano; solos are usually written for the soprano.

I wasn't always kept from stardom in this church. Once, this soprano boy got sick and I was asked to sing the solo part. I think it was the first time I sang before an audience. The music was too high for me. I almost strangled myself. It was the most horrible experience. If someone had told me then that I would spend my life singing high notes, I would have gone at them with my fists.

The church my father and I sang in was very small. It was named after the patron saint of Modena, San Gimignano. I have such fond memories of this church and that beautiful part of my boyhood. Today, when I return to Modena from singing around the world, I sometimes drop by that church to look around and remember.

As I grew older and began venturing more into the center

of Modena, I quickly developed a strong fondness for the entire city, as I had for the old neighborhood. We Italians are funny about our cities. Your hometown may have specific specialties, things you can't find the same way in other places—the fantastic food of Modena, for example, or the Lambrusco wine—but the love we feel can spread to physical characteristics such as our fantastic Romanesque cathedral with its exquisite and majestic tower that dominates the town's center, or the many sidewalks covered with graceful arcades that are so pleasant to stroll along, even when it rains. Of course, these are the superficial characteristics of a love that becomes intermeshed with your own life. If the memories of the early life are happy ones, as mine are, then the love for your own past melds into the ancient stones and narrow streets of your city.

Others talk about Modena's bad climate—cold and rainy in the winter, brutal heat in the summer—or that we are away from the mountains in flat farmland, or that we are not on the sea. Yes, yes—we have all of these failings. If you are a true Modenese as I am, however, you love the city the way you love another person—without restraint, without criticism, without comparisons to rivals.

When I was about twelve, Beniamino Gigli came to sing in our city. He was surely the most famous tenor in the world at that time. I was particularly thrilled as I had been listening to him on my father's records for years. I went by the theater and asked what time Mr. Gigli would be arriving to rehearse. I returned at the time they told me and they let me in. I must have appeared serious and not as though I wanted to make trouble.

Gigli was in his late fifties then but sang wonderfully and I listened enraptured for the hour he vocalized. When he finished I was so overwhelmed I went running up to Gigli and burst out the news that I wanted to be a tenor when I grew up.

Gigli was very nice and patted my head. *"Bravo! Bravo, ragazzino.* That is a fine ambition. You must work very hard."

"How long did you study?" I asked, trying to prolong our conversation.

"You heard me studying now. I just now finished—for today. I am still studying."

I can't tell you what an impression that made on me. He was world-famous, acknowledged by everyone to be one of the great singers of all time; yet he was still working to improve his artistry, still studying. I think about that even now, and I hope I am the same, that I will always keep the desire to become better.

Did I really want to become a singer at the age of twelve? I must admit that I didn't think seriously about it. I was just swept away by my adoration of that spectacular voice and seeing such a famous Italian so close. But as for an all-consuming ambition to become a tenor, I think it would be honest to admit that had Gigli been a soccer player and had I the chance to speak with him, I would have insisted my ambition was to become a professional athlete. I would have believed my own words just as strongly.

It is true I was constantly hearing tenor records at home, but how could I have determined to be a tenor at the age of twelve? God might have made me a bass.

Later that same year when I was twelve, a terrible thing happened. I was sitting at the dinner table with my family when suddenly I could feel nothing in my legs. I came down with a powerful fever and was put to bed. I went into a coma. No one knew exactly what it was, only that I was seriously ill. It turned out to be some sort of blood infection. The year was 1947 and they got for me the first penicillin we had in Italy for civilians. Even that new scientific miracle did not pull me out of the illness. Everyone was sure I was going to die. At my bedside, someone asked my mother how I was. I heard her reply that it

was all over for me. I did not like that at all. They called the
priest and he administered the last rites. I was immobile, almost
unconscious, but I could hear what was happening.

"It is time now, little boy," I heard the priest say, "to
prepare yourself to go to heaven."

I heard someone else say, "He does not have one week
left."

I don't want to make this too dramatic or people will think
years of acting grand-opera stories have affected me. But the
fact is, that at the age of twelve, I looked death directly in the
face. I knew I was going to die, and everybody else knew it too.
Somehow I came through it. The illness ended as mysteriously
as it started. I look on my recovery as a miracle.

The important thing, however, is that such an encounter
with my own death has made me value life enormously ever
since. If I am allowed to be alive, then I want to be *alive*. I
want to live life as fully as possible. Having seen what it is to
die, I know that life is good—even life with much trouble. Even
life where everything isn't exactly as we wish. So I am optimistic and enthusiastic and do everything I do with all my heart. I
try to communicate this outlook in my singing.

DR. UMBERTO BOERI

A Friend's Recollection

Now that Luciano and I are such good friends, it's ironic we didn't know each other when we both lived in Modena. Today, practicing medicine in New York City, I see him often— whenever he sings here. Twenty-five years ago, when I was a medical student at the University of Modena, however, I didn't know Luciano at all. For one thing, he was younger. Also, a kind of snobbery existed between the University students and the town boys. Coming from other cities to go to college, we students felt superior and were careful not to mix. You have that in America too, I think, the "town-and-gown" rivalry.

The odd thing is that I was aware of Luciano, even without knowing him. I would notice him walking through the streets during the *passeggiata*. This is the custom of an evening stroll that is almost a ritual in every Italian town and city. At the end of the working day when the shops close down and workers leave their offices, most of the town turns out into the streets to stroll in twos and threes through the streets in the center of town, converging from time to time into the principal piazzas.

The *passeggiata* is particularly popular with young people because it is the best opportunity for flirting. For the young or the old, the point of the *passeggiata* is to see and be seen. In Modena, with its miles of covered sidewalks, we had the *passeggiata* rain or shine.

A particular corner in front of the Caffè Molinari was a popular spot for the young men to congregate. They gathered there to watch the girls pass by and to pass comment on them or on anyone else of interest. Luciano was always among this pack. He was not a type you could miss. He was tall—as tall as he is now, but slender—and he was strikingly handsome. He would have been in his last year of high school.

It wasn't only his physical appearance that made him stand out and stick in my memory, he was clearly leader of the crowd; he was the most animated, the one the others looked to, whose name you would hear most frequently. Most of those town boys were spirited and full of life, but Luciano more than the others.

During that time I became friendly with Mirella Freni. Years later here in New York, when Mirella was singing at the Met, she introduced me to Luciano. He and I were friends for a long time before I put together in my mind the famous tenor with the boy I'd seen in Modena. One day I saw an old photograph of Luciano from those years and I made the connection.

I have a more specific recollection of Luciano from the Modena days. From time to time groups of opera lovers would charter buses to take them to another city for a particular performance. This is common throughout Italy. One summer there was such a bus going from Modena to Verona to hear *La Gioconda* with Giuseppe di Stefano. The opera was wonderful, and during the trip back to Modena that night everyone's spirits ran high in the bus. There was a lot of singing. Some of it was group singing, but there were many solos as well. I dislike admitting it, but Luciano's wasn't the only good voice on the bus that night. Still, his high B's were extraordinary. I was impressed that this popular, good-looking, town boy could sing like that.

Apropos of that evening, Luciano and di Stefano later became friends. I don't think there is any tenor Luciano admires more. One time many years later, Luciano was in New York to sing at the Met and he asked me to go with him to Carnegie Hall to hear a concert with di Stefano and Licia Albanese. Di Stefano had been on the phone earlier to Luciano complaining that he had no voice that day. Others managed to persuade him to sing.

Before the concert Luciano wanted to go backstage to encourage di Stefano, whom he knew was frantic with worry and nerves. When we got to his dressing room, we found Maria Callas there on the same mission. Luciano knew Callas, but I could tell he was very impressed with her and treated her with great respect, as though he was dealing with high nobility. He has said many times how he regrets never having sung with her. He felt she was such a remarkable artist and did so much to build interest in opera.

Di Stefano was distraught. When the concert began, I realized he was right to be. He was not in voice at all. It is a dreadful thing for a singer not to sound like himself. On that night di Stefano did not sound anything like di Stefano.

Sitting next to Luciano, I could see that he was as upset as the tenor performing. Finally Luciano could stand it no longer. He bolted from his seat to go backstage so he could stand in the wings throughout the rest of the concert to offer his friend moral support.

Luciano was already well known in New York, certainly in musical circles. I've often wondered how it must have appeared to the audience to see one of the most promising new tenors getting up and rushing out during a bad performance of one of the earlier great tenors—a tenor Luciano was, in a sense, replacing.

Friendship is very important to Luciano. He has many close friends among opera stars—Carreras, Freni, Ghiaurov—but he also has numbers of good friends in other fields. Take me, for example, a medical doctor. And he has friends in sports, films, television. I know many of the top opera singers and this is rare. Opera singing is such a strange life with so many special problems, most successful singers retreat into their own little world and see only people who either work directly for them or who, in one way or another, serve their career—conductors, directors, agents. Luciano is the opposite of that. He is interested in every aspect of life—and that means in every sort of person.

It is exciting being friends with Luciano, but you never know what to expect. He thinks nothing of calling at one-thirty in the morning because he feels like talking for a half hour. And he can be a law unto himself. He loves driving at high speed after a concert. It helps him unwind. Once, after singing in

New Haven, he was driving a group of us back to New York in a friend's car. He was going at such a speed his secretary then, Annamarie Verde, warned him that if he got stopped, the police would take his license.

"They can't," Luciano replied happily.

"Why not?"

"I don't have one."

LUCIANO PAVAROTTI

Becoming a Singer

As the time came for me to graduate from the Scuola Magistrale, which is like high school, a major decision had to be made. Should I attempt a singing career? This was a very big problem and, like all big problems in Italy, it involved the entire family in long debates around the dinner table.

If I was going to seek a different, more normal career, I would have to take up further studies after graduating. I hear young people now say, "I don't know what I want to do for a career: I'll go to college and decide later." Money was not so plentiful in our family. If I was going to remain in school, it had to be for a serious and definite purpose.

More school would require an outlay for tuition and my expenses. More important than that, it would put off the day when I would earn money and be able to contribute to our family's support. Several possibilities were considered. I was good at mathematics and liked the subject well enough to entertain the idea of becoming a mathematics professor. That would have meant four or five years at the university to earn the degree I needed to find a position. At least then I could be sure I would be able to earn a salary and pay back my parents for the years of support.

I was also crazy about athletics and still played soccer or other games six, seven hours a day. I was thin then and all muscle and quite a good athlete. My mother learned about a course in Rome that trained you as an instructor of athletics. It would require less time than becoming a professor of mathematics. That was another definite possibility.

Here I must confess something. I wasn't exactly lazy, but I had a good amount of inertia. I loved my life in Modena and I didn't *want* to go to Rome. That is one of the principal reasons I leaned toward the singing career.

My mother was optimistic about my chances as a singer and encouraged me. She said, "When you sing, your voice touches me. Try it." My father was against it. Out of every thousand who try, he said, only one manages to make a living at singing. The risk was too high. Of course, my father's voice made him even more skeptical. He knew better than anyone that a beautiful voice did not guarantee success.

My sister Gabriella was fourteen and was refused the vote. I offered my parents this proposition. They would support me till I was thirty. If I hadn't established myself as a singer by then, I would give up the idea and support myself in whatever way I could.

When I say "support" I mean simply allowing me to live at home and eat at their table. What money did I need? I still spent most of my free time playing sports during the day or playing cards with my friends in the evening. Our favorite games were briscola, conciccina, tressette, and sette e mezzo. When I was twenty, my father gave me the equivalent of one dollar a week pocket money. It was enough. He had a motorbike and he would let me take it for the whole day once a year—in the summer when my fiancée would hang on the back and we would drive it to the beach or to the spa at Viserba. It would be hard for kids today who have their own cars at sixteen to imagine what pleasure that one day a year gave Adua and me.

It is not my nature to yearn for things I don't have, but I worried that my parents who had supported me for so long would have to continue to do so. They were both willing—my father was against the singing career only because he was afraid I would be disappointed.

So with my father saying no to the singing career and my mother saying yes, naturally the decision was yes.

In 1954 at the age of nineteen, I began serious vocal study with a professional tenor who lived in Modena, Arrigo Pola. I had taken a few music lessons with a Professor Dondi—more really with his wife, who taught me some of the fundamentals of music. Dondi thought I had a chance as a singer and suggested I sing for Pola, who also had a reputation as an excellent teacher.

My father knew Pola and took me to sing for him. I remember I sang *"Addio la madre"* and one or two other songs. Pola immediately agreed to take me on as a student. Knowing the Pavarotti family's financial situation, he said he would teach me gratis.

Maestro Pola was enthusiastic about my voice. He says now that he could see right away that it was an important one and that I had the other qualities to become an artist. If that is true, he saw more than I did. Still, I went at singing with great enthusiasm and seriousness mainly because I am that way about everything I do.

I wasn't a fanatic about learning to sing—not quite. Everything Pola asked me to do, I did—day after day, blindly. For six months we did nothing but vocalize and work on vowels. We did elaborate exercises with vowels for the purpose of opening up the jaws, making the voice bigger and, of course, making clear, exaggerated pronunciation of vowels automatic. Then we vocalized—hour after hour, day after day—not music, just scales and exercises. There are many things a nineteen-year-old Italian would rather do than stand endlessly singing scales and mouthing over and over A, E, I, O, U.

I think I am fortunate to be able to develop a curiosity about whatever I do. While studying with Pola, I became fascinated by the voice and the way it responded to different vocal techniques. Many singers find studying voice—the *solfeggio*, the endless vocalizing, the exercises—very boring. I didn't. I became intrigued with the entire process. I was interested from the detached point of view of an experimenter as well as from the point of view of one who stood to profit from the lessons' progress.

Pola quickly discovered that I had perfect pitch. I hadn't realized I had it or how fortunate this was. Many incredible voices are lost because of faulty pitch. If you don't have an accurate ear, there is nothing to do, because you do not conquer pitch problems. My father has a little difficulty in this way. Sometimes he doesn't quite reach the note he wants, yet he doesn't hear he is off pitch. If you don't know you are making a mistake, how can you correct it? I suspect the reason my three daughters do not sing is not because they don't have voices, but because they inherited bad pitch from their mother. That is all right; they inherited enough other good things from her.

About the same time that I was starting studying with Pola, I was at a party with some of my friends. The group was having fun making guests attempt various opera arias. A pretty girl I didn't know was trying to sing something from *Rigoletto*. It was terrible. "That girl needs my help," I said.

Her name was Adua Veroni. She was a Modena girl who was about to become a teacher. She was full of fun and very pretty. We started seeing each other and became engaged. I had never been serious about any one girl, so this was a new experience for me. In Italy it is the custom to become engaged early in relationships because it is not considered proper for a young man and woman to spend time alone together regularly unless they plan to marry. Breaking these "engagements" is easy—and frequent. Very soon Adua and I realized our engagement was not like that.

At a time when my friends were either going off to college or starting in jobs, I settled down each day to singing scales with Maestro Pola. In a little while I got a part-time job teaching at an elementary school for the astounding salary of $8 a month. I was more of an assistant teacher overseeing the boys' outdoor activities, occasionally teaching. At one time or another I taught classes in music, religion, the Italian language, and gymnastics. The last was the most frequent—happily, as I still loved sports.

I would like to be able to say I adored my students and they adored me, but it was not like that. They were absolutely wild, screaming all the day. I did not have the authority of a regular teacher and the little monsters did whatever they felt like. I wanted to kill every one of them. I think I would love to teach, but in an orderly, systematic way. Not like that. I did it for about two years while I was studying voice. It was a terrible experience.

Through the school, a better way of earning money came along for me. I began selling insurance for a company that had an arrangement with the school. The school authorities would notify the families of the students that I would be calling on them. When I arrived, it was not as though a total stranger was appearing at their front door. I had the endorsement of their children's school.

I would arrive just at mealtime. To be sure to find them at home, I would catch them as they had the fork to their mouth. It always started with them saying, "Oh, I don't want anything, no, no, no . . ." But after I talked to them, they often came around. Or they would tell me they would think it over. I was very persistent because I believed in the policy I was selling. It was a good one—not total risk, something in between where their families collected a good amount if the person insured died, but even if the insured person lived, they still got money when the policy matured.

More and more often one of the boys would come up to me in school and say his father had thought it over and had decided to buy the policy and wanted me to come around to see him again. It was very easy. I started making good money. I stopped teaching and devoted myself to selling insurance.

Before long I was making about three hundred dollars a month. In the late 1950s in Italy that was a lot of money, certainly more than I had ever had before. And I was earning it working only a four-hour day. It was too good to last. After some months, I noticed that all that speaking from my sales talks was damaging my voice. Talking can be harder on the voice than singing. Toward the end of 1960, I ended my career as a salesman.

Even though I was making good progress with Maestro Pola toward becoming a singer, my vocal talent was not in great demand. The only use I put it to that I can remember was to help a guy in my neighborhood court his girl friend. She was very romantic and loved singing. He asked me to stand out of sight under her window while he pretended to serenade her. Just like Don Giovanni or Cyrano. I remember singing *"Di quella pira"* from *Il Trovatore.* I don't know what made him think that would melt her heart—it's about as romantic as the *William Tell Overture*—but it was a famous showpiece—every Italian schoolboy tried singing it—he wanted to dazzle her.

When Maestro Pola moved to Japan to teach and sing there, I began commuting to Mantova to continue my voice studies with Maestro Ettore Campogalliani. This wonderful teacher had been the choice of Maestro Pola. Happily for me, my childhood friend Mirella Freni, who is now one of the world's greatest sopranos, was also studying with him. I had seen little of Mirella in my teenage years, since her family had moved away from our neighborhood when we were quite young and Mirella had gotten married at an early age. But now we saw a lot of each other. We would often ride to Mantova on the train together for our lessons. Sometimes she would get the use of her husband's car and we would drive. We constantly talked over our progress, then talked about the careers we would have. Mirella and I are still doing that.

When I started studying voice I had allowed myself ten years, or until I was thirty, to establish myself, but secretly, of course, I was hopeful something would happen sooner than that. I actually thought I'd be able to prove myself within a year or two. I was too optimistic. I worked extremely hard with Pola for those two and a half years, and I worked just as hard with Campogalliani for another four years, and still nothing happened.

Eventually I got one or two concerts, recitals really, in small towns, but I was never paid for them. I was studying hard and singing hard. My morale started to go down and down.

I had been studying voice for almost seven years and had not even started professionally. My friends were all getting married, settling down and establishing themselves in careers. I wanted to get married too, but financially it was out of the question.

The most discouraging aspect of this course was that I had no idea when it *would* be possible. When you study to become a lawyer or doctor, it may require many years, but at least you know with some certainty when the study will be over and you can begin earning money and living your life. With something as uncertain as singing, you start out with no idea how many years it will be before you start earning your living—or if you ever will.

Of course I knew this when I decided to try to become a singer. You acknowledge these problems, yet deep inside yourself you always believe that, with you, it won't be too bad, that you will have some sort of success in a few years. But six years with no success? My optimism had run out.

Probably because of my discouragement, I developed a nodule on my vocal cords. I sang a concert in Ferrara that was a disaster. I sounded like a baritone who was being strangled. Not only was I an unsuccessful singer, now I was not even a good singer.

That night after the concert I said to Adua, "It's no use. I have one more concert to do in Salsomaggiore, then I am going to give up singing completely."

Something quite mysterious happened. Making the announcement that I was quitting seemed to release a strange energy in me. Maybe it was because I thought it was my farewell concert at the age of twenty-five and I was no longer frantically concerned with how well I sang. Or maybe something inside me wanted to prove my idea of giving up was a mistake.

Whatever the reason, the concert at Salsomaggiore was the finest singing I had done up till that time. The audience was thrilled, though not as much as I was. It seemed that everything I had learned from Pola and Campogalliani, all my work and study for six years, came together with my natural voice to make the sound I had been struggling so hard to achieve. There wasn't a trace of the nodule.

I said to Adua, "*Ci siamo* (We're here). Perhaps I've found the right form."

I did a few concerts, programs that included other singers, in towns around Modena. The voice seemed to be holding up and my confidence was returning. Almost immediately something happened to put my recovery to the test. I was to sing at a concert in the Salle Ariosto in Reggio Emilia, the capital of our province. My selection was to be the aria from *Rigoletto*, "*Parmi veder le lagrime*," one of the most difficult tenor arias ever written. When I walked out to sing, I immediately spotted sitting in the first row the great tenor Ferruccio Tagliavini.

Tagliavini is from Reggio but, of course, was and is famous all over the world. He must have been in his late forties then. He was one of my idols. It is difficult to explain the sensation, the emotion you feel when you are about to have the audacity to claim to be an operatic tenor and to be looking into the face of one of the foremost operatic tenors of the day.

I almost passed out from nervousness. You are always frightened before singing but to add to the usual anxiety an extra cause for worry can sometimes make the whole experience unbearable. It is the extra jolts—these unexpected problems—that either drive you from the field or teach you to conquer your nerves. You must learn this and, if possible, learn to harness the energy they release for your benefit. It is as much a part of learning to be a singer as learning to breathe correctly.

I had a very good friend who was also studying voice with Campogalliani named Bindo Verini. He was a marvelous kid with a motorcycle and was always a little sick. Bindo had a beautiful baritone voice. Everyone said he had as good a chance at an operatic career as I did.

But he never did it. Bindo now sings with the Florence Chorale Society. We are still very good friends. Not long ago he told me he could tell, even when we were students together, that I had the other requirements besides voice to be a singer—primarily the ability to conquer my nerves—and he did not have them. He said it with no envy or regret, just a statement of the truth as he saw it.

(I think Tagliavini's presence at that concert is the reason some people say he was present at my operatic debut in Puccini's *La Bohème* in Reggio Emilia a short time later. He might have been, but I assure you I was so nervous at my debut performance and so completely focused on what I was doing I wouldn't have noticed if the twelve apostles were lined up in the first row.)

The concert in Salsomaggiore was the psychological turning point in my singing career. Next came the other kind of turning point. Early in 1961, I entered a singing competition, the Achille Peri competition for singers from all over Emilia. I won first place. The prize was the role of Rodolfo in a production of Puccini's *La Bohème* to be given in Reggio Emilia that April.

ARRIGO POLA

Teaching Pavarotti

When Luciano's father brought him to sing for me in 1955, I knew right away that this was an exceptional voice, and I took him on as a pupil. Every day for the next two and a half years, he came to my apartment in Modena and we worked—sometimes he would even come on Sunday.

I felt it was essential that he learn very well at that age correct vocal technique—correct placement of the voice, correct breathing, which underlies all singing. For a long time we just worked on enunciation and did vocalization, to make good pronunciation and the right technique automatic. Eventually, after some months, we began working on musical scores—*Rigoletto*, *La Bohème*, and the other major tenor roles.

Luciano went at all this with enormous enthusiasm. I was having a reasonably successful career as a tenor and he was a fan of mine. Perhaps this increased his eagerness. In any case, I found him a wonderful pupil. He worked hard and with great intelligence. After the voice itself, his intelligence is his most important attribute as a singer. If I would tell him something or demonstrate a way of producing a tone, he would pick it up right away. It was not tiring to teach Luciano: he got things so quickly.

I worked on him to develop a technique that was pure, natural, spontaneous—I think that is what you hear today.

Nowadays there is a certain confusion about vocal instruction. There are many teachers, each with their own teaching system. This is unfortunate. The only right method is the one that adapts to the student. It is impossible to make a voice do something that nature did not intend. One should arrive at a way of singing similar to the way of speaking. When Luciano speaks, you understand every word. It is the same with his singing. He enunciates with great clarity and this is very important to the public.

One of the instructor's biggest jobs is making the student

realize his capabilities, making him understand what is within his reach and what is beyond it.

With Luciano there were really few problems. Often a student comes to you full of bad methods and habits. Even if he hasn't studied before, he has surely sung before and has already fixed in his mind a way of doing it. If this way is fixed firmly and is wrong, it is very, very difficult to correct—sometimes it is impossible. Many potentially fine voices are lost this way. But Luciano had very few fixed habits and no disastrous ones. I was able to build his technique almost from scratch; most important, he was impassioned about singing.

After working hard for a year Luciano had two octaves of his total range in very good shape. Gradually he expanded the range both upward and downward, achieving the same control at the outer limits—the high and low notes—as he had at the middle. Today he is the complete master of his voice. No one can fault his technique, his breathing, his pronunciation, his phrasing. It was also a big help that Luciano was born musical. There is only so much you can learn. If it is all done by remembering the lessons, done from memory, it won't be music. A good part of it must be natural reflex.

Of course the biggest teacher of all is the stage. When you are singing a performance, you are out there all alone. There is no maestro to guide you. Only you can discover what works best for you. You can also learn much singing alongside excellent and experienced singers.

Once you have developed the right technique, a technique that is correct for your natural vocal equipment, it becomes an automatic reflex, and your voice will be preserved much longer. I can remember when I was singing *La Bohème* at San Carlos in Naples, Gigli was also singing there. He was about sixty years old and he sang both *Cavalleria* and *Pagliacci* in the same evening. He sang them beautifully with no sign of vocal strain.

Luciano can look forward to the same long vocal life. If you have learned correctly, whenever you need it the voice is there.

After Luciano had studied with me for two and a half years, I contracted to go to Japan for several years, so I took him to the best teacher I knew in the area: Ettore Campogalliani in Mantova, who continued with Luciano where I left off. There are many people who can coach singers in particular roles, but there are very few who can teach how to sing. Campogalliani is one of those who can teach. He really knows the voice.

From the start, I never doubted Luciano would one day be a very great tenor. It wasn't only the voice, it was his approach to the work—he was dedicated, mature, alert. He wasn't dabbling, he was totally serious about perfecting his voice.

ADUA PAVAROTTI

A Tenor's Wife

It is odd I should end up the wife of an opera star. I was never very fond of opera and that makes me a scandal in our family. I remember being sick for a long period when I was a child and becoming fascinated by the opera stories. I read all the librettos and knew the story of every opera, but I never cared very much for the music.

Of course, that is completely changed now. If something is truly beautiful in itself, as you become familiar with it, you can't help but come to appreciate it. Now I love opera—and have grown very critical. I get upset if it's not done well. After all, opera as a form is out of date. If it is to be performed at all in the present time, it should be done extremely well—with the finest sets, direction, singing, conducting. If it is done in a half-hearted way, it should be left in the nineteenth century. I know Luciano feels this way too.

Those first years, we didn't worry too much about the quality of the productions Luciano sang in. It was enough that they would let Luciano sing before an audience and pay him something.

Even though there were some difficult times, I was never anxious about Luciano's opera career. I thought he had a good chance of succeeding in an important way, but I didn't agonize over what would happen if he didn't. I knew he could always make a living at something. I was working at that time, too. For a while I taught in the same school in which Luciano taught, then later I worked in the school office.

My small teacher's salary was what got us through that first year or two. I kept working until our second daughter, Cristina, was born. Then, with two babies at home, I decided I could no longer work. Fortunately Luciano was now making enough to make it possible for me to give up my job.

There were some bad moments but there were some wonderful ones too. One time Luciano had been away a number of weeks singing performances in a small opera company in Holland. The company had financial problems, so they didn't pay the singers until the very end of the run. Instead of getting little amounts of money every week, Luciano got one big pile of cash at the end.

The day he arrived back in Modena, I was at school teaching. I got home that evening to find Luciano had taken the money and covered our bedroom with it. There were bills everywhere—over the bed, the dresser, the chairs—he had even stuck money to the wall.

Another particularly happy moment I remember was when he first got a definite offer from La Scala. Luciano had already sung at Covent Garden with terrific success as well as in other opera houses around Europe. For a long time he had been in touch with La Scala, but they either wanted him to understudy or take a role that he didn't feel was right for him to sing. This was very frustrating. Even though his career was going well, La Scala, especially for Italians, is in a class by itself.

One day I was in our apartment and I heard Luciano calling me from outside. I looked out the window and saw him in the garden below our window. In one hand he was waving the Scala contract. It was famous for its pink color and I would have recognized it from twice that distance. In the other hand he was holding a metal orange-juice squeezer. It was a silly gadget he had wanted for a long time but didn't think we could afford. Thanks to La Scala the Pavarottis had plenty of fresh orange juice from then on.

Since Luciano has become successful, I do pretty much what I always did. I run the houses—Modena and Pesaro—plus do a lot of other tasks concerned with Luciano's singing career. I read all the Italian mail and answer those letters that need answers—requests for photos, for specific information, for an autograph.

This takes up more and more time. Luciano now gets mail

from all over the world—everything from women sending sexy photos of themselves (some men too) to heartbreaking letters from old people, sick people, invalids, people who say Luciano's singing is the only joy in their lives. Many have written that hearing Luciano has rescued them from despair. Luciano wants all of these letters answered. Recently, he has been getting more and more letters from children, particularly in America. Many of these are wonderful.

Another job I've undertaken is to keep the scrapbooks—all the photos, press notices, articles. I love doing this, but it takes time. And I keep a record of all his performances. It is so easy for this sort of information to get lost in all of the excitement of the moment. Then someone—a journalist or a writer for a theater program—urgently needs a date or some other fact and no one knows. I have appointed myself the official Pavarotti archivist.

Luciano has turned me into a businesswoman. He feels he only has a limited number of years to earn the large fees for singing and he is most anxious to invest as much of the money as possible. It is incredible the expenses connected with the life of a successful opera star. Considering the large fees he earns, he is remarkably thrifty. Even so, it is not easy for him to save some of the income, but he is determined to. Because Italy has strict laws about taking money from the country, most of our investments are around Modena. I look after these business affairs.

For a while we owned a vineyard, but we sold that and have invested in other things—mostly real estate. We now have a few apartment buildings in town. There are constantly matters to see to in connection with these ventures. I enjoy handling our business interests. We Italian women are good with money.

Our daughters have grown into healthy, attractive young women. The oldest, Lorenza, was born in 1962. Cristina came along two years later; she was born when Luciano was singing in *Idomeneo* at Glyndebourne. Three years later we had Giuliana.

Lorenza is the only one of our girls old enough to think about a career. Right now she is considering becoming a dress designer. None of our daughters is particularly crazy about lyric opera. They enjoy going to hear their father sing, but I fear it is because it is their father and not because it is Verdi or Puccini. Lately, however, I've seen signs of more genuine interest. Not long ago they took a large group of their friends up to Milan to hear Luciano sing *La Bohème* at La Scala.

For a long time their father's success made little impression on them. After all, the heroes of their generation are not opera singers. Few of their friends had any idea who their father was— or, rather, that their father was anything special. Part of this was that Luciano became famous in America before he became widely known in Italy.

Now he is known in Italy as well and this has changed things for the girls. Suddenly their friends are hearing about Luciano. People ask them questions about him; others pay more attention to the girls than they would if Luciano was just another man. I think they are growing a little cynical about it. They say they can tell if people are playing up to them because of Luciano. I hope this doesn't make them too suspicious of people.

With so much of Luciano's work outside of Italy, and with the political unrest Italy is going through right now, many foreign friends ask why we don't consider living somewhere else. I always laugh and say it is because we are *cretini sentimentali*, sentimental morons. Of course it is more complicated than that.

Naturally there are the reasons of family ties. Our Italian families, his and mine, are so close-knit and the connections go trailing off so far it is sometimes hard to see where family stops and close friends begin. The important thing is that these ties are mostly in Modena.

There are also practical reasons for staying—the girls' schooling and the problems of taking money from Italy. One of the main reasons we stay is our feeling about Modena itself. First, Luciano and I both love this city; it has been our life, it is in our blood. Then, too, we know Modena so well, we know our fellow Modenese, we do not feel fear here. Those terrible things that happen in Milan and Torino—that is another world. It is not Modena.

Luciano is a complicated person. He thinks of himself as a highly controlled machine. He is very concerned about his physical condition. He has one of those gadgets for taking blood pressure and takes his own frequently. When he does, he takes the blood pressure of anyone else who happens to be around. He wants everyone to be healthy.

From time to time, when he is singing in Italy, he will sneak off to a spa for a day or two to purge his system. He has all kinds of theories about health. I feel sorry sometimes for the doctors taking care of him or one of us. Luciano has as many ideas about what is wrong and what should be done as the doctor. I think they find him a little overbearing; but of course he means well.

When my father was almost dead with heart trouble, Luciano got a medicine for him that they had developed in the United States. Luciano had heard about it, but we didn't have it here in Italy yet. It saved my father.

Luciano is very much a creature of habit. He does not like changes—around the house, in the way we do things, all the arrangements for our living and his getting around. For instance, when he goes back to a city to sing, he likes to stay in the same hotel, even the same room, if possible. He has gotten more this

49

way over the years. I am sure it has something to do with his moving around so much, of trying to feel at home in Milan, London, New York, or Boston.

He doesn't like to be at the mercy of other people. I mean even with little things. He doesn't want to have to ask where the elevators are; he wants to *know* where the elevators are. You see this in his eagerness to drive an automobile himself, even when he's in someone else's car. Friends in cities he visits often, like Chicago or New York, will offer to drive him to a singing engagement or to a social event. Very frequently, Luciano will ask if he can drive. He is not one to sit back and let other people guide him around.

Another aspect of Luciano's personality that sets him apart from many people is his terrific need of friends. He must have friends around him at all times—not just when he's home in Italy but any place he goes. It is very lucky he's so good at making friends, because he can't get along without them.

People who have met Luciano only once are often amazed at the details of their lives he remembers after a long period of time. Someone will come to his dressing room after a performance in Philadelphia or San Francisco and Luciano will ask him how his redheaded wife is or if his broken arm has healed or whatever memory Luciano might have of the individual. But he will have *some* recollection.

Luciano has an incredible memory, and this is part of his constant effort to convert fans into friends. He is very good at it, and he seems to have time for an unlimited number. Even if he doesn't make friends out of fans, they are still very important to him. He feels a bond with them, made up in large part by the gratitude he feels for their loyalty. Some people think it is a pose, but there is one management in an American city that learned it isn't.

After singing a concert in this city, he said he wanted to greet his admirers backstage as he always does. The concert's

Here I am, three years old. The ball is typical of my childhood, the costume is not. CREDIT: Dante di Pieiri

With my soccer team in Modena. I am in the back row third from the right.
(*above*) This picture of me was taken at the time of my operatic debut in
Reggio Emilia, April 29, 1961. I was twenty-five.

The *Bohème* company of my debut took our production to Modena after the 1961 opening. I am third from the right. CREDIT: Franco Vignoli (*above*) My 1954 appearance as Idamante in the Glyndebourne production of Mozart's *Idomeneo* was a fantastic experience for me musically and artistically. CREDIT: Guy Gravett (*below left*) I finally was asked to sing at La Scala in 1965. Here I am trying to look as though I belong there. CREDIT: Publifoto (*below right*)

Adua and I were enough encouraged by the success of my debut to get married a few months later, on September 30, 1961.

Next to Rodolfo, I think I have sung the Duke in *Rigoletto* more than any other role. Here's one of the earliest, the 1966 La Scala production. CREDIT: Piccagliani (*above*) Dr. Arturo di Filippi, founder and director of the Miami Opera, was the first impresario to bring me to America. Here I am in my Edgardo (*Lucia di Lammermoor*) costume at the time of my 1965 American debut. CREDIT: John Pineda (*below*)

When I sang *Lucia* with Joan Sutherland in Miami in 1965, I had already sung with her several times at Covent Garden. CREDIT: John Pineda (*above*) My childhood friend, Mirella Freni, and I have performed together many times over the years. In 1967 we sang *La Fille du Régiment* at La Scala. CREDIT: Piccagliani (*below*)

My manager, Herbert Breslin, and I often confer in strange places. Here we are in the parking lot of Philadelphia's Robin Hood Dell West before a 1979 concert. CREDIT: William Wright (*above*) My father and I are always giving each other singing lessons. CREDIT: William Wright (*below*)

It would be as difficult for me to explain why I love Modena as to explain why our cathedral is an architectural masterpiece. CREDIT: William Wright

that because they are teenagers they need a live-in policeman, only that it is a time when young people are experiencing so many major changes in their life, they need a parent nearby, even if the young people like to think they don't.

In any case, I feel I should be with them and Luciano agrees. As a result, he and I are separated much of the year. Sometimes I wish I'd married a bank clerk who is always at home. But when I think about it for a minute, I change my mind. Because of this wonderful gift Luciano has to give to the world, I know it is all worth it.

LUCIANO PAVAROTTI

The Working Tenor

Reggio Emilia is about twenty-five miles from Modena. As in most of the cities in this part of Italy, the people are very enthusiastic about singing. They take opera very seriously, are highly knowledgeable about it and have strong opinions. Food and opera—these are the two passions of the province of Emilia.

It would be hard to imagine the joy I felt at finally getting an opportunity to sing in an opera. Never mind that I wasn't being paid anything. I was at last getting a chance to perform—and not just any role, but Rodolfo, one of the greatest creations for the lyric tenor and very good for my voice. I threw myself into the work like a madman.

The company was mostly young singers with little experience or, like me, none. The management put us up in a very simple hotel where I shared a room with the male singers and the ladies were in another room on the same floor. We all shared a bathroom at the end of the hall.

Each one of us was so excited and happy, so full of the fun of being young and already doing the precise work we wanted to do. We lived in that hotel just like the characters we were portraying in *La Bohème*—penniless young people with artistic aspirations, full of optimism and *joie de vivre*.

Our work schedule was painless. We would rehearse three days, then have a week off; then another three days of rehearsal and another week's rest. Finally, the last week, we rehearsed the entire week. The stage director was Mafalda Favero, the famous soprano who had retired from singing. She was a marvelous woman and a good director, although that *Bohème* was, I believe, the only opera she staged. I followed her directions with much love.

We never saw the principal conductor toward the last days. For the rehearsals our conductor was a man named Renato Sabione. He was very good with us, very patient. He understood that we were all making our debuts, so he took extra pains with us. Only two rehearsals remained before the opening when the conductor arrived. He was Francesco Molinari-Pradelli, who was important in Italy's opera world. He never heard any of us sing until those last two rehearsals.

Those final days before the opening were so exciting, I was living in a dream. One thrill, however, stands out from the many others: singing for the first time with a full orchestra. All those years of studying and thinking of yourself as a singer—there is always an orchestra there, in your mind. But the first time it is *really* there—it is an experience, impossible to describe to someone who hasn't dreamed for years of becoming an opera singer.

At the dress rehearsal, Maestro Molinari-Pradelli stopped the orchestra after my first-act aria and said to me, "Young man, if you sing like that at the performance tomorrow night, you will have a triumph."

I could feel my knees almost give way. Mafalda Favero said to me later that the conductor was a very difficult man to please and wouldn't make a compliment to his mother. It was very encouraging to me.

During the actual performance, I was concentrating so hard on what I was doing, I was barely conscious of what was happening. I was frightened of the conductor. I was also frightened by the audience. There is a big rivalry between my city of Modena and Reggio Emilia. I knew they would like nothing better than to see a Modena tenor make an ass of himself. After "*Che gelida manina*," I could feel that the audience liked me very much.

You can tell if an audience likes you by the size of the applause, but, even before that, I always know if I sing well or not. Also my friends from Modena who came for the opening, if they don't like my singing, they are not one little bit shy about telling me. But on this night they all gave me nothing but praise, which made me certain I had sung well.

So I had the triumph that Maestro Molinari-Pradelli predicted. But was he happy for me? He was furious. I learned right away about the envy that plagues the opera world.

It would have taken far more than that to dampen my spirits that night. While everyone sang well, it had been my evening. Except for the conductor everyone was very happy for me. We had a big party that night after the performance and I have never felt more like celebrating. At one point, however, my father pulled me aside and said, "It was very nice, Luciano, very nice. But you still don't sound like Gigli and Schipa. You must work some more."

I got even with him. Several years later I was singing *La Bohème* in Modena and my father was singing the small part of Parpignol, the toy vendor who has only a few phrases in the Café Momus scene. As usual my father was terribly nervous. During the dress rehearsal, his voice cracked. Afterward I took him aside and said, "Father, I think you should go home and study some more."

The day after the first Reggio Emilia *Bohème*, the papers were more favorable about my debut than my father had been. The *Nova Gazette di Reggio Emilia* said: "The tenor Luciano Pavarotti sang with estimable good taste and with vivid musicality, likewise displaying vocal equipment both penetrating and flexible. He was liked perhaps more than his colleagues." The other papers who reviewed the opera were also complimentary to me.

As with any successful career, mine has had a good amount of luck. One of the luckiest strokes of good fortune happened the night of my debut. In the audience was an important agent, Alessandro Ziliani, who was also a tenor. He was associated with a Milan talent agency but had a considerable reputation of his own in the opera world. He was present that night, not to hear me, but to hear the bass Dmitri Nabokov, who is the son of the famous writer.

Perhaps because he himself was a tenor, Ziliani was more

interested in me and switched his attention away from Nabokov. In any case, Ziliani rushed backstage after the performance and introduced himself. I was in such a state of elation that I am surprised that I remember meeting him or that I made any sense when we talked. I am a very exuberant person, but part of me always knows what's going on. He wanted to know my plans. I said that I intended to learn well about four or five roles before attempting to launch a career. He said that as soon as I felt prepared, I should contact him and he would represent me. This was very important for me; Ziliani was known in all the opera houses in Italy and many throughout Europe.

It is interesting how important to every career are these endorsements from other professionals. Someone with real standing in your field—an agent, a critic, an important maestro—tells you you are good; they confirm what you yourself have been thinking, or hoping, all the years you are preparing yourself. You store these accolades as fortification against the bad things—no phone calls for jobs, an audience that remains unmoved, whatever.

If the encouraging things aren't enough, or aren't strong enough, they may not be sufficient to help you over the bad places and you give up. You always hear about struggling artists having faith in themselves. Well, I had faith in myself. I had worked hard for six years without earning a penny. But it is much easier to keep up that faith when it gets recharged by someone from the outside who knows the profession you are trying for.

With each artist you see—good or bad—you never know what little sack of encouragements they carry around with them to support their career, what pats on the back from which hands, what newspaper clipping, what word of hope from what teacher. I suppose the so-called faith in ourselves is the foundation of our talent, but I am sure these encouragements are the mortar that holds it together.

In the case of Ziliani liking my voice, it was more than just support for my morale, of course. He was a man in a position to get me jobs singing in opera houses throughout Europe.

I was so heartened by the debut in Reggio Emilia—the audience response, the reviews, the important agent asking for me—that I decided the future looked promising enough to get married. Adua and I were far from certain that I could earn a living as a singer. After all the congratulations and bravos cleared from our heads, we remembered that many others with modest successes such as mine had never been heard from again. Adua was more confident than I was; I think women have a nose for this sort of thing.

Even to me, my chances looked far better than they had before winning the competition, so we decided to take the chance. Adua was working as a teacher and, if all else failed, I could go back to selling insurance. On September 30, 1961, just five months after my debut, Adua and I got married.

For a while it looked as though I might be one of those tenors you never hear from again. When I went back to Ziliani to say I was ready to start looking for parts, he was good to his word and began selling me. It was not easy for him. One success in Reggio Emilia does not make you a box-office drawing card.

Every opera house manager, like people who buy talent all over the world, feel safer and happier with established artists. Even if it means taking someone they know is second-rate, they feel more secure with known quantities. If someone suggests that the tenor or soprano they are presenting is not very good, they can shrug and say, "What can I do with my budget? I can't afford Corelli and Tebaldi."

The fact is, there are always young Corellis and Tebaldis around who will work for very little; the impresarios only must trust their own ears. It is sad how many people are in positions of importance in opera who don't know whether or not the singing is beautiful until they see the singer's name.

Ziliani's phone was not ringing away with requests for the young tenor from Modena. For a while it looked as though he was going to have to sell me in what we call the *scatola chiusa*— that is, the "closed box." I think in America this is called blind booking.

An impresario comes to Ziliani and says, "We must have Mario del Monaco for our production of *Tosca*."

He replies, "I will let you have him if you will also take a young tenor of mine named Pavarotti for a few recitals." I believe Ziliani actually got me a concert this way.

This timidity of managements can make an influential agent very important. Ziliani was known to have very high standards, particularly as far as tenors were concerned, since he was a tenor himself. If he went to a management saying he had a tenor who was out of the ordinary, they were inclined to believe him.

In this way he got me my first paid role: a *Bohème* that was to be produced in Lucca, Puccini's hometown. I know I was given the part through Ziliani's persuasion. When I arrived for rehearsals the conductor said to me, "If Ziliani says you are a good tenor, you must be a *very* good tenor, because he never speaks of any tenors with the enthusiasm with which he speaks of you."

One odd thing about my career is the bad experiences I had with colleagues at the beginning. For almost twenty years of constant singing and performing in opera houses around the world, I have generally had the most cordial, warm relations with the people I've worked with. But that conductor at Reggio was not nice to me, and now I had difficulty with the soprano at Lucca.

She was a woman who had been singing for years and was reasonably well known in Italy. In 1961 she was definitely at the end of her career and was not singing well. I think she knew this. She was afraid, others told me, that my "*Che gelida manina*" would receive more applause than her *"Mi chiamano Mimi."* Whatever the reason, she resented me. With her, I could do nothing right.

A few years later, when she came to sing an opera with me in Modena, her voice had become even worse. She sang so badly, the audience booed her. She sent her husband to me and accused me and Mirella Freni of having organized the boos. I suppose their reasoning was that we were both from Modena and didn't allow other singers to sing in our city. Sopranos can be afflicted at times with odd thinking.

It was a farce, but I still felt terrible that she and her husband could think this. Then at one of those Modena performances, something happened to her voice and she sang very well. For once the audience didn't boo and they applauded her with great warmth. It was like some divine intervention had sent her one good performance to prove to this soprano and her husband that the audience was *not* doing something Mirella and I had paid them to do. The audience was simply responding to the singing. If she sang well, they would show their appreciation.

I was so inexperienced at the time of that *Bohème* I just suffered through the soprano's bad feeling. I'm not sure that more experience with divas would have helped. When a soprano gets angry with you, there is little to do but wait for the anger to go away—like a bad storm. At the time, she had me upset—mainly because I don't want to be the cause of anyone's unhappiness. I did not let it affect my performances, although I suspect she would have liked that to happen.

She need not have worried. My Lucca *Bohèmes* were not great triumphs. The wig I had to wear made me nervous; it was a different conductor, different singers. Maybe I was afraid to make the soprano unhappy with good singing. I don't think so. My top notes were just not as sure, the whole voice not as pure as it had been at Reggio.

Considering my showing, I was overwhelmed after the first

performance at Lucca to receive a visit in my dressing room from the great tenor Tito Schipa. He was quite enthusiastic at what he had heard and gave me a lecture. "You have a beautiful voice," he said. "You should sing just as you are singing and don't listen to anybody. Do not push your voice to sound like someone else."

Like everyone else, I had great admiration for Schipa and had listened to his records for years, so these kind words were very thrilling for me. In addition, what advice could be more welcome than being told *not* to listen to advice?

Even with this unpleasant soprano and not singing my best, the Lucca Rodolfos went well and were a good experience for me. After all, it was the first time I had been paid to sing an opera—80,000 lira for two performances, about $50 a performance.

In the next months, thanks to Ziliani, I got to sing twice in Ireland—*Butterfly* and *Bohème* with an opera company in Dublin; later I sang *Rigoletto* in Carpi, the town near the farm where the Pavarotti family had lived during the war. Carpi is not a large town but they have a beautiful opera house there.

Even before I fulfilled these engagements, something very important happened. Ziliani had learned that the great conductor Tullio Serafin was looking for a tenor to sing the Duke in a production of *Rigoletto* being mounted for the Teatro Massimo in Palermo. Ziliani arranged for me to audition for Serafin the day after my last Lucca performance in *Bohème*.

Serafin was then eighty-three years old and a god in the operatic world. He was a top conductor, having conducted at all the great opera houses, including the Metropolitan. In addition, he had been musical director of the Rome Opera and later La Scala. This was the first time I would be seeking the approval of a major musical figure.

I was extremely nervous when I took the train down to

Rome to see Serafin. Our appointment was for four in the afternoon; I arrived at his apartment building at two. I was like a mule from nerves, pacing up and down in front of his building for two hours. I went into a cafe to drink something for my throat. Then at four on the dot, I went to his door and rang the bell.

A maid answered and said, "Are you the tenor from Modena whom the Maestro expects?" I said that I was. She showed me into a large salon with a grand piano, then said, "I will announce you right away." Very soon Serafin entered and greeted me in a businesslike way. He then turned to the maid and said, "Rosina, bring a glass of water for this young man."

"Don't trouble yourself, Maestro," I said quickly, "I stopped at a bar before coming up. I'm not thirsty."

He ignored me and said firmly to Rosina, "The glass."

Serafin sat down at the piano. I expected him to ask me to sing *"La donna è mobile"* or some other aria from *Rigoletto*. Instead he started on the first page of the score and had me sing through the entire opera. At the end of the second act, I was exhausted.

"I am thirsty," I said.

"I told you that time would come," he said, smiling for the first time. He nodded toward the glass of water.

As I was singing the final act, I began to feel that Serafin was satisfied with me. He never said so, but at one point he stopped me and said, "Now you understand that Maddalena is a whore. The Duke *knows* she's a whore. When you come to Palermo I want you to sing 'Bella figlia dell' amore . . .' the way Caruso did, with exaggeration, irony, not sincere . . ."

When I come to Palermo! That was the first I knew I had the part. I was beside myself with elation and could barely get through the rest of the opera.

That night taking the train back to Modena, I had ten thousand lira left to my name. What was that worth then?

About sixteen dollars. It was all the money that remained from the Lucca fee. I had to go second-class in a very dirty train, but I knew for a certainty there was no happier man in all of Italy that night.

Working under Serafin in Palermo was a marvelous experience. He was collapsing with age but such a brilliant musician, a *grandissimo capitano*, everyone had enormous respect for him. I respected him too, but I was also twenty-seven years old and a bit full of myself.

At the end of one of my arias, I made some variation—a higher note, or holding it too long, I forget what. Serafin forbade me to do it. At the dress rehearsal, he told me to go ahead if I wanted. He was usually so definite about everything, so rigid. I was surprised and asked him why he changed his mind.

"It seems to work for your voice," he said. Then he added dryly, "Don't forget, half of your ovation will be mine."

The soprano was Gianna d'Angelo. She had a beautiful voice and was a wonderful Gilda. She sang at the Met for a brief period. I've heard she went on to teach in a university.

One cloud hung over the company. The famous bass Ettore Bastianini was singing Rigoletto. He was not singing well and Serafin was very hard on him. In addition, Bastianini's behavior with the rest of the company was odd; he was short-tempered and unfriendly. We later learned that he was dying of cancer. He knew it, poor man, though none of the rest of us did. He sang for another year or two, but it was all over for him.

The performances went very well. Serafin was pleased with my singing and so were the people of Palermo. I was beginning to feel like an opera singer.

JOAN INGPEN

Discovering a Tenor

In the early 1960s I was working at Covent Garden with the title Controller of Opera Planning, which meant I was responsible for casting the repertoire. I later did much the same thing for Rolf Liebermann when he took over the Paris Opéra. I'm doing it now for the Metropolitan. In 1963 we had scheduled a *Bohème* with Giuseppe di Stefano. Our company tenor was on vacation, which worried me because di Stefano had a history of canceling performances at the last minute.

In Europe we don't always have a cover standing by for each role as they often do in the States; the distances are not so great. You can usually get on the phone and produce a replacement for just about anyone in a matter of hours. Usually, but not always. Since di Stefano was chancy and our regular tenor was not around, I saw us headed for a disaster.

I asked Covent Garden's administrator, Sir David Webster, for permission to search for a young Italian tenor—someone of Covent Garden quality but unknown enough that he would be willing to come to London just to cover, with no assurance he would get an opportunity to sing the role. Sir David told me to go ahead.

Dublin has an interesting organization called the Dublin Grand Opera Society which does a two-week season twice a year. At that time, the fall season was usually English singers; in the spring it was nearly always an *ad hoc* company of Italians. It was then the time for their 1963 spring season. I am Irish and enjoy running over from time to time, so I said to myself, "Suppose I go over to Dublin to see if by any chance they have a tenor this year."

When I got to Dublin in June, I came in to a *Rigoletto* performance and there was this large young man—not as big as he is now, but big—who was, at that time, very inept on the stage, singing a bit to the gallery and hanging on to his top notes—but, my God, what vocal material! A curious sidelight is that the

Rigoletto in that performance was played by a young unknown baritone named Piero Cappuccilli.

I announced to the friends I was with that I had found what I had come to Dublin to find. One of them said, "You can't mean that tenor! He doesn't know what he is doing on stage." I said I was aware of his faults but the incredible voice more than made up for them.

There is a funny sidelight to that Dublin *Rigoletto*. The Pope at that time, John XXIII, was gravely ill and expected to die. The manager of the Dublin company was on tenterhooks all day because there is a custom in Ireland that if the Pope dies during the day, performances must be canceled; if he dies after the first interval, the performance is completed, and the *following* day's performances are canceled.

The manager was frantic because if he had to cancel the *Rigoletto* he would have to return the ticket money but would still have to pay the fees. The Pope did die, but somehow the manager kept it from everyone until the opera had begun, then they created an interval after the prologue and made the announcement.

Much later, Luciano told me that the company knew all day that the Pope had died. Backstage at that opera house they couldn't understand why it wasn't announced earlier.

Luciano was so unknown, he was delighted to come to London for a modest fee. To make it more attractive for him, we promised Luciano he would definitely sing the last performance if he would cover di Stefano for the others. He came a little early so we could give him some extra stage coaching before the regular rehearsals began. The result of all this was, if I recall correctly, that di Stefano sang one and a half performances, canceled, and Luciano sang the rest—and with enormous success.

He made such a hit at Covent Garden that we asked him back immediately. That was the fall of 1963. In those days, you didn't book as far in advance as you must today. Now when you encounter a promising new singer, you have no parts open to offer him or her for three years.

We all took to Luciano personally as well as vocally. He spoke almost no English, but it didn't seem to matter with that personality of his. I remember we called him "Lucky." I haven't called him that for a long time, although I doubt if he'd mind if I did. We always maintained a special affection for him at Covent Garden because of the way he came to us—taking over someone else's role at the last minute and establishing his reputation.

One important thing for Luciano that grew out of the Covent Garden *Bohème* was a Glyndebourne engagement. The directors heard about his success as a replacement Rodolfo. They came up to hear him and offered him the part of Idamante in a production of Mozart's *Idomeneo*. Glyndebourne's approach to opera is the opposite end of the spectrum from the provincial Italian school that Luciano grew up in. And Mozart was a departure from his usual repertoire. It was funny watching them coach him in Mozart, but they are terribly good and very serious—which Luciano was quick to appreciate—and when Jani Strasser was in charge of musical preparation there, Glyndebourne was a marvelous place to polish vocal technique. Jani had a big influence on Luciano. This was an important step in Luciano's musical development.

The most significant thing to come out of Luciano's Covent Garden debut was his connecting with Joan Sutherland and her husband, Richard Bonynge. Before going to work for Covent Garden, I had been Joan Sutherland's manager—this was before she made her big hit in 1959 and became world-famous. We've remained good friends over the years.

In 1963, when I found Luciano, I rang up Ricky Bonynge and said, "I've got a tenor who I think is very good. I'm quite sure he can sing Joan's repertoire and, what's more, he's tall.

Height is a constant problem with Joan's leading men; there's always the danger they'll look like her little boy alongside her. But Luciano is taller than she is. The Bonynges, of course, loved him and persuaded managements to hire Luciano to sing a *Lucia* with Joan in Miami and then tour Australia with her. It turned out to be a marvelous thing for them all. Now, with his voice growing heavier, he's moving into other repertoires than hers.

I saw him only once when I was doing casting for the Paris Opéra. We offered him a *Bohème*, which he did. I didn't see him again until I came to work for the Met. By then he was a very big star and unhappy with the Metropolitan Opera. As far as I could tell, it was because he felt the Met was doing special productions for others but not for him.

When you have only four new productions a season, you choose them on all sorts of musical grounds rather than for a particular singer. The singers never see it that way. They see only that so-and-so is getting a new production and they are not; therefore, so-and-so must be considered more important than they are. It's always that way when you have two or three big stars concurrently. Look at Tebaldi and Callas. One always feels the other is being favored by management.

What it really came down to was that Luciano felt unloved by the Metropolitan. Had this been true, he would have had every reason to be angry, as he has the right to be loved, both as an artist and as a man.

I decided the whole thing was most unfortunate and that I should try to do something about it.

I phoned Luciano and asked if I might come talk with him at his apartment in the Hotel Navarro. He said he would give me lunch—he would cook spaghetti in spite of his diet. We didn't eat until about half past two. After lunch, when I tried to get down to serious talk, he kept trying to avoid it—he'd get up to answer the telephone and leave the room for one reason or another. I sat it out. A good friend of Luciano's later told me that Luciano had deliberately tried to wear me down, to annoy me, but I stood firm.

I was convinced that the misunderstanding was stupid, that he *had* to sing at the Met and that most of what bothered him wasn't true. We discussed what it was he most wanted to do; it was not out of the question. We are, in fact, going to do it soon.

Luciano is now a very big star. He is not stupid and he knows he's a big star, so he tries quite naturally to insist on what he wants, but, then, so do a lot of lesser singers. *Au fond*, I think he is a nice man with his colleagues and I understand that he in return has tried to help a number of young singers. I think he is not at all competitive with the singers he works with. I think he wants them all to be as good as possible. This is not true of all of *them*, I fear.

Since that first *Bohème* at Covent Garden, Luciano's stage work has improved enormously. It has developed little by little as he worked with different directors. He came up through Italian houses where acting and directing have never been too important. You can get away with things in Palermo that you can't do in London. For Italian opera lovers, it's enough that you can sing. I've particularly noticed a big improvement in his stage work since he's been directed in a few productions by Jean-Pierre Ponnelle.

Luciano is also very musical and picks things up quickly. When he repeats a mistake in a passage, he sometimes must have it pointed out, which doesn't always please him, but more often than not, before anyone says anything, he will say, "I think I'd better have a call on this. I know I always make a mistake here." He's really very serious about getting things right. And if he's doing a new role, I've never known him not to be thoroughly prepared.

In spite of his size, he always has great charm on the stage. I think it has something to do with his face. It registers an openness, a sincerity. Whatever it is that shines through in the face, it is something that has evolved as his career progressed. He didn't have it in the beginning. Maybe it has something to do with confidence and enjoying what he is doing. Whatever it is, that something in his face makes you forget the figure.

One way I think Pavarotti differs from many tenors is the extremely intelligent way he has handled his voice. I mean his waiting until his forties to attempt the heavier roles. The only thing I regret is that he no longer sings *The Daughter of the Regiment*. He still does *L'Elisir d'Amore*, but he was fantastic in *Daughter*. That production was done first in London for Joan Sutherland, and the critics didn't like Sandro Sequi's direction. The Met brought it over to America and New York loved the whole thing. Of course, they loved Luciano in London as well as in New York. How could you not? That incredible aria with nine high C's—and every night you sat back and didn't worry— it was always bang on. They went wild.

I understand there are opera houses so eager to get Luciano they let him select the other key members of the production. The Met can't do this. Naturally, we would never force artists who did not like each other to work together. I can understand Luciano's not wanting to accept a role until he knows who the conductor will be. But we could never let a singer say, "I will only sing on condition that I have X, Y, and Z." As far as I know, Luciano has never tried to do that. It's surprising that big stars also want to take on that impresario responsibility. Callas would always select her tenor and her conductor. One can't run a serious theater and allow that to happen—particularly if it means taking people one doesn't think are right.

Considering what a big star Luciano now is, he has very few of the star failings. I remember going to a large reception for him after one of the first concerts he did in New York. It was before I went to the Met and we started working together again. He was the hero of the moment and all the beautiful girls were lined up to meet him.

He saw me and came right over to me and said, "Of all the people who say they discovered me—I haven't forgotten—it was you, really."

After all these years and with his enormous success, I was very touched. You'd be surprised how many singers won't acknowledge who helped them when they were struggling to get established. Maybe the stardom makes them resist admitting they *ever* needed help. No matter how great the talent, there's usually one person whose support was essential to the success they later earned for themselves. Most prefer to forget this. Luciano never has. Maybe the feeling of gratitude he has toward me helped when I persuaded him not to stay angry with the Metropolitan.

JUDITH RASKIN

*Glyndebourne
Colleague*

I had a chance to sing in the Glyndebourne *Idomeneo* with Luciano in 1964 when he was just getting started, but it conflicted with something else I wanted to do more—sing in *The Rake's Progress* with Stravinsky conducting. I couldn't do both. At least I was there at the same time.

I regretted it at the time. I regret it more now. All of us at Glyndebourne in those days knew that Luciano was something special. People from the *Idomeneo* company would come pull us from rehearsals saying, "You've got to come over and hear this young Italian! He's incredible."

They had Luciano singing Idamante, a role usually sung by a mezzo-soprano. I thought the tessitura would be too much for him, but he handled it with ease. And, of course, there was that glorious sound!

I got to know Luciano at the parties the Christies would give for the visiting artists. The Glyndebourne Festival Opera is run by George Christie on his family's ancestral estate in Lewes, East Sussex. The Christies had young children and Luciano loved to play with them. Even without that, you couldn't help but notice Luciano when he walked into the room. He was so good-looking. He had a little bit of a bulge around the waist, but it was more a burly look, very athletic.

One thing that struck me right away about him was his eagerness to learn English. He didn't speak it very well in those days, though he was trying like mad to improve it. He would put together difficult questions, then ask you to correct his mistakes. So many Italian singers I know are reluctant to learn English. They claim it will damage their singer's diction or hurt their legato or something. I often suspect it's just laziness.

This was not Luciano. When we would encounter each other at these parties, he would make an agonized effort to converse with me in English. I'd known German singers who were conscientious about learning other languages but never an Italian.

79

Another aspect of Luciano that set him apart was an intellectual capability. This was quickly apparent, even in party conversation in flawed English. He had a curiosity about everything, but most particularly anything that related to his work. He was struggling hard to improve his artistry. The Mozart music did not come as naturally to him as the Puccini and Verdi music he was accustomed to. In his *Idomeneo* part, he had to work extremely hard, and you could see he was eager to.

George Christie commented on this aspect of Luciano. He recognized a dimension in him and an instinctive ability that was lacking in other Italian artists, one that enabled him to assimilate all that was being taught him. Like everyone else there in those days, the Christies were very fond of Luciano; George Christie refers to Luciano as "one of nature's virtues." Luciano's eye for all the pretty girls around the opera house earned him the nickname "Passion Flower."

His voice was somewhat lighter then but very beautiful. Now he likes to project his top notes in a way that gives a very penetrating, focused sound. It is highly effective but a little risky, because it puts you in danger of cracking. The terms "open" and "closed" are confusing when talking about vocal projection. To describe the way he hits those notes, Luciano uses the word "*stretto*," which means something like "tight" or "firmly grasped." A few critics have grumbled about the way he sings those high notes, but not the public. Regardless of who is right, the high notes are quite secondary to his incredible musical line. His phrasing alone would make him one of the greatest singers of our time, if not the greatest.

LUCIANO PAVAROTTI

Making a Name

After those first successes in the strange world of opera, you trade one set of frustrations for another. Audiences that seem to have lost their minds give you ten-minute ovations; the critics kiss their fingers and say, "Not since this or that great singer have we heard . . ."; the management throws itself at your feet and tells you how wonderful you were. Then you go home to await the cables and phone calls with job requests. And nothing happens.

It is part of that mysterious process of building a name, becoming famous. In opera, as with any other performing art, to be in great demand and to command high fees you must be good, of course, but you must also be famous. They are two different things. The first thing always happens well before the second. Occasionally the second, fame, never happens for good talents. (And very rarely it happens without talent.)

Sometimes, with good voices, fame is so slow to arrive that by the time the artist becomes widely known, he or she is no longer good, or not as good as they were. I think this was a little true with the great Maria Callas. By the time she became well known in New York, that is, when New York opera lovers learned of a remarkable singer named Maria Callas—a phenomenon in their midst whom they should not miss hearing—her voice had already deteriorated from what it had been during those remarkable years when she sang at La Scala.

It is possible that it takes longer to become famous in the opera world than in other fields. I am not talking about fame for opera singers outside the opera world—that is very rare and happens only to a few singers a generation. I mean fame establishing a name with the relatively small number of opera lovers. Even here the trip is discouragingly slow.

In more popular fields like film acting and popular singing, the performer makes a movie, records an album, or appears on a national television show. The entire public gets a chance to experience what the person has to offer and can decide "yes" or "no."

In opera you can have a triumph at a major house like Covent Garden. People in New York probably won't hear about it, but if they do, they may say: "Yes, but maybe it was a fluke evening," or "Perhaps the soprano made him sound good," or "Maybe they were starved for a decent tenor." It is easy for people to dismiss the reports unless they hear the singer themselves.

As for the impresarios, most are too busy to fly off to another country to hear every new singer they get good reports about. Important casting decisions are often made by conductors and music directors. This group is more frantically busy than the impresarios. Unless a James Levine or a Claudio Abbado happens to be conducting in the area where you are having your success and is urged by others to go and hear you, you are likely to be ignored by these powers in the opera business for years.

There is a network of sorts that spreads news about singers. Rudolf Bing used to have a man in Europe, Roberto Bauer, whose judgment he relied on about singers, and I understand that artists were occasionally signed to the Met, or at least brought over for an audition, merely on this man's recommendation.

And Kurt Herbert Adler, who directs the San Francisco Opera, valued the opinions of the late Otto Guth about promising singers. I suppose other impresarios have similar scouts, but for the most part they don't assign major roles unless they are personally familiar with the singer. Making your voice familiar to the top decision-makers in opera can take years.

You can't always count on the network, however. As an example, when Joan Ingpen invited me to sing at Covent Garden, it was because she happened to hear me in Dublin and liked my singing. She certainly had never heard of me. I had already made a promising debut in Italy, sung in several Italian opera houses, and had a big success with Tullio Serafin in Palermo. But Joan, who was responsible for finding new singers for one of the world's most important opera houses, had heard nothing of this. There is little reason why she would have. As with most fields, you must be discovered, not once, but again and again before you *stay* discovered.

It takes even longer to make yourself known to the opera audience. If your first successes are in Europe, Americans, for example, might read a favorable review in *Opera News* or one or two similar publications that cover opera internationally. Even if people in other countries should happen to see the review, the most they might do is make a mental note to watch for you when you show up at their opera house.

Then if through some incredibly lucky circumstances management is persuaded to try you and you are hired by the opera house in their city, you must sing better than Caruso and Gigli combined in order to make an impression. Just singing well will not do it. I sang at the Metropolitan for a number of years before the New York audience at large became aware of my existence. It was not enough to sing beautiful high C's in *Bohème* or *Lucia*. I had to sing *nine* high C's in a row in *The Daughter of the Regiment* before I won their attention.

The year after my debut, 1962, Ziliani got me a number of jobs singing around Italy. My repertoire was now three operas: *Bohème, Rigoletto,* and *Traviata* and I sang these roles in a few big cities like Genova and Bologna but also in a number of small ones like Forlì and Rovigo. My first appearance outside Italy was in Amsterdam in a role new for me, Edgardo in *Lucia di Lammermoor*. That was early in 1963.

That was a big year for me for building a reputation outside Italy. I sang *Bohème* at the Staatsoper in Vienna and the

Rigoletto in Dublin that led to Joan Ingpen's inviting me to cover for di Stefano at Covent Garden. (Just before Dublin, I had sung Pinkerton in Belfast.) All of this was 1963. Of course these significant appearances were interspersed with more routine ones in Palermo, Reggio Calabria, Naples—even a *Traviata* in Barcelona.

As for any particular excitement to singing in foreign countries, in those days I was concentrating so hard on my singing and the performances that I gave little thought to whether I was in Amsterdam, Belfast, or wherever. I am still a little like that when I sing in a new place, hardly knowing where I am until *after* the performance. And in those days I had no money to spare for staying over a few days to be a tourist. As soon as my engagement was finished, I would shoot right back to Modena to be with Adua and my baby daughter. Very soon it was two baby daughters.

While I had certain degrees of success in those appearances around Europe, the British were the first to accept me as a singer. I really think of myself as having been discovered in England. It started when Joan Ingpen of Covent Garden hired me to cover for Giuseppe di Stefano, who was to sing *La Bohème* there and who was an idol of mine. He had not been too well and often had to cancel. As everyone feared, he canceled after one and a half performances, and I sang the remaining ones. The London audiences were wonderful and made me feel like an important new star.

During those first weeks in England, I was living in a hotel and was quite lonely. I had studied English for four years in school and considered it my best subject. Years earlier when I went with my Modena chorale group to sing in Wales, I was horrified not to understand a word. Someone explained to me that the people in Wales were not speaking English, they were

86

speaking Welsh. I was relieved that my four years had not been a waste.

When I arrived in London to sing at Covent Garden, everyone still seemed to be talking Welsh. People would speak English to me; by the time they were on the third word, I was still on the first. It was awful. I started carrying a grammar around with me and worked hard on my English.

I spent much time alone in my hotel room watching television. I couldn't even understand that, so I would talk to the set in Italian. I got tired of that and finally had to shut up and listen. I think listening to so much television helped my English. Little by little my ear became accustomed to the sounds.

I had a few friends. When I am working in a strange city, I can usually establish contact with people—maybe not real friends, but companions with whom to eat and pass time. In those days, if they spoke Italian, I fell on them like lost relatives.

Sir Georg Solti, the music director of Covent Garden, had a secretary, a wonderful person named Enid Blech. She died recently, and it is a great loss. Enid had three grown children but had time to organize the complicated life of Sir Georg. She spoke many languages and could fly her own plane. I became good friends with this remarkable woman. She had a little cottage south of London in Sussex where she would invite me for weekend house parties.

One weekend while I was appearing in that initial Covent Garden *Bohème*, I went out riding a horse for the first time in my life. It was a rough experience, and I thought I would not sit down for a week. I was looking forward to returning to Enid's house and sitting in a cold tub for several hours, then having a nice dinner with Enid and her friends. I needed a quiet evening to recover from the horse.

I arrived back at the house to find everyone terribly excited. "Quick, Luciano," they said, "you have only a few minutes to change and get to the station. Di Stefano has canceled an appearance on 'Sunday Night at the Palladium,' and they want you to replace him."

I said I couldn't possibly. My behind was too sore and I was very tired.

"No, no," they cried, "you don't understand. 'Sunday Night at the Palladium' is the most popular TV show in England. It is like 'The Ed Sullivan Show' in the States. The whole country watches it. You must hurry."

I hurried. As they hustled me into the car for the station, someone shoved a steak sandwich into my hand, saying it was for my strength. I wanted to sit on it to cushion my pain. I arrived at the studio in time for one rehearsal before going on the air.

I never sang better. Maybe it was all the rushing—I was so happy to be allowed just to stand and sing—or maybe it was the excitement of such an important show . . . Something made me sing my best and the audience went wild. I think that TV studio audience was more open-minded than some opera audiences and certainly more so than some opera professionals. They had never heard of me, they were not opera lovers, but they went crazy. I learned later it was the same with the huge at-home audience.

That one television appearance made me known in England. So, in a sense, I was discovered twice in England—at the opera house and on television, one after the other. The producers of the television show were very pleased and invited me to come on the show again the next time I came to London—not to replace anyone, but as guest of honor myself. It was a very happy experience.

Other good things happened as a result of the Covent Garden appearance. My career picked up momentum. The directors of

the famous Glyndebourne Opera Festival heard that my singing in *Bohème* was worth a trip up to London. After hearing
me, they signed me to sing Idamante in Mozart's *Idomeneo*.
This was very different music than what I was accustomed
to singing. The musical change was part of what made singing
at Glyndebourne a wonderful experience for me. I learned to
sing in the Mozart style—*piano* and *legato*. Also, the Glyndebourne people have a very pure, almost cold approach to
opera; this was a good counterbalance to some of my Italian
excesses. Looking back, I realize I was a little bit wild when I
began. I was so thrilled to have a voice, I used it with little restraint and a lot of exuberance. The English are frank and don't
stand on ceremony, at least in professional matters. They didn't
hesitate to point out my faults. For that I am most grateful.

It was at that time that I met Joan Sutherland and her
husband Richard Bonynge—perhaps the most important encounter of my singing career. They asked me to audition for
them, then contracted me to join them on an opera tour they
had planned for 1965, almost two years later.

Ever since my debut in Reggio Emilia and signing with the
agent Ziliani, I had been having a flirtation with La Scala.
Shortly after my successful Reggio debut, Ziliani was trying
hard to sell me to the Scala management, and they were aware
of my voice and mildly interested but not enough to cast me in
a role.

I must say one thing about opera in my native country that
may sound bitter. Italians never let performers, singers in particular, be better than when they began. By that I mean that they
never allow for improvement, development of talent. When you
make your debut, if you are not acknowledged immediately as
the new Caruso, they immediately lose interest, dismiss you.

There is another problem. (Maybe it's because we were a

dominated people for so long.) Italians are skeptical of anything native, particularly tenors. On the other hand, anything foreign wins quick respect whether it is toothpaste or singers. It is sad that so many Italian singers must go abroad to achieve their success and are passed over in their own country.

I had been approached by La Scala, thanks to Ziliani, but nothing definite happened until *after* I had that success at Covent Garden. It was as though they were saying, "Ziliani says he's good, the critics in Emilia say he's good, Tullio Serafin says he's good—but they are all Italians. Now *Covent Garden* says he's good! He *must* be good."

I don't mean to belittle the importance of the Covent Garden success. It was the first time I had been hired by one of the great international opera houses. But I think it says something that it was not *my country's* great international house.

American colleagues tell me it used to be exactly the same in the States. Young American singers had to make a success in Europe before they were accepted at home. This is equally ridiculous, but it is a little more understandable because Europe was the home of opera. I think it is shocking that it ever was true in Italy, and still is.

And while I am in this sour mood, I must say one thing about my beloved Modena. This city never gave me any encouragement. In fact, one time I tried for a role in a production planned in Modena. It was a part I would have been perfect for, one I had already sung with success in far more important opera houses both in Italy and abroad.

There is a rule in Italy that a provincial opera house must hire local talent, and may go outside for singers only if there is no suitable local person available. When I offered myself to the Modena managers, they wrote me a letter saying they would not hire me as they did not think I was as good as another tenor they wanted to hire.

When I started out, there were many young tenors around who sang better than I did; this gentleman was not one of them. He has never been heard from since. So this letter from the Modena opera people made me angry. I try not to make comparisons, but when you are faced with a letter as nasty as this one, you can't help it. If I thought all the time about who was better than me, who was worse, I think I would have given up early.

I once heard my father asked by an interviewer what he enjoyed most about my success. Without hesitation Fernando replied, "Proving to all my Modena friends that they were wrong. They used to tell me that Luciano had a nice voice but not good enough for a career."

My relations with Modena are not as bad as Caruso's with his native Naples. Because of a cold reception one time, he refused to sing there again. He never did and announced that the city was only "for eating spaghetti." My feelings toward Modena are nothing like that. I have since sung there many times and would sing more if my schedule allowed. Still, there is a curious antagonism between the cities and the native sons who try for international fame and glory. The touchiness exists, I am sure, on both sides.

When I began my career, there were at least thirty tenors singing around the world who were better than I. I could probably name them all now if I had to. The great ones were del Monaco, di Stefano, Corelli, Bergonzi, Raimondi, Gedda, Vickers, Tucker. But there were many more who, if they were singing today, could have very good careers—better careers than they had then. Among tenors today, there are a few wonderful ones, but the top level is not crowded as it was at that time.

It is odd, because at the second level there are a great many today who sing beautifully. When I started out, there were more top-level tenors and fewer good second-level ones. Now the second-level has many who can go into a first-class production and not seem out of place.

When I was finally contracted to sing at La Scala, it was not, I am sorry to say, because of any enthusiasm toward me on the part of the management of that opera house. Although I had not performed at La Scala the directors knew me and my singing. At that time La Scala had a reciprocal arrangement with the Vienna Opera that they would supply singers—*speranzi* or young hopefuls—to fill emergencies. Often I would be sent up to cover for their tenors. Though they were in no hurry to have me sing from their own stage, the La Scala management didn't mind sending me to sing from Vienna's.

A prominent tenor at that time, Giuseppe Zampieri, was popular in Vienna and with the opera's music director, Herbert von Karajan. Zampieri was getting older and had so much money he didn't have to worry about singing all the time. They cast him in many of their productions, but he was not in good health and often canceled. I received a number of assignments in this way, and von Karajan became familiar with my voice. Through the same arrangement I was able to sing a concert in Moscow at this time which was an incredible success. How strange to succeed in Moscow before Milan.

For two years La Scala had been doing a production of *La Bohème* conducted by von Karajan. Many different tenors had sung Rodolfo in the various performances of that production. In 1965, toward the end of the second year, they had run out of tenors. Von Karajan asked me to sing the last two performances. So for my first appearances at La Scala, I had von Karajan to thank, not the directors of La Scala.

La Scala's audience, which is not the easiest, was enthusiastic about my Rodolfo, and the directors of La Scala also were pleased. We started discussing other roles I might do for them.

They asked me to sing Rossini's *William Tell* and were willing to pay what for me was an incredible fee.

It is not difficult to imagine how much I wanted to make a proper debut at La Scala, but I declined the role. I told them that if I tried to sing that part it would ruin my voice and I would have the shortest career in the history of opera. They replied that it was enough for them that I sing *William Tell*.

Ziliani was more understanding and asked me what I wanted to sing instead. I told him *La Sonnambula*. He was surprised and asked why. "Because," said I, "I want to prove to you and to myself that I am not afraid of challenges—provided they are within the range of possibility for my voice. But I would not run the risk of ruining my voice with a role that is too heavy for me—even to get to La Scala."

Finally, La Scala put me to work singing the Duke in *Rigoletto*. I sang it many times. Eventually the Scala directors offered me, not *Sonnambula*, but a later Bellini opera, *I Capuleti e i Montecchi*. So it was in the role of Tebaldo in this opera that I did my first full-scale La Scala production; that is, where I created a leading role in one of their productions.

So my first appearance in a major international opera house was due to an Irish woman, and my first appearance at La Scala was due to an Austrian. It is only because I am Italian and know our faults so well that I am sensitive to them and take pleasure in nagging about this.

Although I regarded von Karajan as my champion, even he had only asked me to replace another tenor. While this is better than *never* being invited by him to sing, it is not the same as if you were first choice. Finally it happened.

The following year, von Karajan was assembling a production of the Verdi *Requiem* that was to be a memorial concert at La Scala for Arturo Toscanini. The concert would take place in January 1967, ten years after Toscanini's death. Von Karajan asked me to be the tenor. You must be a European, perhaps a singing European, to know what it meant to me to be selected by this great conductor for such an important musical event. It made me very, very happy.

With this step on the ladder, I had come a long way in the six years since my debut. I had made successful debuts at both Covent Garden and La Scala. In 1965, the year following my first Covent Garden appearance, I had sung *Sonnambula* with Joan Sutherland and *Traviata*, both at Covent Garden and both big successes for me personally. And now Europe's top musician had selected me from all the world's tenors to sing in a concert honoring one of the greatest conductors of all time.

Professionally, I could now feel that I had arrived. But if I wanted to be considered an opera singer of truly international rank, there was still one important area where I had yet to make a mark: America.

JOAN SUTHERLAND
AND
RICHARD BONYNGE

Interview at
Les Avants

BONYNGE: The first time I heard Pavarotti was at an audition he was doing at Covent Garden in 1963. I was surprised by that extraordinary voice. It was fat and had a ring to it and went sailing right up with no trouble. It was also in very good technical condition, even in those days. As soon as I heard him I asked Frank Tate, who was managing an Australian tour we had coming up in two years, to engage him for that tour. Early in 1965, several months before the Australia tour, we were in Miami to do *Lucia* and our tenor, Renato Cioni, was asked to go to Paris to do *Tosca* with Callas—obviously a very exciting thing for him to do. But it was a big problem for us. There were only a few weeks to go before the performance; not much time to find a replacement. Miami opera people are very name conscious; they wanted to get a big name to replace Cioni, but they couldn't find one. They rang everyone under the sun. I told them they should get this young boy Pavarotti. They didn't want to at first but eventually they were so stuck, they agreed. That was how he came to make his American debut. Of course, he had an enormous success. The public loved him—the public always loves him. That was the beginning of his love affair with America—and that love affair has paid off very handsomely.

SUTHERLAND: His stage work was very limited in those days— very limited indeed. But when you are talking about opera, the acting is secondary. When someone has a voice like Pavarotti's, how he deports himself on the stage is not all that important. And Luciano was so *appealing*. He was intensely sincere in everything he did. Being an athlete, he had a youthful grace about himself. From his background in sports, he was coordinated so that he moved well. And a final thing that is important to me, for a tenor, he is incredibly tall.

BONYNGE: His only weakness was his lack of experience. The voice was already first-rate. It is the kind of great natural voice that comes along once in a century. If such a voice had not been abused, and Luciano's had not, it merely must develop naturally

97

—and he's allowing his to do that. To a very great effect. His father is a marvelous singer. I can remember his father singing in Italy; we would all be together at a restaurant and Fernando would get up and sing. He had a wonderful sound—complete with the top C and everything. So, singing is obviously in Luciano's blood.

The Australian tour that we took Pavarotti on was arranged by a venerable old firm called J. C. Williamson's. For years the company had been run by four Tate brothers. Three of them were deceased. The last brother, Frank, was a very, very old man. At the beginning of his career he had been involved in the famous tour of Australia that Melba had made with the company in 1911; that tour was a major milestone in Australia's cultural history. He decided he wanted to conclude his career by bringing Joan on a similar tour. Of course, this sort of tour—an entire opera company wandering around Australia with sets and costumes for seven operas—is almost totally impractical in these days, so we had to do the tour on a shoestring. Frank Tate was a very tough manager but he was marvelous to deal with.

SUTHERLAND: Frank wanted us to do *Bohème, Butterfly*—all the operas he knew the Australians would flock to. He was terrified of the works we wanted to do—*Sonnambula, Semiramide*. Finally, he let us do what we wanted.

We had only a three-week rehearsal period. We opened in the first week with three operas, then added an opera a week. That meant every minute during the first weeks we were either performing or rehearsing the next opera. I don't think any of us have ever worked so hard before or since.

At the tour's beginning, it looked as if Frank Tate had been right about doing more popular operas. The first performances with me and Pavarotti singing the leads were not sold out. After the first two or three, however, you couldn't get a ticket for anything. They'd never heard *Sonnambula* before, but with a

98

voice like Luciano's—and with me singing the soprano—well, the audiences loved it and spread the word. It was the same with *L'Elisir d'Amore*, which Luciano sang with another soprano. At first it wasn't all that sold out, but people loved Pavarotti and told others. Soon, tickets for that were impossible to get, as well.

BONYNGE: The operas we did in addition to *Sonnambula* and *L'Elisir* were *Lucia* and *Traviata* also with Luciano, then *Semiramide*, *Faust*, and *Eugene Onegin* without him.

I don't think any of us will forget that last performance in Melbourne. It was *Sonnambula* and both Joan and Luciano were in top form. I don't think Australia had ever seen anything like it. Frank Tate said the tour was the culmination of his career in management. He died only a few weeks after that.

Sir Frank told us that it was the happiest company they had ever had. Others connected with the tour said the same thing. For all the backbreaking schedule, there were amazingly few problems. For one thing, it was the only Australian opera tour that actually finished what it set out to do. We had eight performances a week—not one was ever canceled. Everyone got on remarkably well. A few people dropped out, but most everyone else stayed and had a good time. We even had a few romances grow out of that tour. Some of the people are still together.

SUTHERLAND: And Luciano loved it all. He had enormous fun. He'd be out on the beach playing all sorts of games, doing handstands, throwing people around. He was so athletic.

BONYNGE: Originally, we were going to do five cities, but we had to cut Perth because of finances. It was too far away. The tour ended up being Sydney, Melbourne, Adelaide, and Brisbane. The company was interesting from another point of view besides being important in Pavarotti's development; it formed the nucleus of what is now the Sydney Opera. All of our chorus and orchestra was made up locally and about a quarter of the lead singers were Australian. A good many of them now sing with the Australian opera. A number of the other members of this

company have gone on to important international careers—
Elizabeth Harwood, Alberto Remedios, Clifford Grant, John
Alexander, Joseph Rouleau, Spiro Malas. Actually, the Australian opera was just forming at that time and they disbanded
temporarily to join forces with us on that tour. Some of their
principals sang in our chorus. One of the girls in the chorus
went on to sing Brünnhilde at the Coliseum in London. Another
boy went to Germany where he had quite a big career. Luciano
got along well with all of them and he was good to work with—
very amenable to direction and quick to pick up things.

BONYNGE: We all thought he sang marvelously from the start
but, like all *real* singers, Luciano was never satisfied with himself
and worked to improve his singing. He admired Joan's technique enormously. Everytime I'd turn around, there he'd be
with his hands on my wife's tummy trying to figure out how
she supported her voice, how she breathed. Luciano is dead-
serious about singing and worked constantly to get better. He's
continued to do so throughout his career.

SUTHERLAND: But it was coaching by example only. I never
taught anybody in my life. Whatever he learned from me he
learned from observation and close contact—physical example is
really the best instruction. Neither Richard nor I ever doubted,
from the first time we heard him, that he was sure to have an
important career.

BONYNGE: Luciano began to relax and enjoy the rigorous singing schedule, just as we all did. He was thrilled when, after singing "*Una furtiva lagrima*" from *L'Elisir,* the audience made him
sing it a second time, then a *third* time. Pretty soon he would
get upset if they didn't ask him to sing it three times.

SUTHERLAND: I don't think he'd mind if he didn't have to sing it
so many times today. The aspect of his voice that most struck us
was its distinctive quality. If you hear a lovely voice but have no
idea who is singing, it's just a sound. But with him, you knew
immediately that it was Luciano singing.

BONYNGE: If anything, the distinctive quality has become more pronounced over the years. And the voice has become bigger, there's no doubt of that. It always has the brilliance, but it grew in volume. Some people worry over all the ballyhoo about him being the world's greatest tenor, but he enjoys it, I think. He seems to get fun out of it. And why shouldn't he? It's probably the truth.

SUTHERLAND: Besides the Australian tour, another episode stands out in our work with Luciano over the years. That was *The Daughter of the Regiment* which we did in London in 1967, then again in 1972 in New York. It was marvelous for both of us. He loved the role and had fun playing it. Then he had the brillance of those nine high C's in one aria which he could ping out without any sign of effort.

BONYNGE: He and Joan together in that were something quite special. Here she was, the mature lady skipping around playing the regimental sweetheart and he was a big Italian boy playing a teenager. They had a lot of fun. Joan and Luciano work extremely well together—they both have big voices, they listen to each other and they blend very well. Also, they are the right size for each other.

SUTHERLAND: There have been other high spots with Luciano besides *The Daughter*. The first time we did *Trovatore* together in San Francisco, he was fantastic. His *"Di quella pira"* was unforgettable.

BONYNGE: Luciano has been very intelligent in managing his career. For a long time he sang the very high roles and made his big reputation. Now, as he becomes more mature, he has started gradually and carefully to undertake roles in the dramatic repertory that he can tackle. He doesn't do anything without first giving it a great deal of thought. So far, he has not put a foot wrong. He's brought off *Gioconda, Turandot, Trovatore*. These are all very tough roles. Where many other tenors have been tempted by *Otello*, Luciano has not been. He certainly could sing *Otello* later—he could sing it today if he wanted to, but I think he is very smart to wait; he will last longer. His voice still has all the bloom, all the blossom, and he'll keep that for a long time. He cares about singing and he's very conscientious about the way he sounds.

SUTHERLAND: And he makes these decisions himself. He's the master of his own career. His manager, Herbert Breslin, has given him much good advice and I think his old singing teachers in Italy, Campogalliani and Pola, were an enormous influence on him about using and taking care of his voice.

BONYNGE: But Luciano himself has tremendous intelligence about the entire thing. He knows how far he can push people, he knows what he can get from people, he plays with his audience—I mean, in a good way. I think he enjoys his career. He's terribly career-oriented. He loves singing; he loves the response he gets back from the audience. He loves the financial rewards; he loves everything about it. Why shouldn't he?

SUTHERLAND: He's worked very hard at his career; anything he gets out of it, he deserves. He enjoys life and he takes his breaks —which is more than I can say for *some* people, Richard.

BONYNGE: I know there are those who say we helped Luciano get started. He didn't need any help from us or anyone else. Other than getting him hired for Miami and Australia, we didn't do anything special for him. Of course, after Australia, we frequently asked him to sing opposite Joan through various managements, but his career started moving so fast, it rarely worked out for us to be together.

I mentioned him to the people at London Records, but like most record companies, they don't want to sign anyone until he or she is a big star. Eventually, they signed Luciano, however, and I'm certain they're glad they did.

SUTHERLAND: I'm very gratified he's been able to do as many performances with me as he has.

BONYNGE: There are other things we admire about the way

Luciano has handled his career. He lives well, but he's careful with his money. This gives him a great security. He doesn't have to rush around the world singing every role that's offered him. He can sing what he wants to, what is good for him.

SUTHERLAND: He's very smart about not jetting around too much. We were just talking about that—how many careers have been shortened by the jet. Management always tries to make it appear a simple matter to fly to this country or that to sing one or two performances. They say, "It's only a two-hour flight," or "It's only three hours . . ." or "It's only a six- or eight-hour trip from New York to Europe." But these journeys take a great deal out of you.

When I started out, it was much different. I would stay a good length of time in one place and I would always allow myself a breathing space so that, once I got to a new place, I didn't have to perform straightaway. Some years ago in Australia on the tours of the music clubs you popped in and out of places, but there the hops were small—just from one town to another. That is very different from singing at the Metropolitan, then shooting off to Los Angeles to sing a performance, then back to the Metropolitan. Or, being in London and flying off to Vienna for a day or two. It really is exhausting, terrible in every way.

When I was getting started, I used to travel by boat. If I was coming from Europe to America, I would take a ship from Southampton or Genoa. In those days I used to travel with costumes. The companies often didn't want to bother with making me a costume for this one or that one, so I had my own costumes. That was a lot of stuff to carry; another reason for taking a ship. So, you had an enforced rest; from Genoa, it was over a week. I try to apply that sort of sensible schedule to the jet age, but it is not easy. Luciano does it, I think.

He stays for a good period in one city before flying off to another part of the world. And he doesn't do nearly as many of those short in-and-out appearances that others do. Of course, younger singers starting out don't have that much choice. There are very few real companies where young singers can settle down, work regularly, and learn their trade. Beginners must take the jobs available. But in a way, the newcomers must share the blame for what's happening. They all want to be stars overnight. People like Caballé, Pavarotti, and me—we all worked extremely hard for years before we got broad recognition. Caballé was singing away in Germany and Switzerland for years, doing fantastic performances, I'm sure, and no one paid much attention.

I was seven years at Covent Garden learning my trade. Pavarotti sang in smaller houses around Europe and in places like Miami and did grueling work like our Australian tour. That tour didn't make him famous. But it was marvelous for him at that stage of his career because he was able to consolidate four big roles; later this stood him in good stead at the Met and other big houses.

BONYNGE: The trouble with the young singers is they don't have the patience, for one thing, and they don't know how to say no.

SUTHERLAND: But also, Richard, the companies don't exist in the same fashion. They use guest artists everywhere. There are no real companies except maybe in Germany. Covent Garden is not the sort of company it was—neither is the Met—although the Met was never really that much of a company—it is an international house that uses guest artists.

Some of the Americans are very badly treated, some who should have had important careers there and never did. For young people starting out, it's much tougher now for them to develop as they should . . .

BONYNGE: I don't think it's any tougher at all, my dear. There are *good* artists and there are *bad* artists and there are *mediocre* artists. The good ones, who know what they are doing and know how to look after their careers, have great careers.

SUTHERLAND: That's always been true and always will be. But I think many want to be great stars too soon and in their late twenties are singing roles that are way beyond them.

BONYNGE: This is also the fault of the managements.

SUTHERLAND: And that's where Luciano has been so sensible because he has never had any difficulty saying no. When the managements have come to him and said, "Don't you think this or that would be a terrific idea for you," he says no. Then he will politely suggest something else. He usually gets his way. But if he doesn't get something he feels is right for himself, he passes up the engagement entirely.

I hope we can work out an opera with Luciano soon again. Right now we don't have any stage plans together. Of course, there is the televised concert with Marilyn Horne.

BONYNGE: We were asked to do a *Lucia* for television with him in Houston but, unfortunately, we were engaged in Holland at that time; something we couldn't get out of.

SUTHERLAND: The first television concert we did from Lincoln Center in 1979 was such an exciting night. We were all three terribly nervous, I think, because none of us had ever done anything quite like that. We did some very nervy bits, but I think it came off well. Someone later showed me a slide of the *son et lumière* they had in front of Lincoln Center before that concert. Two gigantic pictures of me and Luciano. They were *huge;* they covered the front of the whole opera house! I said, "Oh, life-size is big enough!"—but it was quite spectacular.

BONYNGE: Aside from loving his voice, we greatly enjoy working with him. He is a nice, gentle person to work with. He knows what he wants, he doesn't say yes to everything you ask of him, but he's got a certain humility. He knows what he can do—and does it—and he's got great charm. Working with him is a pleasure.

SUTHERLAND: He can take a stand on doing something his way— but you can always work it out with Luciano.

BONYNGE: I never ask him to change his way of doing something unless I have what I feel is a very sound reason. Usually, the reason will be that I think the change will be better for him and his voice. He is always open to suggestions—and he is not shy about making them about my part of the work. Sometimes he will say to me, "Ricky, why don't you take it a little slower in this spot . . ." Often he is right. He has a great innate musical feeling.

One problem about Joan and Luciano working together is that, except for the biggest theaters like the Met, few opera houses are able or willing to spend the money to have them both together at the same time. Even when they can, it's so difficult to coordinate schedules. If we had our choice, they would sing together much more.

LUCIANO PAVAROTTI

Journeyman in Miami and Australia

Everywhere I go to sing an opera, they have a different approach to productions. The criticisms of my early performances are true, I didn't pay attention to my stage work, and concentrated only on my singing. Glyndebourne and Covent Garden helped me develop these other aspects of operatic production, but I still was a long way from being a brilliant stage actor.

Many things have led me to improve as an actor. First among them was my growing security about the voice. As the vocal technique that was correct for me became automatic, I could give more attention to my acting performance. Even today, I must concentrate quite a bit on the musical side of things, but only on interpretation, much less on voice production; there is some mind left over for the characterization.

I was influenced and improved by many of the outstanding directors I have worked with. Each time one of a number who have directed me as Rodolfo, for example, gives me something to do that strikes a note of truth in me, it becomes a permanent part of my interpretation—provided, of course, subsequent directors don't persuade me to eliminate it.

It is such an odd thing about being an opera singer. It takes years and years of the most difficult and dedicated work to develop your voice, assuming you have a voice, to the incredible degree of proficiency and training to be able to negotiate the scores of Puccini, Verdi, Mozart. You finally make your debut and the world says, "Not bad. Let's hear you in this opera, now that opera . . ."

You have arrived as a working singer on the international opera circuit. All those years of struggle are now to be rewarded. You are accepted in your chosen profession, you look forward to many years singing as well as you can, perhaps improving your singing as you earn a good living. But they tell you, "Wait. Singing well is not enough. You must also be highly skilled in another profession. You must be a good actor as well."

It is not as though they were requesting a supplementary talent that was related to music—a good ear for harmony, for instance, or a firm sense at rhythm. They are asking you to be accomplished in a totally different performing art, one as difficult and demanding, in its way, as singing. Many Italians feel it is an unreasonable demand and don't make the effort. Others think it is beneath their dignity to try anything that might not be done at the same high level as their singing. They would rather be non-actors than bad actors.

I was a little like many of my fellow Italian singers in this regard when I started out. I thought it was enough if I sang well and gave an approximation of the character. I was also afraid, if I tried acting too strenuously, it might make a worse effect than trying very little. But I soon changed. I don't like doing anything badly, if I can improve. Also, I can't stay near anything too long without wanting to throw myself in it. I have worked very hard on my acting over the past fifteen years and I think I have made progress. Now I almost pay as much attention to the acting as I do to the singing.

I always keep in mind one thing, however. It is not necessary to be Laurence Olivier to be a good opera performer. You must be believable and definitely "in" the character, but as for pulling emotion from the audience, in opera that is more the job of the music and your interpretation of it. Laurence Olivier must do it with his acting alone. Also, I find that singers who get highly involved in their dramatic performance often allow the vocal part to suffer.

The director of my first opera in America, the *Lucia* in Miami, with Joan Sutherland, was a nice American of Italian extraction named Anthony Stivanello. Rehearsal time was short, as it so often is. When you are doing a standard opera like *Lucia* and it is not a big-budget production, directors have reason to assume the singers will know the part and be able to deliver a decent performance with little rehearsal.

I guess Stivanello did not feel my acting as Edgardo was decent. He took me up on the roof of my Miami hotel, the McAllister, and worked with me for hours. We went through the entire opera, scene by scene, just the two of us working frantically to reduce my awkwardness. He was a great help to me and I think the extra trouble he took has had results in all my later performances.

I was still a long way from being a polished actor. Certain of my roles—Rodolfo and Nemorino, for example—are particularly close to me and are less difficult for me to get into. But other characters are further removed from me, and I have to work harder. Not always with success, I might add. A critic once wrote about my acting: "Mr. Pavarotti never went out of character. Then how could he? He never got in it."

I was invited to Miami at the request of the director of the Miami Opera, a dear man named Arturo di Filippi, who had been a tenor himself. He had never heard me sing so I imagine he asked for me at the suggestion of Ricky Bonynge and Joan Sutherland, but I shall always be grateful to him for giving me that chance merely on the recommendation of others. This Miami *Lucia* in February 1965 was a last-minute assignment. Immediately after hearing me at Covent Garden in 1962, Ricky Bonynge signed me up to sing four tenor roles in a fourteen-week tour of Australia that he and his wife were then planning far off in the future—the summer of 1965. The Miami *Lucia*, therefore, came about *before* the Australian tour; the invitation was given me long after I had been signed to sing with Joan Sutherland in Australia.

I was excited about Australia, but Miami would be my first performance in America and I was very excited and very anxious to do well. I am happy to report that the opening was a great success. The critics were very nice about my singing and Dr. di Filippi, who had treated me like a son throughout the rehearsal period, was so pleased he gave me a bonus. Since most opera companies work on a tight budget, such gestures are not common.

Naturally the Miami audiences went crazy for Joan, but they liked me very much too. It is so much easier to become enthusiastic about a singer's performance if you have been told in advance that he or she is something special. The Miami operagoers had heard nothing about me. Still, they gave me their approval without reservation. For that reason, I will always have a warm spot in my heart for Miami. (I have many such spots but I like to think there is plenty of room.)

One of many nice things that resulted from that first Miami appearance was meeting a lively young woman named Judy Drucker who was singing in the opera chorus. Judy and I became good friends and have remained friends over the years. Today she runs the Great Artists Series sponsored by Temple Beth Shalom in Miami Beach. These concerts of hers are probably the most important cultural events in Miami each season; she presents such artists as Vladimir Horowitz, Isaac Stern and —I am pleased to say—Luciano Pavarotti.

Since Judy has become so important, and today hires me to sing, I make it a rule always to be particularly nice to the ladies of the chorus.

Miami is a wonderful city with a vigorous cultural life. I am always happy to go back today, not only because I like nice weather and playing tennis. I have many, many Miami friends and I think of it warmly as the first place in the United States to welcome me so wholeheartedly. Of course the major American cities for opera are San Francisco, Chicago, and New York. While in Miami I felt I had established a beachhead. I had to conquer those three cities before I could consider myself a success in America.

In the meantime, I had a great deal of singing to do in Australia.

In June 1965, just four months after our Miami *Lucia*, I met Joan Sutherland and Richard Bonynge in Australia to begin rehearsals for the four operas I would sing on their tour: *La Traviata, La Sonnambula, Lucia di Lammermoor,* and *L'Elisir d'Amore*—each with a difficult tenor role. The tour would also present (without me) *Faust, Eugene Onegin,* and *Semiramide* to make seven operas in all. If I was eager for work, I now had it.

I saw in this impossible schedule a very big opportunity for me. Despite the successes I had been having in opera houses around Europe, one thing about my singing still bothered me. It was the consistency of my vocal quality. Some nights I sang well, but too many nights I sang less well. All singers have this problem to an extent, and no one can eliminate it completely. The voice depends on too many variables besides the basic equipment. Your mood, your physical health, your confidence, your anxieties—all of these things can affect the sound that comes out of your mouth.

I mentioned earlier how important I felt it was for people attempting singing careers to master their nerves. Well, it is important to master all of these other variables as well, or else singers should at least be able to minimize the ability of these external elements to alter the voice. I did not feel I had done this sufficiently. It is very frustrating to sing badly when you know you can sing well. I knew I had a voice, but I did not yet feel I was its complete master.

Joan Sutherland has one of the most remarkable voices of our age, perhaps of all time. It was amazing for me to watch her, night after night, on that backbreaking schedule of performances sing the most difficult music written for her voice, and never vary in the superb level of her singing. I said to myself, "She must know something."

I wanted to learn her secret, to be able to sing as well and as strenuously without showing signs of wear. Until I could, I would not feel comfortable in an opera career. I would spend half my time worrying that I might lose my voice, the other half worrying because I *had* lost it.

I began studying her and asking her questions. She was wonderful about it, but warned me not to try it her way unless my body was ready, unless I was in the proper physical shape. Basic to her method was the support she gave her voice from the diaphragm. Joan is a big woman and she is very strong. Her torso muscles work hard when she is singing. She seems just naturally strong and doesn't appear to work at it, but she knows others are not so lucky; they must first develop the muscles needed for support.

If your body is not in shape to sing this way, she told me, you will push and push but keep falling back on your throat to make the sound. This will ruin your voice. That is why you shouldn't try it, unless you are in the right physical shape.

She showed me a number of exercises that would strengthen the key muscles. I worked very hard at them. I also watched her constantly, often putting my hands on her rib cage to feel what was happening when she sang. (I did this only off stage; I doubt the action would have helped our director's conception of *Lucia*.)

All voice students hear of the importance of strong support and correct use of the diaphragm. If you are young, however, and blessed with a strong, beautiful voice, you don't worry too much. Why work so hard when the sound that emerges pleases everyone? The answer is that without working hard and supporting the voice from below, it will tire quickly and it may not be there the day you need it. Then eventually it will not be there at all.

On this Australian tour I needed my voice all the time.

Everytime I turned around, it seemed, I was making my entrance for another four hours of death-defying singing. Joan could do it; I was determined that I could too.

That Australian tour was a great period for a self-improvement attempt by me. In addition to vocal technique, I continued to work hard on my acting, although our director didn't think so at one point. As we were approaching our first performance of *L'Elisir*, he pulled me aside and said, "You know, Luciano, it is not enough to sing the role well, you must act it too."

I said to him, "Please don't worry. I have been working on the music during rehearsals, but the acting, the way I'll portray Nemorino on the stage, has all been accumulating inside me. It is all in my head. In the performance, you'll see what I mean."

And my performance was a fantastic triumph. The critics applauded my characterization as much as my singing. The director was very pleased. He was a trusting man; in that instance, at least, he didn't regret it.

I also worked very hard on my English during those months in Australia. The big effort, however, was to perfect my singing technique. When I finished the tour my diaphragm was much stronger, my use of it more automatic, and my vocal cords were in far better physical shape.

When I got home, the doctor who looked after my vocal cords was delighted. He always worried that after strenuous singing they looked pallid, a little sick. Now he found them looking pink and healthy. He said, "You are singing correctly, you are breathing correctly . . . the strength comes from your diaphragm, not your throat. You are no longer straining your throat; it is at last healthy again."

I think that this tour of Australia was the final important experience of my education as a singer. I have learned a lot since, and I hope I go on, like Gigli, studying and learning till I

stop singing forever. But with Joan's diaphragm-support technique, I was able to sing at the level I knew was my very best,
and do it night after night without signs of strain.

My voice still gets tired and I still must be careful not to
sing too much (or talk too much), but since Australia the
amount I can sing without wearing myself out is far greater than
before. I am grateful to Joan for many things, but most of all
for that.

LUCIANO PAVAROTTI

*An Assault on
New York*

When I made my San Francisco debut in *La Bohème* in 1967, it was very important for me to have a big success. The city has a strong tradition of opera, and their company, under the direction of Kurt Herbert Adler, is one of the three in the United States, with Chicago's Lyric and New York's Metropolitan, that is of top international standards. For an opera singer, success in America is almost as tough as winning the Triple Crown is for a horse. To win the Derby, the Preakness, and the Belmont Stakes is like a singer making a big success in San Francisco, Chicago, and New York.

For one thing, the three companies watch each other carefully. If word travels across the Atlantic that a singer has made a good showing at one of Europe's opera houses, there is something a little abstract about the information. But if the Metropolitan Opera management learns that a singer has conquered San Francisco or Chicago, they seem unable to shrug off the news.

The San Francisco *La Bohème* was with Mirella. Working with her is always a good experience for me. So is *La Bohème*. And so, it turned out, is San Francisco. I fell in love with the city, quickly made many friends there, and have never stopped feeling at home the many times I have returned. Luckily, on that first visit, my voice did not let me down, so that the people of San Francisco returned the love I was beginning to feel for them.

I still had Chicago and New York to go. The San Francisco Opera asked me to return the following year, 1968, to sing *Lucia* with Margarita Rinaldi and, at last, the Metropolitan's director, Sir Rudolf Bing, invited me to make my New York debut in *La Bohème*, also with Mirella, immediately after I finished the San Francisco *Lucia* performances.

While singing in San Francisco that fall, I contracted a case of Hong Kong flu that I was unable to shake. The illness grew so bad, I had to cancel one of the *Lucia* performances. I proceeded on to New York, growing more and more nervous as the date for my Metropolitan Opera debut drew near and the flu got worse rather than better.

I have since had my ups and downs with the Metropolitan, yet it is impossible to overestimate the importance of a success at the Met in the career of anyone hoping to reach the top of the operatic profession. Put most simply, it is almost impossible for a singer to have an important international career without making a resounding success at the Met. Some have. Beverly Sills, for example, was an established star well before she sang at the Met. For the most part, however, it is extremely rare to be considered a top-rank singer by the American musical establishment without the Met's stamp of approval.

That, alone, is enough to make any singer paralyzed with fear about a Met debut. In my case, I knew that reports of my San Francisco success had reached New York and that the New York opera public was waiting to hear if the favorable advance reports were justified. Part of you is happy that you arrive with a history of success, but part of you would prefer to sneak into town, sing your role as inconspicuously as possible.

You reason that if you are good, you will quickly become conspicuous, but if you sing less well than usual, no one will notice. Of course, this is a fantasy. Rudolf Bing and others at the Met will notice because that is their job. The same is true for the critics. In any case, my hope of slipping into New York unnoticed, however unrealistic that may have been, was out of the question with my San Francisco acclaim. Now I was to make my Met debut in November of 1968, in *La Bohème*. New York, always skeptical about non-New York successes, was waiting for me.

I knew very well that I have had much good luck in my career: the agent Ziliani coming to my Reggio Emilia debut to hear another singer; Joan Ingpen coming to Dublin to find a tenor for Covent Garden when I happened to be singing there; Joan Sutherland eager for a tall tenor to take on tour. Now I was to pay for it all, these strokes of good fortune, by an illness I couldn't shake before this crucial date.

I know there are plenty of other professions where an everyday illness can be a disaster—a sick businessman might miss an important meeting, a salesman a rare sales opportunity, or an athlete a crucial game. But it would be difficult to find anything comparable to an opera singer facing his debut at the Metropolitan Opera with a bad case of the flu.

Behind all the anxieties, which become crushing as the moment approaches and you still feel miserable, is the knowledge that, should you be forced to cancel, everyone will assume you did it from fear. Nothing less than the sight of your dead body laid out in Lincoln Center Plaza will convince the public otherwise.

I coughed constantly, my throat was sore, and my fever was running to 102. My old friend from Modena, Mirella Freni, was singing Mimi to my Rodolfo. Mirella, adorable creature that she is, was as upset as I was at the disastrous timing of my illness. She was also terrified of catching it. One sick performer on stage was bad enough; two would strain the audience's sympathies.

Even with her fear, Mirella tried to take care of me. She cooked minestrone and other soups for me. When she brought them to me, I would open my dressing room door a crack and take them without even seeing her face. I could hear Mirella saying, *"Povero ragazzo, povero ragazzo."*

Instead of canceling altogether and going home to Italy, which is probably what I should have done, I took a middle ground by postponing my debut one week. The week passed and I still felt terrible. The day of the performance, November 23, 1968, I phoned Bob Herman, who was one of Sir Rudolf

Bing's top lieutenants in the Met's artistic administration. I asked him to meet me in a rehearsal room at the opera house with an accompanist.

When we were together there, I made him listen while I sang through the most important parts of the *Bohème* score for the tenor. I wanted to know if he thought I could do it. He said I sounded fine. Maybe I did, then.

Somehow I got myself into makeup and costume and out onto that major goal for every singer—the stage of the Metropolitan Opera. It was a Saturday matinee, and, fortunately for me, it was shortly before the first nationwide radio broadcast of that season. My indisposition would not be flashed into every American household. Any other singer, if they should sing badly through illness will be forgiven by an audience who has heard him or her before and knows the sound they are producing is not the usual one. But if you are singing in a city for the first time, they know nothing of the kind. They have every right to assume, if you walk out onto the stage as I had just done, that the voice they hear is your normal voice.

Anyway, there I was—and there they were. The New York audience. We have since become involved in a love affair, one of the most satisfying of my life, but then we were total strangers.

The conductor that day, an Italian whose name I prefer to forget, did not help me at all. There is much a conductor can do to assist a singer—giving a strong phrase in a weak spot, allowing the singer to breathe, anticipating trouble, and other technical matters. But more important even than these things is the feeling a conductor can give a singer that he is on his side, is thinking of his well-being, is supporting him.

Many conductors do this, but there is another kind: the conductor who works only for himself and his vision of the music. He is getting his direction from On High and regards the singer, if he regards him at all, as another one of his obedient instruments. It is very demoralizing to look down from the stage and see that the person you are relying on to get you through cares not at all if you live or die. This dependence of singers on conductors is always true, but particularly so when you feel dreadful and are not in voice.

Mirella was wonderful. She bravely snuggled up to my Hong Kong germs during our love scenes and would whisper words of encouragement to me throughout the opera. I managed to get through the performance. The audience was warmly appreciative, though the reception was nothing to what I had been given elsewhere and later would be given in New York.

Amazingly enough, the reviews were quite favorable. They wouldn't have been if I had been writing them. Peter G. Davis in the New York *Times* said, "Mr. Pavarotti triumphed principally through the natural beauty of his voice—a bright, open instrument with a nice metallic ping up top that warms into an even, burnished luster in mid-range. Any tenor who can toss off high C's with such abandon, successfully negotiate delicate diminuendo effects and attack Puccinian phrases so fervently is going to win over any *La Bohème* audience and Mr. Pavarotti had them eating out of his hand."

Very nice, but if they had eaten out of my hand, they would have caught flu. No matter what the circumstances of your debut—your health, your state of mind, your nerves, your talent—you always hope that everything will come together to give you the explosive, history-making reception of legends, the kind of dream success that kept you vocalizing for six years. My debut was respectable, perhaps a little better than that, but I know how I could sing and I knew I hadn't sung even close to my best.

At least I could console myself that the New York critics liked me better than they liked Caruso after *his* Met debut.

I tried to do the next performance but could not go through with it. I sang two acts, then was unable to continue. I was replaced, I think, by Barry Morrell. I wanted desperately to return to Modena and go to bed. In order to do this, I had to cancel all the rest of my engagements in New York, including some twenty or thirty more performances I was scheduled to sing at the Met. Sir Rudolf Bing was very understanding, for which I am grateful.

In the seven years that I had been a professional opera singer, I had many joyous returns to my home in Modena. I love my family very much and always miss them terribly when I am away. It is so strong, this feeling, that I can't carry photographs of them. If I were to see a photograph of Adua and the girls when I am singing in a foreign country, I would drop everything and take the next plane to Italy.

When I finish my work and am able to return home, it is a very happy time for me. I always arrive with arms full of gifts for my wife, my daughters, my parents and sister—and I've been lucky enough to bring back a bouquet of favorable press clippings or other mementos of a successful engagement.

This homecoming was very different. Adua tells me she thought the New Yorkers must have thrown tomatoes at me, I looked so dejected and defeated when I came into the house. I went right to bed and was sick for almost three months. Some people have suggested that this fever was a result of my nervousness at making my Met debut. For me, illness is illness, and there is nothing you can do about it. Maybe other people get fevers and sore throats from nerves, but I don't think I do. I think a very nasty little San Francisco germ did not want me to win over New York.

I had been in New York once before that unfortunate debut. A year or two earlier I had been touring in *Capuleti* with La Scala for Expo '67 in Canada and stopped off in New York at our

While my new Modena place was being rebuilt, I would check progress each time I got back to Italy. CREDIT: William Wright

My mother and my sister Gabriella in front of our first apartment. CREDIT: William Wright (*above*) With my parents in front of the Modena apartment where I was born. CREDIT: William Wright (*below*)

Our house on the Adriatic at Pesaro is the one place I get to each year where I can completely relax. CREDIT: William Wright (*above*) Halfway through this book, I checked the blood pressure of my collaborator, Bill Wright. He was still all right. CREDIT: Gildo di Nunzio (*below*)

In Pesaro during the summer of 1979 with my three daughters: Cristina by my side, Lorenza above my head, and Giuliana beside Lorenza.
CREDIT: William Wright

The Metropolitan Opera's Gildo di Nunzio came to Pesaro to work with me on Rossini's *William Tell*. Instead I got him to try painting.
CREDIT: William Wright

I keep a small boat in Pesaro for fishing and to take my daughters water-skiing. CREDIT: William Wright (*above*) A normal after-lunch period in Pesaro in, believe it or not, a normal hammock.
CREDIT: William Wright (*below*)

I always ask for a piano in any hotel room I stay in. Before a 1979 concert in Miami, I go over the program. CREDIT: William Wright (*above*) The baker's son appears with the coal miner's daughter, Loretta Lynn, and Hal Holbrook on the 1980 ABC Omnibus Special.
CREDIT: William Wright (*below*)

Getting some air during a rehearsal break at the Temple Beth Shalom in Miami Beach. CREDIT: William Wright

P A V A R O T T I

tour's end to cover for Carlo Bergonzi, who was singing the Verdi *Requiem* with von Karajan there.

My first impression of New York was terrible. The weather was sad—cold and dark. The tall buildings depressed me. Everything looked dirty. I saw no sky, no greenery. And I hated my hotel; people were disagreeable, no one smiled.

As soon as von Karajan's arm was raised and I was sure Carlo was present and in good voice, I rushed to the airport to get away from New York as fast as I could.

I can talk frankly about this bad first impression without fear of offending anyone as New York has since become one of my favorite cities in the world. I think I have as many good friends there as I have anywhere with the exception probably of Modena. The city is a place of endless fascination for me and I always feel a surge of exhilaration when I return to it.

After that disastrous first showing at the Metropolitan, however, I wasn't sure there would be a return. Sir Rudolf had confidence, and was good enough to invite me back in 1970 to sing Alfredo in Verdi's *La Traviata*. This went very well, but it wasn't until my next appearance at the Metropolitan in *The Daughter of the Regiment* with Joan Sutherland in 1972 that I had the success I had dreamed about having in 1968.

125

LUCIANO PAVAROTTI

On Singing and
Interpretation

You cannot have studied singing or sung as long as I have without developing strong convictions about how it should be done. As others have pointed out, there are as many theories as voice teachers. Beyond that, each voice is a little different—like a signature or a fingerprint—and presents the teacher with special problems. But some things are fundamental to all voices.

First among the basics is the support and the breathing. I knew this in theory for many years but I didn't master it or learn how essential it was to an important career of constant singing until I made the tour of Australia with Joan Sutherland in 1965.

For me, Joan Sutherland is the dream singer because she has such a strong build. She has a large body, and it is well distributed and well constructed. Another singer who has the physical requirement is Franco Corelli—he is not skinny, but a full-sized man. These two people possess incredible voices and incredible diaphragms for support. A violin can't be a little tiny thing and produce a great sound. Important voices usually go with the important body (I will avoid saying the fat body).

The support from a strong torso is so important because it takes the strain from the vocal cords, which are small sensitive membranes, to the diaphragm, which is a large muscle development and, if you develop it correctly, a strong one. If you support the voice correctly from below, you can sing far longer—in one evening and in one life—without signs of strain.

The best illustration of this is a baby crying. A baby can cry all night without letting up or without any loss of volume because he is crying from the diaphragm, not the throat. Of course, the baby has an advantage: he picks one note and just sticks with that one. Still, he teaches us something about singing.

The sound comes from the stomach area—the lungs, really —and not from the throat. It is so simple and so true, yet how many singers forget this? You must work and exercise until there is a natural reflex of support from the diaphragm. You must also work to suppress any obstacles to that column of air you are forcing up from deep down in your diaphragm to your vocal cords. There is, of course, great variation between one set of vocal cords and another. That is why some people have beautiful voices and other people not so beautiful. But below the vocal cords, we are all constructed pretty much the same. Anyone, if he or she works at it, can develop the correct diaphragm support to be a singer. But even the most celestial vocal equipment will not reach its potential unless the breathing and support are so thoroughly trained that each time you sing, the column of air, which is the fuel for the sound you make, is automatically sent up with the correct force and without restrictions.

The next most important thing for a singer is concentration. It must be complete—not just on how one is singing, but on what is being sung. If I find myself touched and moved by a singer, I look, and, without fail, that singer is completely immersed in what he or she is singing. The singer who moves me is not thinking about how well he just sang that last high note or how attentive the audience is; he is thinking only of the song and his expression of it. Then and only then will he move other people. Without total concentration, the finest voice in the world will leave people not fully satisfied.

Terribly important also for any singer is enunciation. We are, after all, always singing words and if the words are unclear, not only is the poetry lost, but the lack of clarity communicates something negative to the audience about the singer. It is so easy for singers to be careless about this because they are concentrating so hard on the difficult business of singing.

That is why good enunciation should be worked on and worked on—slaved over, really—until it becomes so automatic, the singer doesn't have to give it any more thought. Unless this is done early, however, it is very difficult to learn later.

To me, an example of superb enunciation is that of Giuseppe di Stefano. I like many things about this great singer but high among them is his fantastic diction. With him, you hear every syllable. All the time people ask me who is the singer I modeled myself after. There is no one singer. I admire different things about different singers. For diction, however, my model is di Stefano.

One of the most difficult things for a singer to master is the *passaggio*. Most every singer has not one voice but three different voices—a lower, a middle, and an upper. When you are singing and move from one of these voices into the other there is often a noticeable changing of gears. You can hear where the voice is moving from one of these vocal areas—you call them registers—to the next.

The first thing a singer must do in connection with these shifting places on his or her scale is to learn where they occur and work to control them with extra care so that the vocal change is as small as possible. The ideal is to control these *passaggio* places so that listeners do not notice them at all, so that your voice sounds like it is all of one piece from the bottom of your range to the top.

Singers vary on this. Some singers have only two registers so they only have one *passaggio* to worry about. I have heard that one of the many things that make Ethel Merman's voice so remarkable is that she has no *passaggio;* her voice is all one register. She never has to shift gears but can sing right up to the top of her range in the exact same vocal quality that she has with the middle or lower notes.

The *passaggio* is also very important in connection with singing the highest notes. If the shift-over from the middle to the upper register is done correctly, it opens up the top much more effectively and those high B's and C's have a better chance of being hit solidly and well.

I am not sure why this is so, the important thing is that it works. It is a little like breaking through the sound barrier. If you do it in the right way, it affects what happens on the other side. Apart from the importance of the *passaggio* on top notes, it is also an important area because of the danger of breaking or making another unpleasant sound. For this reason, too, these notes must be kept under tight control. You should even close the throat a little. Then once you are safely past the *passaggio* you can open up again and give full volume to those showy top notes with far less fear.

By working hard on the *passaggio* of students I have taught, I have given them top notes they never thought possible for themselves.

Does all this sound too technical? I thought it would be interesting for nonsingers if only to show the many complicated things a singer has to master before saying that he or she has really developed the voice. And, of course, if we had to think of this and many other things while we are singing before an audience, we could never make our songs sound like music. It must be worked on so hard and so long that it doesn't have to be thought about at all, but happen automatically.

People have asked me how you can study singing for years and years without being ready to perform. That is how.

There are other ways a singer can help his top notes. To reach those nine high C's in *The Daughter of the Regiment* is not impossible if I am cautious with my voice during the rest of the piece. It is a matter of careful phrasing and control to avoid driving the top voice. If you use a good technique with all levels of singing, the top may not be easy but it is possible. If you push and try to force out a sound that is bigger than what naturally belongs to the voice, you have a problem. Many tenors have trouble because they do this.

I would be creating a very false impression if I suggest that, using the correct technique, you can toss off those nine high C's in *Daughter* without a care.

The first time I sang them in Covent Garden I was so scared I think there was another set of muscles in my body I used more than my vocal cords. They told me that no tenor had attempted that aria in the original key—without transposing down, that is—since Donizetti's day. I didn't decide whether or not I would try it in the original key until the dress rehearsal. When I did it as written at that rehearsal, the orchestra stopped and applauded. It was a wonderful moment for me and made me decide always to sing it as Donizetti wanted.

The whole business of top notes for a tenor is sad and a little ridiculous. You can sing badly all evening, but come in strong with your high C and the public will forgive you everything. On the contrary, you can sing like an angel for three hours, but one cracked top note will ruin the whole evening. Somebody said, "An evening never recovers from a cracked high note." It is exactly like a bull fight. You are not allowed one mistake.

I don't know how the opera public became this way. I suppose there is something undeniably exciting about a grown man singing full out those difficult, unnatural high C's. It creates a wild, almost animal excitement. Then, too, there is the excitement of the matador danger, the closeness of sudden death.

Singing extremely high notes full voice came rather late to opera. In the early days, the top notes were sung falsetto. It was in 1820 that a tenor named Domenico Donzelli sang an A in his full voice. The public loved it. Shortly after, another tenor, Louis-Gilbert Duprez hit the high C's in *William Tell* with his full voice, prompting Rossini's famous remark about Duprez's note sounding like a capon having his throat cut.

The opera audience disagreed with Rossini, and tenors ever since have been trying for high C's. I don't know whether to thank Duprez or curse him. To make so much of the high C is silly. Caruso didn't have it. Neither did Tito Schipa. As a matter of fact, Schipa didn't even have a great voice, but he was a great singer. He had a great line. For producing music, that is ten times more important.

Line or phrasing is the way you shape the music within the beat the conductor gives you. I think for the most part, this is a matter of instinct: you either have a feeling for it or you don't. With me, all of my singing is, I feel, about 50 percent intellectual and 50 percent instinct. But there are things a singer can do to create excitement in the musical phrase. For instance, at some moments it makes a good effect if you anticipate attacks on a note, coming in a fraction of a second ahead of the beat. At other times, the opposite works well, hitting the note a split second after the orchestral beat.

A singer must be very cautious about such deviation, even ones that small. The best example of a deviation that can ruin a piece of music is bad *portamento*. That is when a singer slides into a note. When he jumps from a middle note to a high one, he will jump to any note somewhere in the vicinity of the one he wants and slide his voice into the correct pitch. It is incredible to me that some singers do this deliberately for an effect. It sounds awful. If the composer tells you to go from middle C to A, then that's where you should go, hitting the notes precisely, with no stops in between.

There is a reason why this is such a common failing of singers. They are constantly being told to try for the melodious *legato* line. In striving for this, they give in to the temptation to slur their notes, to slide from one to another. Here again is an example of one of the many things that makes good singing, which seems so effortless, so difficult. Yes, you must develop a flowing *legato* musical line and, no, you may not slide from one note to another.

My first vocal coach, Maestro Arrigo Pola, drilled this law about *portamento* into my head from the very first lesson. He hated passionately the sound of a singer coming into the note from the back door. He drilled it into me until I had a choice either to develop the habit of hitting each note squarely or to go crazy from his scolding. Now, I think I have learned well his lesson and I am just as determined to drill this into my pupils as he was with me.

You can teach very little about phrasing. You can take a singer over and over a phrase until it sounds the way you think it should, but if he doesn't feel it within himself, he probably won't be able to repeat it the next time. Also, to do this kind of line-by-line coaching with an entire opera would take years. Phrasing must come naturally and grow out of the singer's sense of what he is doing. It must come from the singer's feeling for the music and what the music is saying. For this, the concentration I mentioned earlier is essential, but concentration alone will not produce good results if there is nothing in the head and the heart to concentrate with.

For a tenor, choosing the right roles is crucial to both his success and his longevity. I mentioned earlier how I turned down an offer to sing Rossini's *William Tell* though I was frantic for a chance to make my debut at La Scala. The role would have ruined my voice. I finished recording *William Tell* for London not long ago, but we made the recording over two years and my voice is stronger after eighteen years of singing. I still would not want to attempt *William Tell* on the stage.

Another time, I canceled an engagement to sing *Così Fan Tutte* at Covent Garden with Sir Georg Solti conducting because I felt my voice was too heavy for that music. (Also, I couldn't see myself in a white wig.)

I can't remember how many times I have turned down *Aïda*. Impresarios are always trying to push you this way and that. Not just impresarios. A friend of mine came backstage after I had sung *Tosca* and said to me, "When are you going to sing *Aïda* or Wagner?" My friend was a Wagner fan, but God help me if I tried to sing Wagner.

Wagner involves a different-sounding voice and a different way of singing. A few people have been able to sing both Wagner and other roles but very few. Joan Sutherland originally studied to be a Wagnerian soprano. However, once she decided her voice was better suited for more lyric music—and it was lucky for me she did—she has not gone back in any serious way. Jean de Reszke, who was the world's greatest tenor for the decades before Caruso, decided well along in his career to undertake *Siegfried*. It was not a success, but more important than whether he was a good or a bad Siegfried, his vocal life ended about two years later. Many are convinced that the effort to sing Wagner brought about the end of his vocal greatness several years before it would have happened if he had stuck to his natural repertoire.

A tenor can damage his top notes by forcing his voice into music that is too heavy for him. I was blessed with a lyric voice, not heavy, with an easy top. It was well suited for a large repertoire of operas, primarily the *bel canto* works of Bellini and Donizetti. Interviewers often ask me what music I like and I tell them, "My voice likes Donizetti."

I also have been able to sing some of the Verdi and Puccini roles without much strain. But certain tenor roles, even within the Italian repertory, will always be out of my reach: Verdi's *Otello*, for example, and Giordano's *Andrea Chénier*. I like the image about the voice that my friend Umberto Boeri uses. He says the voice is like a sheet of rubber: if you pull it one way, it loses something in the other dimension. If I push my voice into heavy, dramatic roles, I would risk losing the quality of the top.

As tenors grow older, there is a natural tendency for the voice to darken, to grow darker like a baritone's vocal quality. This doesn't necessarily mean you will lose your top, just take on a natural darker coloration—and I emphasize *natural*, as that is very different from straining to achieve this coloration. This development generally occurs around the age of forty. So I waited until I was forty before taking on Manrico, the bravura tenor role in Verdi's *Il Trovatore*. I was forty-four before trying Enzo in *La Gioconda*.

Verdi created a broad range of tenor roles, yet there seems to be a logical progression from the lighter ones to the heavy. The last act of *Luisa Miller*, for example, is as heavy as *Otello*. When I first did *Luisa Miller* in 1974, it made me think that I was perhaps approaching the time to sing Radames in *Aïda*. I have agreed to sing *Aïda* in San Francisco in 1981. The public will let me know if my voice has arrived at this capability.

My voice has changed over the years in a way different from coloration. My wife insists it always had a beautiful sound, and I like to agree with her. (May I discuss my voice in this frank way? It is, after all, a gift from God, so it is not a matter of conceit, but gratitude.) Over the years, the quality of the sound has changed little, thank heavens. It has, however, grown bigger, more secure, more from the diaphragm. In the early years, my voice was a little more "flying"—it was too much in my throat and not under complete control. I think I have it tamed now.

I did not push my voice in those early years doing heavy roles that were beyond me. Because of that caution, my voice has remained the voice of a lyric tenor, a little spinto perhaps, but basically lyric. I can sing *Turandot*, but also *L'Elisir d'Amore* and *La Sonnambula*. Manrico in *Trovatore* is a very heavy role, very spinto. When I sang it at the Met, I proved I could do it, but it remains at the outer edge of my range.

Occasionally I worry that my voice is not "brown" and rich enough, though it is not really my desire to have a brown, dramatic sound. I really want to have a clear voice, with a strong metallic sound, but not like a castrato.

With the natural darkening of the voice, I am moving more toward operas like *Un Ballo in Maschera, Luisa Miller, Tosca.* And one day I would like to do Don José in *Carmen.* A special dream of mine is to sing *Werther,* but I will not do that romantic role on stage unless I lose weight.

Certain of the roles I sing put a severe strain on the vocal cords. *I Puritani* is like tightrope walking. Almost the entire opera is full-volume singing for the tenor in the upper part of the voice. There are two D's and an F. *Il Trovatore, La Favorita,* and others also create stress even with the most correct diaphragm support. After you sing one of these parts, you need a good rest for the vocal cords to rebuild themselves. For them to regain their strength and health, the muscles around the cords that support them and the blood vessels that irrigate them need at least two days to recover, maybe more, depending on your age.

Concerts can do even more damage to the voice. After singing twenty pieces, music of many different styles, my voice needs a rest for several days.

La Sonnambula has always been an important role for me. I undertook it early in my career to master what I thought was one of the most difficult *bel canto* roles and to prove to my agent I was not lazy or afraid of challenges. I have been cautious about roles, though not from fear of hard work. I have never taken the easy way.

With *Sonnambula,* the tenor cannot bluff. It is more difficult than *Puritani* in one sense. If a tenor has an easy top, he doesn't have to be a great singer to do an incredible *Puritani.* But *Sonnambula* requires great, great phrasing in the middle as well as the top. I knew that if I could sing *Sonnambula* as it was meant to be sung, I would know *bel canto.*

Dramatically, there are two roles I identify with quite a bit: Rodolfo in *La Bohème* and Nemorino in *L'Elisir d'Amore.*

Rodolfo is intensely romantic; I think I am too. I give romantic interpretations of most of the roles I sing. Perhaps I have a special feeling for Rodolfo because with him I made my debut, and so many subsequent debuts in other places.

I love Donizetti's *L'Elisir*. I think it is a masterpiece. The plot is inspired and the music expresses it perfectly. Nemorino is half comic, half sad, just like life. He is also a simple country boy, yet he is not stupid. He figures his way over the obstacles and gets what he is after in the end. I like to think of myself that way too. As for my friend who accused me of singing in operettas, he may have had a point about *Tosca*—the role of Cavaradossi is not too taxing for the tenor—but he would be wrong about *L'Elisir*. Nemorino is on stage all the time and he has a great deal of difficult singing to do.

There are a number of roles I have a special feeling for—the roles like Rodolfo and Nemorino for which I think I am well suited vocally and temperamentally—but if I was told that I would only be able to do one role for the rest of my life, that role would be Riccardo in Verdi's *Un Ballo in Maschera*. I love the part. Without doubt the opera belongs to the tenor, and the fantastic music Verdi has given him provides the opportunity to display many different types of singing.

The first time I saw *Ballo* was, for me, a big disappointment. Not because of the opera itself—certainly not—or even the production. I had gone to see it at La Scala to hear my idol, Giuseppe di Stefano sing, but he had to cancel that performance. The tenor who took over for him—I forget who it was—sang very well, but still the evening stands out in my memory as one of disappointment.

The first time I got to know the opera thoroughly was in Dublin in 1963 when I was singing in a different opera. The same company was mounting a production of *Ballo*. I went to all the rehearsals and, I think, all the performances. I studied it very carefully and of course came to love it. I knew I was, at that time, a long way from singing Riccardo myself; the role sounded so heavy for my voice as it was then. Even so, I made a serious study of the role, both the character of Riccardo and the music. I knew I would sing it one day, but I figured it would probably be toward the end of my career.

By 1969, however, my voice had changed enough that the role was within my reach. (I hope that doesn't mean my career is almost over.) I won't say the part was easy for me, because "easy" is a word that doesn't really exist on the operatic stage. But the music of Riccardo felt comfortable for me, and I hope I sang it in a way to satisfy people who love that opera as much as I do. The critics were very enthusiastic—even one critic who always finds something about me to criticize—and that made me very happy.

As an example of the demands *Ballo* makes on the tenor, look at the second scene of Act I, the scene in the fortune-teller Ulrica's den. In that scene Riccardo has three different stretches of music alone and a difficult trio—each in a different musical style. Each calls for a different sound and a different phrasing and a different dramatic mood. That is just one scene.

The love duet in the second act is incredible. The only duet I can think of that matches it in intensity is the one in *Tristan und Isolde.* The love duet in Verdi's *Otello* is a masterpiece, of course, but a different kind of love is being expressed. For direct, immediate passion, I know of nothing like the *Ballo* duet in Italian music.

That aria ends with a high C for the tenor. Generally when I approach a high C I think of little else, but in the *Ballo* duet the music is so sensuous and exciting that I generally get carried away and forget about the high C until just before I must sing it. Maybe Verdi thought about this, because in the music he gives the tenor and the soprano a few seconds to collect themselves before he sends them to that final note.

And there is an interesting point about that duet. Some people criticize the opera by saying that the hero, Riccardo, is too irresponsible, that he is reckless in pursuing his love affair and causes too much harm. Here is where Verdi, with the frenzied passion he has put into his love-duet music, puts a logic into the story that is not spelled out in the libretto. Verdi makes us feel how unreasonable and uncontrollable Riccardo's love for Amelia is.

At the end of that second-act love scene, it is a good thing Verdi makes the husband arrive when he does or I'm not sure Riccardo would be so noble.

I was once in a fascinating production of *Ballo* in Hamburg directed by John Dexter. His concept was to set the action in the United States at the end of the Civil War. Riccardo was a Northerner and Renato was from the South. The page, Oscar, was a black boy. This made sense because Riccardo, being on the side to free the slaves, accepted Oscar as a friend. The conspirators were members of the Ku-Klux Klan. The whole thing was ingenious.

The ball scene at the end was set in New Orleans with all the ladies in those incredible hoopskirts. The effect was sensational. You can imagine how the Hamburg audience applauded that scene when the curtain went up.

The *Ballo* we did for the Met in 1980 took many ideas from that Hamburg production, but not the main one of setting it in Civil War time. The Colonial Boston setting was used. Because the Met production was done with television in mind the director gave more emphasis to the individual performances; most of the audience would be receiving the opera's impact through closeups.

When I select a role, the first consideration is that it be right for my voice, that I can do it without damage to my vocal cords.

Next, I think in terms of a role that interests me musically and dramatically. I think the hardest roles to act are the ones where the character is not clearly drawn.

For instance, one of the greatest dramatic roles for a tenor is Verdi's *Otello*. But the character is so strongly written, we are never in the least doubt—through the music and the story—about what is on his mind. This makes it easier, I think, for the performer, than conveying a character that is less well drawn. With a hazy character, it is hard to make him interesting and believable.

Otello has a few basic feelings and he is driven inevitably to his conclusion by Iago. Similarly, in *L'Elisir*, the part of Nemorino is very definite, very clear—the singer cannot go too far from what is written. In *Bohème*, on the other hand, Rodolfo is a subtle part. He can project a great feeling, but it is up to the tenor singing the role. If he does well, it becomes the tenor's opera. A soprano must be really exceptional, or the tenor exceptionally bad, for Mimi to take the opera from Rodolfo. Other roles I have done that present a challenge to the tenor because of their lack of clarity are Rodolfo in Verdi's *Luisa Miller* and Fernando in Donizetti's *La Favorita*. Aside from these librettos' other failings, the tenor parts are given somewhat confusing characters. Because of the glorious music, it is important for the tenor to make a special effort to render these characters as believable as possible.

As you do one role many times over the years, there is inevitably a change in your interpretation. Sometimes this can be a gradual thing that happens as your perspective on the character and his situation changes. Other times it can change abruptly with a different director's radical concept.

I am not talking about the staging which always changes with different directors, but the expression, the way the drama is envisioned. For instance, the *Bohème* I sang in Milan with Carlos Kleiber in 1979 was totally different from the one I did with von Karajan. It was both dramatically different and musically different. Working with Kleiber, I tried out many new ideas of his that I liked very much. He is an incredible, sensitive musician and suggested nuances of interpretation I found very exciting.

Sometimes I experiment on my own and find new ways of singing an aria or a phrase which I prefer. These I work in to my interpretation of a particular role. It might be something minor like making a smaller pianissimo at a certain point. Or it might be major—the whole tone of an aria or the feeling behind a scene. These opportunities to find better ways of doing something you have done many times can make the ninety-fifth Rodolfo as interesting for you as the first.

When a singer arrives at a point in his career where he can be given a broad choice of roles, matters other than musical ones can affect his decision. It is far more fun to be in an opera where you are at the center of the dramatic action than one where you are standing a bit to the sidelines. Donizetti's great opera buffa *Don Pasquale* is a good example of what I mean. The action centers on Don Pasquale, Dr. Malatesta, and Norina. They are constantly involved in brilliant ensembles and the most comic scenes. Ernesto, by contrast, despite some truly lovely music well suited to my voice, seems to mope around by himself, a bit of a jerk. He is supporting—not like Nemorino, who is never out of the action of *L'Elisir*.

I feel a little this way about Alfredo in *La Traviata*. Verdi gives him some spectacular music, but no matter how well the tenor sings it, the opera belongs to Violetta and Germont. I sang Alfredo many times earlier in my career, but in those days I was happy for any opportunity to be heard.

There is another consideration in selecting roles. As you advance in your profession, you are pressured by people to undertake all the classic tenor roles. There is a little feeling of the labors of Hercules about this. Fans and critics say, "All right, you can do *Ballo*. What about *Trovatore?*" They sometimes make it appear that there are so many hurdles before you can arrive at some imaginary finish line.

They may be motivated by nothing more than the desire to hear you in all their favorite parts. Whatever the reason, there is constant pressure on you to undertake new roles. As long as the role is not out of my vocal category, I will try it. I think it would be a little mean and lazy of me not to make the effort.

This desire to conquer all the major tenor roles within my capabilities was one of the main reasons I did Enzo in *La Gioconda* for the San Francisco Opera in 1979. The tenor in this opera is not given the most intriguing personality in the world; in fact, he's quite baffling. And the overall story of the opera is not the greatest. Even by the special standards of Italian opera librettos, it is farfetched.

Vocally, on the other hand, I find the role quite interesting. As with Rodolfo, the tenor has the ability to make this hard-to-believe character come to life in a believable way by the right kind of expressive singing. I love this kind of challenge. Wagner said something wonderful along these lines when a friend pointed out some illogicalities in the Ring's conclusion. Certain things about the story made no sense to the friend. Instead of defending his story, Wagner acknowledged that what his friend was saying was true—on one level. But, said Wagner, the music makes it logical.

I think I understand what he meant. A performer, too, can bring essential ingredients to a libretto that are not there in black and white.

One of the most difficult tenor roles for me is the Duke in *Rigoletto*. It is difficult because Verdi has asked the tenor to sing in so many different styles—lyric, spinto, leggiero. All these styles are required at one moment or another.

I make such a point of saying how important it is for a tenor—or any other type of voice—not to attempt roles that are beyond them. At the same time, I am a great believer in setting difficult challenges for yourself. I don't think this is a contradiction. Even within a singer's general range of roles, there may be roles that are simply too hard for him at a particular moment in his career. It may require more in terms of technique, phrasing, interpretation, or simple stamina than he is ready for. Here is where I am more reckless. I am a great believer in tossing myself into the water to see if I sink or swim. More progress is often made in a few hours by responding to challenges than with years of hard work in the safe sanctuary of the coach's studio.

Therefore, what I am saying is that I believe very much in challenges, yet I believe very much in staying within your natural vocal boundaries. To lyric tenors like myself who are starting out I would say that *Rigoletto* or *Sonnambula* offer a lifetime of challenges; you don't have to go galloping off to *Otello* or *Siegfried* to prove yourself.

People often ask me how I happened to come to sing the role of the Italian Singer in the London recording of *Der Rosenkavalier*. Sir Georg Solti wanted me to do it. It is such a small part—just that one aria—I asked for my full fee by way of turning it down. They must have been desperate, because they agreed to my request. I wasn't as unreasonable as I may sound. It took us six hours—two full sessions—to record that one aria. Richard Strauss once asked Caruso to sing it, but Caruso never did, as far as I know.

I have an opera coming up on my schedule that is an example of the kind of challenge that stretches me, yet is within the bounds of my natural range. I am very thrilled that the Met has asked me to sing the title role in *Idomeneo* for their 1983 season. Even though I sang Idamante at Glyndebourne in 1964, I have never sung Mozart in America and I am very excited about it. It is always wonderful to show the public, even a public who loves you, that you can do more than what they have come to expect from you.

For the most part, however, I think I have now covered the range of roles that is possible for me, not all the *roles*, but the range. I think I am entitled sometimes to choose a role that is easier for me than some others might be. Before, at the beginning, I looked only for challenges. I still want challenges, I still want to try works that do not come easily—to keep myself in good form. But I no longer want this hard road *every* time I select an opera the way I did in the beginning years.

LUCIANO PAVAROTTI

The Opera Network

Now that I have brought my life up through my Met debut, and find myself singing in opera houses all over the world, I will make some observations about this strange profession I had worked so hard to conquer. It is incredible that opera, as an entertainment, has survived at all. It started out as an esthetic experiment for an exclusive audience of intellectuals and quickly became an elaborate, exorbitantly costly entertainment affordable only by royal courts.

We live in a day when experts predict that live entertainment in general is becoming obsolete. The convenience of watching television, the staggering costs of production, and the relatively tiny audience served by theaters make live performances a doomed species. Even the popular theater such as Broadway has reflected this trend by putting on ever-smaller productions (down to one-man, no-set shows) or big shows of only the widest appeal. The most popular entertainers, if they appear before the public at all, do it in places so vast—Madison Square Garden, the Hollywood Bowl—that they are "live" only in the technical sense of the term.

That in spite of these grim realities there should still be entertainment as cumbersome and specialized as opera is a miracle. Think what is required: a full symphony with an important conductor, elaborate sets and costumes, very often a ballet company, a highly trained chorus, and many singers blessed not only with beautiful voices, abnormally large, but the years and years of training required to learn how to use these instruments and to execute the music. You must add to the enormous expense and difficulty of production. And working against all this —the most popular and greatest operas are fifty to two hundred years old and, by necessity, quite removed from contemporary concerns.

Compare all that goes into this with the popular singer who stands with a microphone and a few musicians and entertains five times the number of people that can squeeze into an opera house. Why go to all the trouble of opera?

I am lucky enough to receive the top fees that are paid in opera today. Not every house can afford these fees, but I would have to be five people to fulfill all the serious proposals that come to me. Someone told me that in the United States alone, over fifteen hundred groups put on opera. Some of these are small workshops, to be sure, but a surprising number are putting on respectable productions with full orchestra and professional singers.

Opera as an art form is flourishing as it never has in its history—not just in the number and quality of productions, but in the widening audience. Now at the opera house you see many young people, particularly in America. Certainly opera is no longer the exclusive property of the rich or highly educated. For years in America, the Texaco Saturday afternoon radio broadcasts brought first-rank opera to every corner of America. And now the televising nationally of onstage performances is building an enormous new audience for opera. It is very exciting for me to be part of this history-making development.

Yet, with all the growing interest in opera and the flourishing state of production, I know that only a small percentage of the population likes opera and is interested in it—maybe ten percent, probably less. Maybe it is because opera's future is threatened, or has been so until recently, that its devotees are so fiercely loyal to it and the people who work in the field so dedicated.

Right now, America is perhaps the best place for a classical musician to develop. There is so much activity and everyone is expected to attain a high level of musicianship. We Italians, for example, are less well educated musically. You don't find as many young people in Italy who have been so meticulously trained. On the other hand, we are, I think, more naturally musical; it is in our blood.

As for the management of the world's leading opera houses, I will say more about that when I stop singing. It is better, I think. But I can say some things. In America you have two wonderful impresarios—Chicago Lyric Opera's Carol Fox and San Francisco's Kurt Herbert Adler. They tell me that Adler can be difficult, but I've never seen that and I've worked with him often. Besides, everyone who achieves anything in the arts is sure to be thought "difficult" by somebody, but often that judgment says more about the person saying it.

Adler has a lively sense of humor and we always have fun when I sing at San Francisco. When I arrived at San Francisco to sing *La Gioconda* in 1979, Adler asked me to sing *"Celeste Aïda"* at a concert they were giving. I said I'd have to think about it. He said, "Don't try to think. Tenors have no brains. Everyone knows that."

That is typical of our conversations. Once I was singing *La Bohème* in San Francisco on the night of my birthday, October 12. For the Café Momus scene in the second act, Adler had the waiters serving us real champagne. Then he came out himself as a waiter. But this is a very different side of him from the side that puts together some of the most beautiful operatic productions anywhere in the world with some of the highest standards.

As for Carol Fox, she and I have had some ups and downs, but she is a strong person who knows what she is doing, knows opera, and knows singing. I admire both Carol Fox and Kurt Adler because they go after the very best and demand a high level. They both have the energy and personality to drive the theaters. They have a good rapport with the artists.

When you become as familiar with opera as I am, you hate to see it done in a careless way. That is why I go to opera so rarely. It is hard to find excellent productions. If it is not excellent, I suffer terribly. Fox and Adler are always trying for the very finest productions possible and, for that, I admire them.

There are many other people involved in the opera world

in America who are very good, but I do not want to be specific. Some are good friends and if I forget one they won't be good friends any longer.

The business of new productions is a running battle between singers and the management. If you have artists like Joan Sutherland, Marilyn Horne, Placido Domingo, the theater should not think they are doing these artists a favor by giving them a new production. They are doing a favor for the opera house and for opera itself.

I'm sure this argument will continue as long as singers and opera houses exist. Of course, a new production is not the sure answer to artistic triumph—it is not hard today to find a director who can destroy a great opera or one of us singers who can destroy it—but the attempts must be made.

It would be easy for me to go on singing Rodolfo and the Duke the same way I have for years in the same fading productions. I would remain as famous and make a great deal of money, but I am far more serious than that about my chosen profession.

The most important way for opera to remain vital among the arts of the twentieth century is through new versions of the great operatic masterpieces, productions that have new insights and a fresh approach that brings the work closer to the modern audience. It is natural that I want, if only occasionally, to be part of this noble effort.

Opera is not in such good shape in Italy right now. It is a sad situation when many of the world's top singers prefer not to sing there, except at La Scala. But even La Scala has political troubles—politics of music, that is. I am Italian and proud of La Scala. It still is one of the best theaters in the world, with one of the best orchestras and choruses for opera. But it must get its affairs straightened out or else it will no longer be at the top.

Something that happened in Italy not too long ago shows

how stupid we Italians can be. The government outlawed agents, the men like Ziliani who were so helpful in getting me started. I would never have sung at Palermo with Serafin if it hadn't been for him, or become known to La Scala so they would send me to Vienna. So many things happened because of his interest in my career, a legitimate business interest. What harm did agents like that do? Outlawing them was idiotic.

And La Scala had better be careful. Nowadays, no country has a monopoly on top opera, nor do the existing top opera houses. The jet plane has scrambled everything. The finest artists are flying here and there. It is not like the old days when a Caruso would sing at the Met and at La Scala and perhaps Buenos Aires and Covent Garden, but no place else. Now you can find a first-rate performance with the very finest voices in Hamburg, Helsinki, or Miami.

Working in opera houses around the world, I sometimes have disagreements with directors and conductors. It is inevitable. Interpretation of music is a matter of sensibility. It can easily happen that the conductor and the singer have a different feeling about a line or a phrase—an interpretation both feel strongly about, both equally valid. It is the same with acting. Only in this way can conflicts between professionals come about. If we singers do not behave professionally, there is no end of ways conflicts can arise.

But if both are working for the same thing—the best performance possible—disagreements can always be resolved. People talk about "difficult" conductors and directors; by this they usually mean demanding. To me, that is not a fault in the performing arts.

Occasionally, there is a collision of egos. I was doing *L'Elisir*, several years ago for a major American company. While we were still in rehearsal, the director gave an interview to the newspapers. They asked if he was pleased with the progress of the stage work. He replied, "We are doing the best we can, considering Mr. Pavarotti's acting."

This made me very angry. I have performed that part all over the world with great critical response for my dramatic characterization. In a sense, he was announcing ahead of time to the critics what they should think of my acting. It was a betrayal and very unfair. I protested to the management. I calmed down, we worked it out, but for a while I didn't want to go through with the performances.

There are many very talented directors working in opera today—Ponnelle is certainly one of them—men with interesting visions of what the operas should be, visions of how to make us see the operas in a new way. In these matters, however, I lean toward conservatism. Sometimes the changes and additions take the work so far from the original that it ceases to be a matter of interpretation and becomes rewriting. It is almost as though the director was embarrassed by the opera for having been written in the nineteenth century and seeks to disguise it so we won't recognize it. Sometimes, too, these radical productions are simply a matter of ego: the directors don't want to present Verdi or Puccini, they want to present themselves.

I have no strong desire to direct an opera, but if I ever do, it will be a very literal interpretation, sticking to what I consider the composer's original intention. You will not see me trying to convert *Pelléas et Mélisande* into *Hair*, or *Rigoletto* into *The Elephant Man*.

Also, I think the people who do the avant-garde new productions should be careful about taking bows *before* the event. So often in New York or elsewhere, you see the creators—the director and the conductor, perhaps some of the singers—going on television to congratulate themselves about their new concept. They talk on and on about how they discovered hidden values and shades of undiscovered meaning in a familiar opera. Everyone gets as excited as *they* seem to be. Then it opens and what do you have? Just another *Traviata* or *Rigoletto*—perhaps not even a good one.

I wasn't working in opera very long before I realized that often you encounter people who do not wish you well. I saw it with my first conductor, then immediately with the soprano in my first paid engagement in Lucca. I suppose there are many reasons for this. First, singers have big egos and often this means nervous egos. We have a lot to be nervous about. It is sad, though, that so often the nervousness is directed against colleagues; we all have the same problems and none of us do any better if the person next to us does poorly.

Not only the fans but people who work in opera are often passionately partisan. They don't love sopranos numbers One, Two, and Three in descending order, or they love soprano One and hate all others who dare call themselves sopranos. There really are some very strange attitudes. And they can add greatly to the backstage tensions.

Often I have seen this bad feeling put into action against my colleagues, sometimes against me. I decided very early to pay no attention to it. I do the best I can on stage and help my colleagues do the best they can. I firmly believe we all benefit if the entire performance is exceptional, not just if *one* of us is exceptional.

But enough complaints and grumbles. I might be selling insurance and not have these problems.

HERBERT BRESLIN

Managing Pavarotti

I was first introduced to Pavarotti in 1968 by Terry McEwen, who was then manager of the classical division of London Records. I'd done publicity for other London artists—Joan Sutherland, Marilyn Horne—so McEwen and I had worked together for some time.

That was the year that Luciano made his Met debut. Terry felt Luciano's career had reached the point where he needed someone to handle his publicity. At that time, Luciano had no one in the United States either for publicity or for overall management. He was singing at leading opera houses both here and in Europe, but he wasn't a star, not in the true sense.

McEwen suspected that Luciano and I would work well together, and he turned out to be right. Luciano was born on October 12; I was born October 1. That makes us both Libras. We have some important things in common; we both love to laugh and kid around, but when it comes to our work, we are both deadly serious. We both have a good bit of energy, and we both dislike letting things drift on the same old way if we think they could be better. Right from the start I thought that, with his talent, his career could be a lot better. He thought so too.

At first I just handled his publicity. (There was a time when that was all I did for any of the artists I represented.) After about a year, I took over the management of his career as well. When I began working with him, he had been singing in the United States for three years but had never sung at the Lyric Opera of Chicago. This suggests how little planning was going into his career. I thought it was absurd for such a fantastic talent to be appearing in such a random fashion, with practically no overall planning. Except for the opera buffs, no one had heard of him. I thought that was even more absurd.

He never signed a contract with me. After all these years together, we still have no formal agreement. Our business relationship is based on a mutual understanding. Sol Hurok never had a contract with Artur Rubinstein. How long were they associated? Fifty years, I think.

I would tell Luciano what I thought he should do—what engagements he should accept, what new ones he should try for. We would discuss it back and forth. We still work that way. I try to convince him of the course I think is best for him. The final decision is always his.

When I took him on, he had sung in Miami, San Francisco, and once at the Met. He was sick for that first Met performance in 1968, so it wasn't the sensation it should have been. He hadn't given a concert or recital in the States, so his American activities were meager. He was not the Pavarotti we all know today.

The beginning of the Pavarotti stardom was his Met performance in *The Daughter of the Regiment* in 1972. That was an incredible triumph and brought about an enormous boost in his artistic dynamic. With those performances the New York audience had to acknowledge that here was a major artistic phenomenon. He got a great deal of attention in the press both in New York and nationally. But it is important to remember that his emergence as a top opera star was based completely on the sheer virtuosity of his singing. Since then the public has discovered other aspects of Luciano, but at the beginning it was the artistry alone that established him.

It is hard to bowl over the New York audience. However, I defy any audience to take Luciano's performance in *The Daughter of the Regiment* in stride. The tenor role in that opera is extremely difficult and Luciano sang the hallelujah out of it. At each performance, he stopped the show with those nine high C's in one aria. He didn't rely solely on his singing. He acted the role wonderfully, too, throwing himself into a zesty, comic characterization.

From the attention turned on him as a result of that amazing performance—the television and newspaper interviews and all the rest of it—the public began to learn that Luciano was also a delightful personality in his own right. The love affair between him and the public began and it hasn't slowed down since.

Many artists are loved, but with Luciano it is something different. He projects a niceness and a lack of guile that people sense right away and they respond strongly to it. I don't know how to explain it. Maybe it's his smile—he has a magnificent smile.

He also reacts to others in a very direct, a very human way. It doesn't matter whether it's an audience or Johnny Carson or the cab driver bringing him in from the airport. With an audience, he's not afraid to show them that their enthusiasm makes him very happy. With Johnny Carson or anyone else interviewing him, he listens to what is said to him and he responds naturally. He's not trying to cut some sort of figure, or to be witty, or to be imposing and impressive. His responses are always natural, unaffected, and personal—one human interacting with others. I think the public picks up on this very quickly—and they love it. I suspect it comes as a big relief after all the phony posturing that pollutes talk shows.

With the cab driver he breaks down any distance between them because Luciano doesn't really think there *is* any distance between them. He has that empathy and respect for his fellow man which is an Italian characteristic but which is particularly strong in Luciano. Luciano has been poor, he's been worried whether or not he could support his family—he knows the other side of things. And he knows that whatever he has to offer as a person—I don't mean his voice, but his personal qualities like his humor, his intelligence, his knowledge of the world—he had this when he was poor and unfamous. So why not allow similar assets to the cab driver, or the barber, or the stagehand? His liking for people is very genuine. This projects in everything he does.

It is remarkable how this personal aspect projects itself immediately when he is performing. No matter how formal the occasion—a recital in white tie and tails, for example—or how new he is to a particular public, he walks out onto the stage and there is an immediate exchange of love between him and the audience. He sings to them, he caresses them. It really is astounding to watch the interaction. Something is happening that goes way beyond singing alone.

Other tenors are admired for one thing or another. Everyone knows what a remarkable artist Jon Vickers is, for example. But it's not the same thing.

When I undertook to manage Luciano, I felt that the most important thing was to get him known, to establish his name with the public. All I had to do was make them aware of his existence. The rest of it, his great talent and personality, were there—he didn't need me to establish *them*.

Now I receive all of the requests for him to sing—for operas, concerts, television, benefits. They all come through me. Also the many other requests that flood in now more and more —appearances on "The Today Show" or with NBC's Tom Snyder, magazine interviews like the *Time* cover story, or the CBS "Sixty Minutes" segment. How long was the latter? Eight, ten minutes on the air? Morley Safer and that crew followed Luciano all over the map for weeks and weeks. They went with him to Israel, to Miami, to Texas. There was much setting up and much coordinating for my office to do.

Then I get all the requests for Luciano to endorse products. I suppose it's an unhappy commentary on our culture, but those television commercials he did for the American Express cards familiarized more people with Luciano than eighteen years of superb singing in the world's opera houses. So these stints are useful for his recognizability.

Some people say that I had a big effect on Luciano, that I changed him, like a Svengali masterminding his whole career. I suppose I've had some effect on him.

One thing I impressed on Luciano when he associated himself with me was the need to follow through on commitments. You can change your mind one hundred times before definitely saying yes, I told him, but once you've agreed to something, you've got to go through with it—unless there is a genuine emergency, of course.

I had nothing to do with the improvement of his stage performing. Remember, Luciano's early career was mostly outside Italy—places like Glyndebourne and Covent Garden where the professionalism and discipline is much stricter than in Italian houses. Luciano hated Glydebourne when he first went there— he found it so serious, so rigid, so dedicated—no fun at all. They had him singing *Idomeneo*, not some exuberant Verdi opera. But he was won over by the Glyndebourne people's approach to opera, and by the end of his engagement he realized it had been an important experience for him, one that taught him much of value about his profession.

In the early days he may have played to the gallery some and done a few things to milk applause, but now he wouldn't think of doing that; besides, he doesn't have to. They just *look* at him and go wild.

After Luciano had that incredible success with *The Daughter of the Regiment* at the Met, I wanted to get him into concerts. It would expose him to more people, consolidate his stardom, and of course one-man concerts can be very lucrative. Opera stars, even the big ones, don't make that much money in the opera houses. It's a lot by ordinary standards, but compared to other top performers, it's not that great.

For opera stars to make the transition to the concert hall can be tricky. Their fans may adore them in costume with a story and dramatic settings but lose interest when it's just the singer and his voice on a platform. Only a very few opera stars can fill a concert hall—Joan Sutherland, Leontyne Price, Marilyn Horne, and Beverly Sills—maybe a few more could sell out halls in New York—but that's about it.

You never know how the singer is going to take to concertizing. The singing is more strenuous than in opera. The men don't get to sit out numbers while the sopranos do their arias. Instead of two or three big arias in the course of the evening, concert singers must do from fifteen to twenty pieces in several different styles. Many fantastic singers simply do not have whatever it takes to enthrall an audience for an entire evening with all the trappings of an operatic production stripped away.

In 1973, the year following the Met *Daughter of the Regiment*, I decided to try Luciano out as a concertizer in Liberty, Missouri, at a small Baptist school: William Jewell College. A local philanthropist set up a trust fund to bring top performing artists to the college. Isn't that an incredible thing to do for your community? Liberty gets the kind of artists you usually find performing only in great cities.

Luciano took to singing an arduous concert program as though he had been doing it all his life. And, of course, the audience adored it. We did another concert in Dallas. It was equally successful—both Luciano and the audience enjoyed themselves immensely. These first concerts went so well, in fact, I was sure we were ready for Carnegie Hall.

To announce Luciano's first New York recital, I took a small ad in the Sunday New York *Times*. By Wednesday the concert was sold out.

Today, Luciano is the highest paid concert singer in the business—which makes him the highest paid in history. He recently filled the Robin Hood Dell West which seats over five thousand under the roof with a couple of thousand more on the lawn. And he did this with just a piano recital—no orchestra. The Medina Temple in Chicago, which he easily filled, seats over four thousand.

The fees vary, but money is, by no means, the only consideration when he decides where he will sing. Luciano feels he has something to offer and he is as anxious to offer it to as many people and in as many different places as possible. He recently did a concert in Rio de Janeiro; his interest in singing there is easily explained: he had never sung in South America before. And when he went to Israel to do the Richard Tucker Memorial Concert the summer of 1979, he was paid a lot less than he could have earned elsewhere.

His records sell phenomenally, too. The album of Neapolitan songs, *O Sole Mio*, has outsold any record by a classical singer. The numbers of these records sold would be considered good for a popular record. *Pavarotti's Greatest Hits* will surely surpass even those figures. For a long time this past year, Luciano had eight records in *Billboard* magazine's list of the top forty classical records. That's twenty percent of all classical records among the top sellers—symphonic, piano, choruses, whatever.

When Luciano and I started out on all this, those years ago, I could see right away that making him widely famous was highly possible. First of all because of his voice and his artistry, but also because of his outgoing personality. It was just his openness and ability to project himself, and what was being projected was so likable and so worthwhile.

What comes across is what he is. Let me give an example. When Luciano sang in *La Gioconda* over national television, he was interviewed during the intermission by Pia Lindström. Pia, as everyone knows, is Ingrid Bergman's daughter and a beautiful woman. She made some reference to the New York *Times* music critic Harold Schoenberg's having said that Luciano's vocal cords were kissed by God.

Without any hesitation Luciano said, "I think He kissed you all over."

Now, every man in America wishes he'd said that. It was also a very deft way of diverting attention from the compliment to himself. I know such compliments make him uncomfortable. The point is, I could have stayed up all night trying to think of some line that would endear Luciano to the television audience, but I never could have thought of anything that good. It was witty, yes, but it was sincere and a little brash—and that's Luciano.

With all interviews, he has the ability to interest whoever is interviewing him. He is interested in so many things himself— everything, in fact. He is remarkably versatile and has the knack of imparting his enthusiasms to others. If it's not on what he's doing, it's on his painting; if not his painting, his tennis; if not on his tennis, it's on his cooking, his walking, his thinking, his seeing . . . There is always something he is eager to talk about and he talks engagingly on any of these things. He is one of the brainiest people I've ever dealt with, but it's more than that. Behind it all, I think, is his fondness for people. He has a hunger to communicate with everyone. If he's not communicating with his singing voice, he will do it with his conversation. But it is all part of the same reaching out, the desire to reach others.

Right now there is what you might call a Pavarotti explosion going on. The whole thing is unprecedented in the history of opera. On that I can simply point to one fact: when Luciano sings one of his nationally televised performances, just one, he reaches a larger audience than Caruso reached in his entire career.

That is just the televised operas and concerts. When he goes on Johnny Carson's "The Tonight Show" the comparative statistics become far more outlandish. Of course Caruso and the great artists of the past did not have this electronic wizardry at their disposal. So my point is not intended to belittle their achievements. It is interesting, I think, that while this mass media capacity has been around for a number of years, Luciano is the first major artist to begin to tap its potential for opera and good music.

So part of the phenomenon is the emergence of television, but a large part is Luciano himself. Consider the incredible impact he has on these vast audiences. After his "Live from Lincoln Center" with Zubin Mehta, over a hundred thousand letters came in to the network. This is unprecedented. Public Broadcast has had these appeals for letters before (usually they request viewers to write in for a printed program of the concert), but Luciano's concert drew many times the response they've ever had previously.

In a three-week period around the time of the Mehta concert, I received six film offers for Luciano. Somebody else wants to write a play for him—a playwright with a long-running hit on Broadway. There are a number of television projects in the works.

I have heard that some people in this business explain away Luciano's phenomenal popularity by saying I masterminded a brilliant marketing plan for him and that such commercialism degrades his artistry.

Both parts of this are totally false. Such allegations are motivated by envy and by people—usually rival performers or their loyalists—who are unwilling to grant how special Luciano is— what a remarkable artist and what a winning personality to boot.

One way to disprove the charge that I am responsible for the Pavarotti mania is to point out that I handle a good many other outstanding artists. If I showed enormous favoritism to Luciano in terms of planning and ideas, I wouldn't have other clients very long. You can't create or manufacture the kind of response Luciano is getting from the public. I would have to be ten times the genius I think I am to do that.

Luciano has another quality that sets him apart from most other artists. He has a willingness to try new things. I handled Placido Domingo for several years. He is a first-rate tenor, but he didn't want to do concerts or some other projects I suggested to broaden his audience. Most artists tend to be very cautious about their careers, but Luciano is willing to try anything he feels is reasonable. He never allows himself to take the easy way, to ride on what he knows he can do well.

He allows himself to be exploited by the media because he feels it is not only good for him personally, but also good for opera if he can show more and more people that a top opera singer is a likable human being, not some august, ivory-tower artist.

Of course, the publicity and fame enhance his earning capacity. Luciano goes after the top dollar. Tell me one artist who doesn't. Heifetz used to make incredible financial deals for himself. Why shouldn't these remarkable artists earn as much as they can? None of them is in it for art alone. They are all up to their high C's in the lusts and greeds of the marketplace.

As for the nonmusical exposure—the talk shows and the like —tell me one artist who would turn down an appearance on Johnny Carson's "The Tonight Show." And with all these side appearances, it is simply not true that Luciano degrades his art. You will never hear him sing anything that is not totally compatible with his artistry.

His appearance with Loretta Lynn on ABC's "Omnibus" special is an excellent case in point. In his banter with her, he never lost his dignity, he never condescended, either. Country and Western music is fine, but as an art it cannot compare with opera, which has a centuries-old tradition, some of the greatest masterpieces produced by man, and a large number of performing geniuses.

Luciano made himself human and accessible and, in doing that, he made his art and opera human and accessible. He does this constantly. He is not invading the world of pop culture so he can become a part of it. He is going in there in the hopes of bringing back a few converts to his field—opera.

If I have done anything in all of this, it simply was to go

with Luciano's philosophy. He loves opera. It would be more accurate to say he is *in love* with opera, and not just because it has been good to him—which it has. He knows he has the ability to win people to opera. He would like to be a catalyst between opera and a broader new audience for the art form. Many of the things he does—the outdoor performances in Central Park, for example—he doesn't need to make himself more famous in New York. What could his motive be?

Too many artist-management firms are nothing more than booking organizations. You want him for two weeks in June? You will meet our price? Okay, you got him. They sell talent the way most supermarkets sell food—not even gourmet class. A good agent should stimulate an artist to his full potential—in terms of artistry and in terms of audience.

With Luciano I don't have to push very hard. Sometimes I push and sometimes he pulls, but he is the one who sets the goals and he's the one who wins them.

WILLIAM WRIGHT

A Pavarotti Week

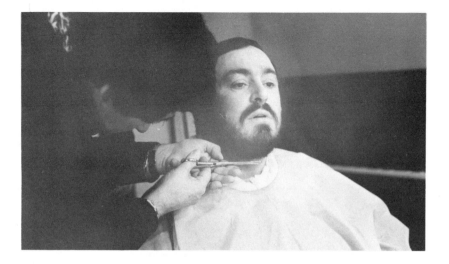

Making up for television is even more painstaking than for an opera. After seeing myself on television the first time, I lost eighty pounds. CREDIT: Susanne Faulkner Stevens (*above*) Hearing young singers for the Philadelphia Opera Vocal Competition sometimes brings delightful surprises. CREDIT: Trudy Lee Cohen (*below*)

Adua likes this blurred picture taken of her at the top of the Empire State Building.

With the television crew, Terry McEwen and I watch the playbreak of his
interview of me during the intermission at the 1978 "Live from Lincoln
Center" concert. CREDIT: Susanne Faulkner Stevens (*above*) They tell me
that one of these televised appearances reaches a larger audience than
Caruso reached in his entire career. Incredible!
CREDIT: Susanne Faulkner Stevens (*below*)

In the 1979 Lincoln Center concert with Joan Sutherland and Richard Bonynge, my secretary and student, Madelyn Renee, sang a scene from *Rigoletto* with us. CREDIT: Susanne Faulkner Stevens

In the many times Joan Sutherland and I work together, we must spend a lot of time waiting for one thing or another. We amuse ourselves as best we can.
CREDIT: Susanne Faulkner Stevens

Working musicians. First cellist, Lorne Munroe, watches Zubin Mehta pull a note from me during a rehearsal for our "Live from Lincoln Center" concert in January of 1980. CREDIT: Susanne Faulkner Stevens

A break during a concert rehearsal. CREDIT: Susanne Faulkner Stevens

The televised Juilliard School master classes I conducted in 1979 were a wonderful opportunity for me to pass along what I know about singing and performing. Here John Wustman and I work with coloratura soprano Roseann Del George. CREDIT: Susanne Faulkner Stevens

FEBRUARY 21, 1980: Dinner at New York's Romeo Salta restaurant with U. S. Navy Commander Jay Coupe who made the high bid of $800 to dine with Pavarotti. This was a fundraising stunt for the Washington Opera Society. Coupe and his five guests were quite late, which didn't bother Pavarotti who is always on time and who usually dislikes waiting for others. No food for an hour and forty-five minutes after sitting down. To one of Coupe's party Pavarotti explains that such delays are why he avoids restaurants—long waits for food and the temptation to fill up on bread. Tonight Pavarotti is unperturbed. When food arrives, Pavarotti tastes everyone's spaghetti, Coupe sings a Neapolitan song. Pavarotti declines requests to sing, claiming to be against impromptu singing. Others sing and the entire restaurant is soon part of the party.

FEBRUARY 22: Pavarotti spends the day in his Hotel Navarro apartment resting for his *Ballo in Maschera* performance. Works on a painting, naps, watches television.

6:00 Leaves for the Metropolitan Opera House.

6:30 Comments to friends waiting in his dressing room on the good cleaning the room has received. Tells them of once returning to the Met after a nine months' absence to find some of his own toenails still in the carpeting. A young woman enters the dressing room for an audition Pavarotti promised her when she approached him in the Green Room after the last performance. The girl sings *"Un bel di."* Pavarotti says she shows promise but must first learn correct breathing.

7:00 With his secretary's help, he applies his own makeup. Gets into costume.

8:00 Performance.

11 to midnight Pavarotti, exuberant from a good performance, greets over one hundred fans in the Met Green Room.

FEBRUARY 23:   Pavarotti cooks lunch (spaghetti alla Pavarotti) in his Navarro apartment for friends from San Francisco and their two children.

4:00 Accompanist arrives to go over *"Celeste Aïda,"* which Pavarotti will sing the following day at the Public Broadcast Gala.

6:00 Visit from "The Waltons" star Richard Thomas, a good friend of several years.

Evening Works on a foreword he promised to write for Rosa Ponselle's memoirs. Spoke at length to his family in Modena making plans about his imminent return to Italy.

FEBRUARY 24:   *1:30* Lunch with Terry McEwen of London Records.

3:30 Meeting with James Levine in the Navarro apartment to go over plans for the televised P.B.S. Gala which Levine will conduct that evening from the Metropolitan Opera House stage.

5:00 Pavarotti rehearses on Met stage with orchestra.

6:00 to 9:00 In the Met dressing room, Pavarotti waits his turn to perform. Because of the large number of stars, backstage security is tight, but a fan has gotten in and asked Pavarotti if he might take one photograph. Pavarotti is having a business talk with his manager but agrees. The man enters the dressing room and takes one photo, then another. When the flashgun goes off for the fifth time, Pavarotti tells the man he is not shooting from the right angle. He should stand over there. Finally the man runs out of film and tells Pavarotti he will be sending him a birthday card in October. Pavarotti thanks him.

9:00 Pavarotti dances onto the stage of the Metropolitan Opera House with mistress of ceremonies Beverly Sills while Levine conducts the orchestra in the "Merry Widow Waltz." The audience is thrilled with Pavarotti's singing of *"Celeste Aïda,"* Pavarotti less so.

174

9:30 Pavarotti leaves the Met before the end of the gala for a dinner party in his honor given by restaurant consultant George Lang.

FEBRUARY 25: *Noon* Pavarotti is brought samples of wine by manufacturers who seek his endorsement. He is cool on this product and later turns down the offer.

1:00 Lunch at the Navarro with his secretary and Hans Boon of the Breslin office to discuss a variety of business matters.

3:00 Meeting at the Navarro apartment with people from the Philadelphia Opera Company to discuss a vocal competition to be established in Pavarotti's name.

6:15 Pavarotti leaves the hotel for the 8 P.M. performance of *Un Ballo in Maschera* at the Metropolitan. He receives friends and goes over fan mail in his dressing room until it is time to get into costume.

Midnight After greeting fans in the Met Green Room, Pavarotti leaves for a supper party given for him by the Associate Concert Master of the Met orchestra, Edmund Jacobsen, and his wife, Ivey Bernhardt, who also plays in the orchestra. Pavarotti arrives with an entourage of six, including two Italian journalist friends who stopped backstage to see him on their way home from the Lake Placid Olympics. Pavarotti is enchanted by the Jacobsens' two-year-old son who is the first American, he says, to pronounce his name correctly. He plays a piano duet with him.

FEBRUARY 26: *1:00* Lunch at the Navarro with old friend Umberto Boeri and Max and Julia Prola. Julia, who first knew Pavarotti years ago in England, reminds him of the time she was taking him to the North of England to visit her parents. She left him in the train compartment while she went out into the London station to buy magazines. At the newsstand, she suddenly heard the famous voice resonating through the vast station calling, "Julia, Julia." He was afraid the train would leave, taking him on without her. Pavarotti reminds her of the time she took him to a posh Saville Row men's store and Pavarotti greeted the salesman with "Have you anything that would fit me?" Haughtily the salesman replied, "A handkerchief, perhaps?"

4:00 Doubles tennis match at the River Club. Evening spent watching television and resting for the next day's concert in Brooklyn.

FEBRUARY 27: *Noon* Sauna meeting with manager Herbert Breslin to go over future plans, particularly the six film projects that have been offered Pavarotti since the appearance of the *Time* magazine cover story on him.

5:00 A limousine picks up Pavarotti, his secretary, and his accompanist, John Wustman, to drive them to Brooklyn College. Pavarotti sits in front with the driver. Madelyn turns on the radio, picking up the overture to Rossini's *Barber of Seville.* Pavarotti asks that it be turned up, then starts conducting the music. At the end he asks who the conductor was. Neville Mariner. Good job. As the car enters the Brooklyn campus, the driver can't find Whitman Hall. Pavarotti tells the driver to pull up by a passing student. Pavarotti asks directions. The student asks if he is Pavarotti. The student expresses admiration and knowledge that Pavarotti is singing that night at Brooklyn College. Pavarotti thanks the student for the nice words and again asks location of the auditorium. The student explains the route. Pavarotti spots a drugstore and asks driver to pull up. He sends his secretary in for Carter's Little Pills, telling her to buy the entire supply so he can take the surplus back with him to Italy. Two women are waiting for Pavarotti at the stage door with flowers. They say they have come from Detroit to hear this concert. Pavarotti kisses both.

6:00 On stage in a leather overcoat, Pavarotti runs through the entire program with Wustman, singing each piece *mezza voce.* Lighting people make adjustments. To test the hall's acoustics, Pavarotti asks his secretary, who is also his vocal student, to sing something. "What?" "*Casta Diva.*" "You're kidding!" "No. Sing it. I'll stand in back." Pavarotti is pleased with her rendition, then goes to change. Two detectives are on guard in the dressing-room area. Pavarotti guffaws when he sees a dressing room set aside for his manager, Herbert Breslin. As Pavarotti leaves the dressing room to go on stage, he stops to tell a long joke to Breslin, the guards, and others congregated outside his dressing room.

8:00 Pavarotti sings the concert to a house that, with chairs on the stage, seats over two thousand. The concert is a benefit with a large number of the seats selling at fifty dollars each. It sold out quickly.

10:30 After three encores, the concert ends and Pavarotti stations himself at an on-stage table where he signs programs for all comers.

11:30 Pavarotti joins the reception being given in another part of the Brooklyn Center for the Performing Arts for college dignitaries and other distinguished guests.

Midnight Pavarotti finally gets to his dressing room to change from white-tie-and-tails. He asks his friend Umberto Boeri to bring him a tray of the reception's exceptional hors d'oeuvre.

FEBRUARY 28: *1:00* A.M. Coming up the west side of Manhattan in the limousine Pavarotti points out to others in the car a waterfront store which he says has fantastic bargains. He has heard that people fly over from Italy to buy merchandise there, then fly back the same day.

177

1:15 The limousine drops Pavarotti at the Hotel Navarro, then takes the others to their homes.

11:00 to 1:30 A complicated meeting in the office of Metropolitan Opera General Manager Anthony Bliss with Pavarotti, Joan Ingpen, James Levine, and Herbert Breslin to discuss Pavarotti's future Met plans.

3:00 Arrive at Manhattan television studios for taping of ABC "Omnibus" segment which Pavarotti will do with country-and-western singer Loretta Lynn whose movie biography, *Coal Miner's Daughter*, is just being released. The makeup man is angered when Pavarotti prefers that his secretary do his makeup. Going over the dialogue he will exchange with Lynn, Pavarotti wants to add a line. Having said to Lynn that his aria *"La donna è mobile"* is about man not being able to trust woman, she replies that she will sing a song about women not being able to trust other women. Pavarotti wants to say, "It comes to the same thing; women can't be trusted." The producer likes the change; the secretary must alter the cue cards. Pavarotti also asks her to spell out the word "hatred" phonetically, as he has trouble with the "h" sound.

4:00 to 7:00 Taping of the fifteen-minute Pavarotti-Lynn segment. There are many run-throughs. During a break, Lynn tells Pavarotti she feels foolish with him in white tie and tails and herself in jeans outfit. "I have lots of gowns," she says, "but they are all in the trailer."

7:15 After leaving the studio, Pavarotti settles in the rear of the limousine. A middle-aged woman, one of a group of fans who have been waiting for him, throws herself into the car on top of him after getting his autograph. She is removed without difficulty.

7:30 Tennis at the River Club with tennis pro Billy Talbot.

10:00 A Chinese takeout dinner at the Navarro apartment with about twelve friends.

FEBRUARY 29: *12:30* Lunch with the Italian Consul at his Park Avenue headquarters.

2:30 Meeting at the Navarro apartment with an accountant.

3:30 Meeting with representatives of R.A.I., the Italian radio and television monopoly, to discuss future projects.

5:00 Sauna meeting with Herbert Breslin.

7:00 Dinner at the hotel. Evening spent packing and phoning friends to say goodbye.

MARCH 1: *11:00* Lunch with old friend Mirella Freni who has arrived in New York in time to see Pavarotti's last performance of *Un Ballo in Maschera.*

12:45 Leaves for the Met.

1:00 to 2:00 Greets friends in his dressing room while signing a large stack of eight-by-ten photographs so his secretary will have a supply to send fans who write in for them while he is in Italy. His secretary opens letters from a sack of fan mail and reads some to him. An admirer has sent him a life-sized woman's leg made of chocolate. Also in the mail are two neckties and a hand-knit cardigan sweater which Pavarotti tries on. It is broad enough, but the length reaches only the middle of his chest. A friend tells Pavarotti it looks like a training bra. Other friends laugh. Pavarotti tells them all to go to hell. Another fan has left a tin of homemade pecan cookies which Pavarotti pronounces delicious. His secretary hides the tin.

2:00 Performance of *Un Ballo in Maschera,* which is broadcast nationally on radio by Texaco.

5:15 Pavarotti breaks his usual custom of greeting any fans who want to come to the Green Room. No one is allowed backstage so that Pavarotti can quickly change from his costume and take a waiting limousine to Kennedy Airport. Pavarotti is disappointed to learn that fellow tenor Giuseppe di Stefano has decided to stay longer in New York and will not be on the same flight as planned. Pavarotti and his secretary go over the many things he has asked her to do after his departure.

7:00 Pavarotti boards the plane and flies off to Milan.

LUCIANO PAVAROTTI

Some Thoughts on Food

I want to pause here and talk about something very dear to me: food. One of the very nicest things about life is the way we must regularly stop whatever it is we are doing and devote our attention to eating. Why not in an autobiography too?

It should be apparent that I like to eat. I do not like being overweight and I fight very hard against it—sometimes with success. I know that my weight has played a part in my becoming well known. It has made me stand out perhaps from the other singers and stick in people's minds.

On the other hand, I think it has hurt my career as much as it has helped. How you look on the stage, even for an opera singer, is important. Also, a big part of being a well-known person today is making appearances on television, either concerts, interview shows, or part of news-oriented programs like the "Sixty Minutes" segment on CBS that showed my trip to Israel. It is so much better to look well for these opportunities and I know that being fat does not look well.

I am not sure how it happened. I started getting heavy in the early years of my professional career, when I was singing in opera houses around Europe and at Covent Garden. I know part of it was the incredible amount of exercise I did as a child. I was constantly playing some sport or other, sitting still only to eat. When my career made this impossible, I think my body had grown used to the large amount of food necessary for constant exertion.

Another factor may have added to this problem. My profession is an enormously demanding one, requiring great discipline. I think I meet these demands professionally, but when I get to the table, I react against the constant restraint. Then, too, in being an opera singer, there is so much pressure, so much strain on the nerves. Some singers react by throwing tantrums. I eat.

I have fought this problem and I will continue to fight it. In the process (both of acquiring and losing fat) I have learned much about food and would like to share some of my findings.

183

For instance, I know the caloric value of every food you are likely to encounter in the civilized world. I am like a doctor in this regard, but I won't bore you with that, as you can find this information in handy little booklets.

First, some general thoughts on controlling weight. I firmly believe that wine with food is ruinous. I love wine. However, something about the way its calories react with other calories seems to magnify the effect. I enjoy drinking, but if a doctor told me I could never again have a drink of hard liquor, I don't think I would mind too much. If he said I could never again have wine, I would die. Still, when I am seriously dieting, I do not drink it. Only diet soda.

There are tricks to dieting. One is to wait as long as possible before starting a meal, or, after starting, between courses. Your stomach is already a little happy because it knows it is about to be fed.

And if you can delay taking more food after eating a little —a bowl of soup to start the meal, for example—that hunger which may still be raging will calm down a little in anticipation of what is to come. When the food finally comes, you are not as hungry.

Another mechanism may be at work here and this is a very useful thing to know about to help you stop eating at a meal before gorging yourself. The appetite, even when it has had enough food, requires about fifteen minutes to "turn itself off." You eat a modest meal but you are still hungry, maybe terribly hungry. Wait fifteen minutes and see if the hunger doesn't go away. It often works.

If the hunger is *still* there after fifteen minutes, you are on your own. Just know that you have my sympathy.

Before you laugh too hard at my offering advice on dieting, stop and think. You don't know how heavy I might be if I didn't have these secrets.

Another thing is to figure out your own strengths and

weaknesses. Some people are capable of eating *half* a piece of chocolate cake, others are not. The ones who are not should not allow chocolate cake to come near them. They must run when they see it. They must leave houses where it is kept on the kitchen counter. They must avoid restaurants where it is a specialty.

I, for instance, adore pasta and would find life difficult without at least some pasta or rice every day. A doctor friend of mine worked out a diet for me which allows a little pasta. It is a wonderful diet and not difficult because it takes into consideration my weaknesses. It forbids liquor and fat, but allows for generous amounts of certain things. It acknowledges that I am accustomed to large portions. So it permits healthy quantities of meat and certain vegetables. Pasta and starch are limited to about five ounces a day. This works well for me because I like everything, including meats and vegetables.

For many years I had as my secretary a wonderful Italian American named Annamarie Verde. She did everything for me, completely organized my life and saw that I arrived where I had to be. One of many things she did that was beyond the call of duty was devising wonderful recipes out of ingredients I was allowed to eat. Annamarie is an inspired cook. Like me, she loves to eat and has a problem with weight. She threw herself into creating variations on my diet with some very happy results. Someday I hope to produce a cookbook with these recipes that Annamarie and I worked out for my diet, plus some I've worked out for my pleasure.

Basically, my diet is measured amounts of protein that is relatively low in calories—veal, chicken, or fish—cooked together with nonstarchy vegetables—zucchini, onions, green beans, celery, carrots, among others—then the whole mixture chilled in the refrigerator.

I eat this concoction with a daily ration of three and a half ounces of rice. Eating the food cold has come to be important to me. This way I can take it right from the refrigerator and eat it. I eliminate that waiting period while food is cooking when the temptation to nibble on whatever is around becomes unbearable. Naturally I adjust the seasoning so that the dishes taste better cold than hot.

If you must worry about your weight as I do, certain facts become second nature to you. For instance, you know that veal has fewer calories than chicken, and chicken has fewer than turkey. I love young, tender veal, but it is hard to find in America; when you do, it is terribly expensive. But most of the things I like most in my diet—red meat, chicken, fish—are readily available in America and quite good.

I am not good at explaining how long everything should be over the fire and other technicalities. I can do it myself, but I am not that precise in telling others. What I am best at is tasting the finished dish and analyzing what it needs to make it better.

I am extremely particular about some aspects of food preparation. For instance, I am convinced parsley chopped very fine adds a completely different taste to a dish—and a far better taste than parsley chopped coarsely. Annamarie kids me about the time she went into the kitchen and saw a big sign I had put up which said: PLEASE, CHOP FINE THE PARSLEY!

MIRELLA FRENI

Two Kids from Modena

Now that Luciano and I sing opposite each other in opera houses all over the world, I marvel at how far back we go together. Even before Luciano and I were born, our families were friends. We lived in the same neighborhood and his mother and mine worked in the same cigar factory. Something about tobacco sours milk, so we both had to have a wet nurse as infants. We had the *same* nurse, Luciano and I, and it's obvious who got all the milk.

The families were very friendly—we wouldn't have dinner together, that's not the way we all did things—but we saw each other every day and we knew all about each other's lives. Then my family moved to another part of Modena so I didn't see Luciano for many years. I don't really have too much recollection of him when we lived in the same neighborhood as we were too small, but the families kept up their acquaintance so as we grew up we were aware of each other.

I started singing at a younger age and one of the first times I remember seeing Luciano as we got older was when I was singing Liù in a production of *Turandot* at the Teatro Comunale of Modena. Luciano was singing in the chorus—so was his father. Luciano wasn't thinking much about following a singing career in those days, but everyone around the opera house said that with such a beautiful voice he should try. So he started studying.

We soon ended up with the same vocal coach, Maestro Ettore Campogalliani, in Mantova. And many times we would drive together from Modena to Mantova in his father's car or my husband's. Sometimes we would take the train together. We often discussed our work, exchanging thoughts about singing, about technique—the things we were studying. We were both learning so much at that time.

It's funny that we were thrown together this way because I had gone to high school with Adua Veroni, to whom he was then engaged and who is now Luciano's wife. We weren't in the same class but we knew each other and saw each other all the time.

I think of Luciano as a brother, truly. And such a loving relationship is very beautiful in careers such as ours where true friends are not easy to find. There is so much envy, so much intrigue. But I have never found Luciano to be the least bit this way—competitive or envious or whatever. And every time we work together in an opera now, we have a wonderful relationship, never any difficulties.

With our singing and our stage work, we are both quick to understand each other's problems. I often ask Luciano's advice or opinion and he has done the same with me. When we are far away in another city, it is marvelous to have a friend you know will understand you, who understands your work, who knows the details of your life, who won't be envious or jealous. When we find ourselves in the same city, Luciano and I have dinner together frequently. We sometimes joke about how we see more of each other when we are abroad than when we are in Modena. Sometimes we are both in Modena at the same time. When this happens our families will have dinner together. But more often than not, when he's there I am away somewhere and vice versa. It is always wonderful for me to learn that Luciano and I will be singing in the same place.

I can't really compare Luciano with other tenors I've worked with because between us there is a special friendship, a friendship I have with no other singer. I was never surprised at his big success. I always thought he would have a major career. I know Luciano was never asked to sing at Modena when he was starting out and that he feels they do not support their own singers, that they favor people from outside. I don't think this is true because my first role was in Modena—I sang Micaëla in 1955—and I sang many things there when I was starting out.

But about Luciano, I don't really understand why. Maybe they are prejudiced against tenors—strange things do happen.

They certainly love Luciano now. When he and I did a concert with the orchestra there in 1979, the audience was equally warm to us both.

The only change I've seen in Luciano personally as he grew more successful was an increase in weight. I've heard a lot of explanations why he grew heavy—from him and from others—but I think it is very simple: he likes to eat.

Success hasn't changed him at all. Our friendship has remained the same, as when we rode the train to Mantova together as students. Luciano is always Luciano.

I don't know whether all this publicity about how great he is will hurt him. It depends on the nerves that one has. I would be terrified. Every time you sing, you must do an incredible performance. Speaking for me, I wouldn't want it. But if his nerves can take it, then I think it's terrific.

LUCIANO PAVAROTTI

Performing an Opera

On the day of a performance, I sleep as late as I can and go to pains to avoid being awakened before my body has taken all the sleep it can possibly use. As always, I start the day with a cup of espresso and artificial sweetener, nothing else. Naturally, my concern is whether or not the voice is there. I might try the voice in the shower like men all over the world, but for me it is not exuberance at being alive and having water splashing over me. Sometimes I do sing for this reason, but not on the day of a performance. The condition of the voice is crucial.

Why is everyone so interested in sex and its effect on the voice? Maybe it's because singers have always looked for excuses when they are not in voice and too much lovemaking is a noble excuse. Or maybe it's because everyone is interested in sex and will use any pretext to bring it up.

Many singers, particularly tenors, believe that having sex before a performance affects the voice. Terry McEwen, who is taking over the direction of the San Francisco Opera, says he can hear it in the voice if a tenor has had sex the day before a performance. One tenor was so convinced it helped the voice, he would often arrange a little something backstage.

My friend José Carreras has the right idea on all this. He says, "Sex is good for my voice, but I can't speak for all tenors. I am never in bed with a tenor."

It is all so silly. Like José, I cannot resist joking about this when interviewers ask the question—and they always do. When *Newsweek*, for their cover story on me, asked how I felt about it, I answered them: "I think sex tunes the body the way vocalizing tunes the voice. I vocalize every day."

If I must be serious about it, I suspect it is better not to indulge before a performance or the day before, but I believe it is better not to exert yourself in *any* way on these days. You can sing badly five minutes afterward and you can sing badly five days afterward. I do not think the connection is so definite as many would have you believe.

195

For a singer, it is better not to let such concerns dominate your life. A colleague of mine at the Metropolitan is very rigid about this. His wife has complained publicly that he won't make love the day before singing or the day after, "And," she laments, "he sings twice a week."

Allow me, for this typical performance day I am going to describe, to leave this matter a mystery.

After I am fully awake and refreshed, I vocalize seriously for two minutes. If the voice is there, I stop and relax until it is time to eat. If it is not there, I still stop after two minutes—relax, then eat. I pass the time painting, perhaps reading. I avoid seeing people; talking is hard on the voice.

After eating, I rest for several hours, then vocalize again. If the voice is still not there, I force it, even screaming if necessary to make it arrive. I keep on vocalizing until I am sure the voice is there. Finally, I leave for the theater. When I arrive, I vocalize again to see if, along the way, I lost the voice.

For a performance of *L'Elisir d'Amore* at La Scala, for instance, I drive myself to the theater in my old Mercedes which I keep in the garage at my hotel, La Residenza Maria Teresa, where I take an apartment when I perform at La Scala. It is a residential hotel, very quiet, very comfortable; there I can get a place big enough for my paintings and with a kitchen so I can put together an occasional meal for myself and my friends.

Downtown Milan is a nightmare of one-way streets going every different direction. I don't know the city well, but I could find my way from the hotel to La Scala blindfolded. I love to drive and much prefer driving to being driven. My friends all know this and often let me drive their cars when we are going someplace together and I am abroad without my own.

After a performance or any other exciting event in my life, I like nothing better than to get behind the wheel of a powerful car and drive fast down an open highway—or sometimes in traffic—*all'italiano*. It is a wonderful way to unwind, but don't tell the traffic police I recommended this. La Scala lets me park in their courtyard backstage, so it is very convenient. I arrive about an hour and a half before the performance time.

On the opening night for my first *L'Elisir* for La Scala, I am more than a little nervous. I am always nervous before a performance. Any singer who says he is not is lying. Certain things make you more nervous than others. For instance, when in America I sang my first nationally televised concert, I was so terrified I hardly knew what I was doing.

The Milan critics can be sadists. You never know when they might turn on a performer or what might trigger their hatred. I suspect it is often an emotional cause unrelated to the actual performance. Word of my successes in America and elsewhere had come back to them and this frightened me. They dislike being told by foreigners which Italian tenors to like and dislike.

Also, on the day of this opening performance, I have a little something wrong with my throat. It isn't a sore throat exactly. Something, however, is not as it should be; just enough out of perfect condition to add to my nervousness.

I enter the dark, wood-paneled dressing room. Hearing my colleagues in their rooms vocalizing tells me that I am backstage in an opera house before a performance. I check to see if my Adina, Mirella Freni, is in her room and feeling all right. She smiles and blows me a kiss from her dressing table.

My dressing room is with the men, on the floor directly above hers. I am greeted by my dresser, a middle-aged woman who has been with La Scala for years. She has my costume ready, but first I must strip down, vocalize a little at the small piano in my dressing room, get cleaned up, then go to the makeup room at the end of the corridor to receive my makeup for the part of Nemorino.

Waiting for me in the brightly lighted room is the professional makeup man with whom I have worked out a good effect for this role at the dress rehearsal. I take a keen interest in makeup and do much of it myself. I sit with my back to the door of this brightly lit room. The door is open to the corridor and as the makeup goes on I exchange greetings into the mirror with colleagues who stop by to watch me turn into Nemorino. Even when I am anxious as I am now, I am always able to laugh and kid with friends.

The director, Jean-Pierre Ponnelle, stops by to go over one or two small changes in the stage business we agreed on after the dress rehearsal. Ponnelle originally directed this production for the Hamburg Opera.

My makeup is complete. I now have a tan to suggest a country boy who spends most of his day under the sun tending his sheep. (Making Nemorino a shepherd is a Ponnelle touch.) A wig of short, curly dark hair is fixed into place and I look pretty good. I don't always feel this way when I'm in costume and makeup. I return to my dressing room and am helped into my costume, which is basically a loose-fitting smock and very comfortable.

Now I am ready and must wait. This is when the nerves start to build with a fury. I sit at the piano and try a vocal run. The voice sounds okay, but there is still something in the throat. This is extremely worrying. Whatever it is may not affect my voice at the moment but might very well affect it very much after an hour of strenuous singing on stage. And there would still be two hours left to sing.

La Scala's vocal coach enters my dressing room as he does before every performance. He says a "*buona sera*" and sits at the piano and hits a chord. I sing the major triad for him. We progress up. When he reaches the C, he stops and turns to me.

"*Va bene?*" he says.

I tell him about the discomfort in my throat. He assures me the voice sounds fine. He leaves.

Now is the worst time. You have done everything you must do but there is still twenty minutes before curtain time. Now you must only sit and wonder how you ever got into this profession where you, a grown man, must get yourself dressed up in a funny costume, walk out onto a stage before thousands of people who may or may not wish you well, and risk making a complete fool of yourself or causing an artistic scandal.

Opera is a fabulous form because it has so many facets. And any one of those facets can defeat the singer, even though he executes the others brilliantly. As the curtain time approaches, lyric opera ceases to be an incredibly rich, tradition-laden treasure house of great art, and becomes a minefield of potential disasters.

Finally, it is time for me to take my position on stage and I begin the death march. My dresser lady follows along behind me carrying a bottle of mineral water, pins, and various other things I might need in emergencies. As we enter the stage area, I search for my bent nail. This is a superstition I have had for years. I don't like to sing until I have found a bent nail on the stage floor. Usually, it is not that difficult with all the carpentry done backstage. The belief is a combination of two Italian superstitions—metal for good luck and bent to suggest the horns that ward off evil.

Everyone laughs at me for this superstition and there have been times when numbers of backstage people have scurried around helping me to find one. It is not true that I send my wife ahead to find me a nail, as I read somewhere. Whoever wrote that has never met my wife. Besides, the habit makes Adua angry because later I put the nail in my pocket and it often tears a hole which she must have repaired. Many people now know about my bent-nail obsession and fans from all over the world have sent me unusual ones—silver nails, even ones of solid gold. All I want is a real nail, right before the performance, to fight bad luck.

I arrive at my post. For the first act of *L'Elisir*, Ponnelle has devised an outdoor village set with a little house for Nemorino at the stage-left proscenium box, a box with direct access to the stage apron in front of the curtain. There is another on the opposite side of the stage for Adina, Nemorino's lady-love. These boxes are usually used by theater managers, but for this production, one of them is my little house. I rarely get to return to this little house, as I am always on stage singing.

I sit down on a small straight chair in the box. I can hear the murmur of the audience, like an ocean capable of caressing or murdering. I am handed the prop for my first aria, a stuffed lamb, a silly little toy not intended to appear real. The conductor arrives at his stand and receives applause. The audience quiets.

These are the very worst moments. There is no turning back now. The performance is starting. I sit there with sweat rolling down my neck and I still have three hours to go. I would rather be in any other profession. I would prefer to be back teaching my monster schoolboys—anything. I pray. I have one good God, but one is not enough to get me through this. I don't think I have an enemy, but if I did I would not want even him to suffer these terrible moments.

As the overture begins, the curtain rises and I know I must soon enter to enact a little pantomime with Adina, who likewise emerges from her little house across the stage. I know from the many past performances that I am blessed with a quality that helps me, when the moment is upon me, shed those paralyzing nerves. As the time approaches when I must make my entrance, something clicks in my mind. I become the character, and everything else leaves my head.

It is like self-hypnosis. It is hard to explain. Part of it is the total concentration I feel is essential to a good performance, whether on the opera stage or in the concert hall. But part of it, I think, is a reaction against the overload of things to worry about. If you let yourself think of everything that lies ahead of you in the next hours—all the hazards, all you must remember, technical details, artistic matters with the music, and the way you and the conductor have worked out a hundred discrepancies in your approach to the score—and the audience, always the audience, that restive, capricious giant—if you allow your mind to wander over even a portion of these concerns, you would have a nervous breakdown.

The total concentration that eliminates everything but what you are doing at the exact moment is not just for artistic excellence, it is for self-preservation as well. You are a simple country boy in love with a girl who is rejecting you. That is all. I have been on stage for long periods of time without being the least aware of the audience. If I am conscious of anything beyond the world that Donizetti and Felice Romani have created, it is only the conductor with his baton waving in the dim light.

With *L'Elisir*, I must begin the opera with a full aria. Alone in front of my little house I stand in a spotlight and, clutching my stuffed lamb, sing, *"Quanto è bella, quanto è cara."* It is a lovely aria, a sweet declaration of Nemorino's love for Adina. It is not without dangers for a tenor, particularly a tenor who has not had an opportunity to warm up.

The aria goes well and the audience makes me aware of them with their applause—nothing wild, but cordial, bordering on warm. It is amazing how you can feel audience reactions to you even before the applause. It is something you sense in an almost psychic way. I have rarely been surprised by the audience's response at the end of a piece—its coldness, its indifference, or its whole-hearted enthusiasm. I can feel it before they show it.

Now I could feel them warm up even more as Mirella begins Adina's simple aria in which she reads to her lady friends the story of Tristan and Isolde. How could any audience not warm to Mirella? She would win them with her petite, appealing beauty alone. That she is also a major artist, a soprano of the very first rank, becomes apparent as she progresses in her aria, but this music does not begin to demonstrate all her capabilities.

As Nemorino, I must watch her longingly from another part of the stage. As Luciano Pavarotti, I watch her and a thought flashes through my mind. The two of us were born within months of each other in the same, small neighborhood, in the same small city. Now we are at the most famous opera house in the world re-creating two of the great roles in the Italian lyric repertoire. What a joy to perform with Mirella! As an artist and as a friend.

The first act progresses well and I can feel the audience relaxing and enjoying themselves more. That does not mean, I know well, that they will give you, specifically, their approval, or that they will not suddenly turn against the whole proceedings. Dulcamara makes his entrance marvelously and sings his delightful sales pitch to the townsfolk. Then I sing my duet with him in which I entreat him to sell me a potion to make Adina fall in love with me.

I adore this duet. The situation is clear and comic: the naïve bumpkin hoping for a miracle and the unscrupulous con artist only too happy to sell him whatever he wants. The music brilliantly captures Nemorino's joy at finding a man of science to help him win his girl and Dulcamara is equally joyous to find an ignorant peasant to swindle. Somehow the happy music connotes the positive aspect of this game—that people may cheat each other but everyone has a way of getting what he wants. I think this wonderful, melodic scene represents Italian comic opera at its best. But there are many such moments in *L'Elisir*.

The first act ends with my lurching desperately around the stage, the entire company jeering me as they prepare for Adina's wedding to my rival. My frantic movements add to my exhaustion as the curtain falls. I head for the dressing room only vaguely hearing the applause which seems enthusiastic but not overwhelming. Milan is not yet won. I am out of breath and perspiring profusely.

I collapse in my dressing room and drink a little mineral water and then some hot tea. My voice seems to be holding up, but there is still much singing to do. My wife comes back and we chat for a while. She tells me the audience loves it, but I cannot relax until I have gotten safely through my big aria in the second act, *"Una furtiva lagrima."* Intermissions are an emotional no-man's-land. You are out of battle for a brief spell, but the war is far from over. Originally I insisted on being alone during intermissions, only letting my wife into my dressing room. I have relaxed considerably about this, though I am not the social animal I am when it is over.

I clean up, repair my makeup, and wait for the call. It seems like no time at all has passed and I am back on the stage renegotiating with Dulcamara for another bottle of love potion. In my drunk scene after I have enlisted in military service to get the money for the elixir, the wine bottle breaks in my hand. I don't notice the blood till I make a brief exit. The dresser cleans the cut and applies a bandage that can't be seen by the audience.

During all the rehearsals up to and including the dress, the wine bottle was plastic. We all agreed this was the safest. For some reason I will hear later, the prop man decided to change what we had all agreed on without telling me. I am out on stage, comfortable in the knowledge that I am dealing with an unbreakable plastic bottle, and it shatters. I am sure there was some reason for switching to glass—the plastic one was lost or some such minor matter—but to discover it during a performance makes me feel betrayed by one who is supposed to be supporting me. Such things keep us on our toes, nervous wrecks, and, sometimes, in a rage.

Compared with many opera singers, some of whom perhaps are accident prone, my career seems to have been relatively free of on-stage mishaps. Once when I was singing in San Francisco, the stage started to shake badly. It felt like it was going to be quite a serious earthquake. Except when I am in an airplane, I am reasonably brave and during this earthquake I kept quite calm—and I was told later I helped to calm others.

Maybe other things have happened that I did not notice. I do wrap myself totally in what I am doing on stage. I do remember one time when I was terribly distracted—almost to the point of ruining my performance. I was singing *La Bohème* in Ankara, Turkey. Since I do not speak Turkish, we put on the opera with my singing the part of Rodolfo in Italian and all the rest of the cast singing in Turkish. It was so strange to hear those familiar phrases coming to me in a completely unfamiliar language. I wanted to burst out laughing. Every time I would adopt the persona of Rodolfo, a Parisian poet of the nineteenth century, I would be thrown into confusion by someone singing at me in Martian talk.

Finally the moment comes at La Scala when all of the *L'Elisir* cast leaves me alone on the stage. I place myself in the center of that vast space and sing one of the greatest of all tenor arias, "*Una furtiva lagrima.*" It is a wonderful aria and a curious one. All of the opera's music up to this moment has been lively and lighthearted, brilliant, to be sure, but always remaining within the realm of the *opera buffa* idiom. Suddenly everything stops for a total change of mood—this one aria of unsurpassing loveliness and seriousness. It is as though Donizetti were saying, "We've been having fun this evening, but in case you forgot, here is a reminder that I am a very good composer and you are listening to very good singers."

As the orchestra plays the sweet, sad introduction, I can only *hope* they are listening to a very good singer. It is difficult to express to others what occurs when an Italian tenor faces an Italian audience to perform one of the great tenor showpieces in

Italian opera. You must understand first what opera means to Italians, how we revere our great composers, how we grow up familiar with their music, how important a part of the national heritage this music is for us all.

Then too, I don't know but can imagine what previous treasured memories the people in front of me have had with this particular piece of music. It is conceivable that they have heard it sung by Gigli, Schipa, di Stefano, Tagliavini, or any of the other great tenors who have sung from this same stage, giving the audience an experience that might have been, for many of them, a high point in their lives. And I am going to have the effrontery to try to do it. As you start the music—softly, quietly —emotion is strong on both sides of the footlights.

The aria is curious in another way, besides its sad isolation in a comic opera. Most of the great tenor arias in the Italian repertoire end with a bravura high note, a note that, if it goes well, can send an audience into a frenzy. *"Una furtiva lagrima"* has no such surefire crowd "activator"—only excruciatingly beautiful music that can show up every flaw of a badly trained voice.

I sing the wonderful melody once with its dramatic and un-expected change of key at the most emotional point, then the music repeats the melody a second time, with very little varia-tion at the end. It is probably the most restrained of all the great tenor arias. From the point of view of getting through it, *"Una furtiva lagrima"* is not a difficult aria. From the point of view of eliciting the enormous emotional potential from the music, it is one of the most difficult.

Suddenly I am on the last note, which I hold. There is a pause. I think it has gone all right. I awake to the most incredi-ble applause. La Scala had gone out of its mind. I stand there, my arms a little out from my side, trying to hold the moment in the characterization. The ovation gets louder and shows no signs of stopping.

So many things course through my mind. Of course, I am delighted I have gotten through it, that it is over. I am glad that they are pleased, that La Scala is pleased, that the critics, I think, will be pleased. The victory has been won.

Another thought comes that may perhaps sound arrogant. I think that a piece of music, even a great piece of music, is not a complete creation by itself. The performance completes the composer's intention. If you feel you have performed it well, then you feel that you are a part of the artist who created it.

The applause goes on and on and I still struggle not to lose hold of my character. At one point in my career, I would acknowledge the applause in the middle of an opera if the ovation didn't seem likely to stop. I would tell myself that it would appease the audience, that they wouldn't stop until I offered a reaction to their enthusiasm. But I have found that if an audience goes wild, as this one is doing, acknowledging the applause, stepping out of character, and in your own personality thanking them—it only excites them more. If you have any hope of getting on with the opera so you can go home and eat dinner, you must just stand there like a dummy, a grateful dummy perhaps, until they exhaust themselves.

The newspapers the next day said that the ovation after this aria went on for ten minutes. This is a long time for people to applaud—I am grateful for one minute. A friend of mine told me that with the singing of the aria that night, I converted the haughty, sophisticated Milanese audience into Neapolitans.

I stand there very happy, very grateful, and a little embarrassed.

Eventually the opera continues. A little more singing with Mirella, then we are in the final scene. When the curtain finally comes down, the passion that the audience displayed after *"Una furtiva lagrima"* again explodes for Mirella and the entire production. With curtain call after curtain call, you are paid back for the agony of those beginning moments. I am sent out alone and the audience goes into a frenzy. I confess I love applause. It is my oxygen.

I am a very loving person and I need lots of love. There is something very special about the love an audience gives you. It is not like any other. With your friends and your family, you can never be sure how much they love you or if the love will last. There are so many complicated reasons for the love between individuals. But between a performer and the audience, it is not complicated. It is very simple. If they love you, they tell you; if they don't, they will not pretend. What is more, as long as you perform as they wish you to, they are willing to tell you every night.

Finally it is truly over and I am in my dressing room. There is my father who has driven up from Modena. He gives me a warm hug. Various friends and strangers rush, push, then squeeze into my dressing room. I let anyone who wishes come backstage to see me. Adua works her way through the people and gives me a big kiss. As her lips are on mine, I am surrounded by beautiful women. A lady journalist from Rome says, "Which one is the wife?" Everybody laughs.

My daughters hug and kiss me, my sister and aunts. Of course, my mother is not here. She has never heard me sing in a theater. She would get too emotional; she says she is afraid for her heart. Mirella and I are singing a concert in Modena in a week and my mother has said she will try to come for that. We will see.

Now the dressing room is jammed with friends and family. People pass in and out. I kiss every woman who greets me—from eight to eighty. I love all this so much; I joke with everyone.

An old man grabs both my hands and kisses them. Another says, "There are no words." I say, "You liked it then, my friend?" And on and on it goes.

After a time I can see that my wife and family, with whom I am planning to go to dinner, are getting impatient, but they know that I will stay here until the last visitor has gone.

Finally we go to dinner at one of my favorite restaurants in Milan. I am never happier than when I have done a performance well and am permitted to eat and have fun with people I love. Of course I eat too much. I can lose as many as ten pounds during a performance, but I gain it right back, especially if I eat as I eat on this night. How can anyone think of a diet at glorious moments like this?

What can I think after such an evening but how lucky I am to be in my profession, to be doing exactly the work I want to do in the way I want to do it. I thank God He allows me to do this.

JOHN WUSTMAN

*Accompanying
Pavarotti*

Pavarotti is, by no means, the first top artist I've accompanied. I've been doing it for twenty-seven years and have worked with many: Nilsson, Freni, Simionato, Gedda, Tagliavini, and others. Luciano and I have been performing together for almost five years.

I love accompanying singers but it's not my principal occupation, which is teaching. I'm on the music faculty at the University of Illinois in Urbana where I teach a course in accompanying. I also coach singers. At the beginning of each year, I sit down with Luciano and his manager, Herbert Breslin, and go over a schedule of the concerts Luciano would like to do. I try to make myself available for each one of them.

You don't get rich as an accompanist. I do it because I love the artists. And Luciano is not like any of the others. That is natural: you don't become as outstanding an artist as he is by being indistinguishable from other artists. It requires a highly personal style, something besides the voice itself that sets you apart from other singers.

With Luciano, you see this individuality on both the artistic and the personal level. Luciano has a way of making each person in the audience, even some of those giant audiences we have performed for, feel that he is singing directly to them. He sets up the most intensely personal lines of communication. It is extraordinary.

Another thing that sets Luciano apart is his musicality. Compared to the other artists I've worked with, Luciano is not a particularly good musician. By good musician, I mean technically proficient—being a quick sight reader, for instance. But he is super, super, super musical. Many are first-class musicians without being musical.

To put it most simply, being musical means that after learning a score you can open your mouth and have it come out music. It is a matter of phrasing and feeling and overall comprehension of the composer's intentions—plus the ability to transmit that intention. Luciano has this to a wonderful degree. He has real feelings, he has soul—and he has no trouble getting these qualities into the music he sings.

I've heard Luciano tell other people that he learns slowly. I've worked with him a lot, and I disagree. He *does* have a problem on his attention span. You measure the periods of serious study in minutes, not hours, when you coach him on a new work. But in those four or five minutes, he really concentrates and learns quickly what has to be learned so that he can give an accurate rendition of the notes. Far more important, he can also translate those accurate notes almost immediately into music.

You can't buy this quality. Or achieve it with years of study. The same thing is true for those other qualities that set Luciano apart as a performer. Those extra qualities are what make great artists.

Something happens between Luciano and an audience that I've never seen with another artist. When he walks out onto a stage to start a concert—even in a new city—I can feel waves of love for him sweeping up from the audience—before he has sung a note. It is so hard to explain, it borders on the mystical.

I've mentioned it to Luciano and he brushes it aside. "Perhaps they've heard me sing before and like me," or "Maybe they have heard good things about me."

That would explain their being receptive and cordial, but I feel real warmth coming up from the crowd. It is palpable—waves of love.

We have had our mishaps while performing. We were doing a group of Tosti songs. We had just finished a happy, lively song and I started the introduction to our next, which was also happy and lively. When I got to the point where Luciano was about to sing, I was horrified to hear him start off on, not the song he was supposed to, the one I was playing, but the song we had just finished. I quickly switched, and we did the same one twice. When you think about it, it's amazing things like that don't happen more often.

I enjoy enormously doing concerts with Luciano. For one thing, I feel we are making first-rate music, so there is plenty of artistic satisfaction. In addition, there is always an excitement about his performances and just being around him—that makes this business of concertizing—which is serious, difficult work—a lot of fun as well.

WILLIAM WRIGHT

Lunch at Pesaro

Once a year, Pavarotti breaks his routine of singing and recording throughout the world and comes to rest at his summer villa in Pesaro, on the Adriatic. These vacations—which started being measured in months, then in weeks, and now in days—are the one stretch of his year when he can cease to be an opera singer and instead be a husband, a father, a friend, a host, a sportsman, a painter, an idler.

Nowhere more than at Pesaro is Pavarotti able to relax and do as he pleases. While he is there, an event takes place that is the focus of each day and that typifies the sojourns. It is the two-hour lunch for never less than sixteen friends, relatives, and career associates who sit with Pavarotti to talk away four- and five-course meals. The lunches are a daily ritual that, for him, go beyond mere socializing and are a daily reaffirmation of his determination not to slip away from the world that produced and nurtured him.

The villa came about in a typical Pavarotti way—a series of circumstances that mixed nostalgia, opera, friendship, and impulse. In January 1969, Pavarotti was singing *I Puritani* in Bologna with Mirella Freni. Among the group of admirers that came backstage after the performance to greet him was an accountant, Cesare Castellani, who had driven up from his home in Pesaro on a bus chartered by an organization called Pesaro Friends of the Opera.

The others on the bus had made the trip to hear Mirella Freni, who, unlike Pavarotti, was already popular with Italian opera lovers. Castellani, on the other hand, was more interested in the young tenor whom he happened to have heard on the radio and whose voice impressed him.

Pavarotti's performance as Arturo lived up to Castellani's expectations. When face to face with the tenor, Castellani was profuse in praising him. Pavarotti engaged the older man in conversation, as he often does with well-wishers out of friendliness, but also with the purpose of neutralizing the idol-idolator cast of these encounters. Learning Castellani was from Pesaro, Pavarotti became expansive.

"I know Pesaro well," he said. "It is a beautiful city on the Adriatic where my family sometimes took me as a small boy. I have not been there in years."

Castellani urged Pavarotti to renew his acquaintance with Pesaro, assuring him that, should the Pavarotti family decide to visit, he would do all in his power to make them welcome and comfortable. As a result of that suggestion, Pavarotti took Adua and his daughters to Pesaro for a holiday the following summer, staying in one of the seaside hotels. He looked up Castellani and the friendship began.

Pesaro is on Italy's east coast, fifty-five kilometers north of Ancona and eighty kilometers south of Ravenna. The old town sits a few hundred yards back from the beach, which is now a solid phalanx of moderately high-rising hotels and apartments. Like many Italian towns, the old section is a concentration of ancient *palazzi* hovering over crooked streets.

Pesaro has two claims to the notice of the rest of the world. Rossini was born there in 1792 and it is today a popular summer resort. In the hot months, its broad, flat beaches are covered with rows of colorful tents, endless and geometrically precise. Prides of German and Scandinavian families descend here to remove most of their clothes and sit in low canvas chairs inches away from Italians, equally naked and equally well chaperoned by small children.

For Pavarotti and his family, summer outings in Pesaro soon were annual events. Paravotti became so enthusiastic about the city that he told his friend Cesare to keep a lookout and to let him know if a good house should appear on the market. Almost immediately a choice property became available. It was an old farmhouse that perched on a hillside directly over the sea at the north end of town, just after the coastline loses the concrete apartment houses and reverts to untouched green hills dropping abruptly into the sea.

The paved road that curves along the water becomes dirt-surfaced as it continues behind the beach about two hundred yards before ending at the gate of the property. Inside the gate, the road makes an immediate hairpin turn and rises, straight and steep, to the house—a commodious, sturdy villa that sits on an expanse of level ground terraced into the steep hillside.

Pavarotti bought the house in 1974 and promptly undertook its renovation. His intention was to keep the original contours but modernize and restructure the interior. Now, when you approach the property from the beach road, you encounter a new gate with a sign: *Villa Giulia.* Pavarotti named the place after his grandmother, his mother's mother, whose favorite he was and whom he worshipped as a child. If the gate is closed and locked, the visitor must ring a buzzer, speak on an intercom and be scrutinized on a closed-circuit television. Such elaborate precautions, however, are counter to the Pavarotti easy-come summer mood, and during the day at least the gate usually stands wide open, all the electronic apparatus going unused.

Pavarotti has paved the steep drive to his house, which climbs in a straight line, then swerves around the sea flank of the villa, passes just below it, then circles back to emerge at the far end of the building. Because this is the side of the house with the swimming pool, the garden, and the covered piazza where meals are served, visitors arriving by car usually do so in full view of all the other guests.

Since its renovation, the house is pristine white plaster with shutters and trim of royal blue, a roof of red tile. The blue Adriatic dominates the view, but if you walk to the edge of the terrace, you can look down on a public beach and some six-story modern buildings slightly below to the right. For miles northward, to the left, green hills drop off to the sea.

One end of the house is a large salon with eight heavily upholstered chairs, an upright piano in one corner, a table permanently set up for playing cards, and modernistic fluorescent lighting built into the ceiling. The end of the house, outside this room, is a broad covered terrace with a dining table that can, without strain, accommodate twenty-four.

Just beyond this terrace, in a flat area of the hillside, bordered by the sweeping driveway and parking area, is a six-foot-high, Pavarotti-designed fountain, four horses holding up a water-spouting bowl. This flat area also has some flower beds and a generous swimming pool with a diving board and, floating in the green water, two inflatable blue rafts. Around the pool are white oleanders, marigolds, red geraniums, grass in need of cutting, and a good number of weeds.

The overall feeling to this villa is one of comfort, recreation, and affluence. The slightly unkempt garden gives the impression that love for the place rather than obsessive fastidiousness propels the casual maintenance.

In permanent residence at the Villa Giulia is a housekeeper, Anna Antonelli, who came with the property and who turned out, with a stroke of luck, to be an exceptional cook, even in a part of the world rife with good cooks. There are also three dogs and a cat population that fluctuates around twenty-two.

Each summer since the renovation was completed, Pavarotti comes to the Villa Giulia with his wife and daughters for a vacation that is constantly shortened by invitations to sing that are difficult to refuse. An example would be the request in July 1979 to sing in Israel where Pavarotti would be the principal guest artist for the gala Richard Tucker Memorial Concert at the Frederick Mann Auditorium in Tel Aviv. This summer event would delay the vacation's start.

At the other end, his holiday would be cut short by a concert he had agreed to sing in Philadelphia's Robin Hood Dell on

August 22 to honor Marian Anderson and to raise money for a scholarship fund at the University of Pennsylvania in her name.

This year's vacation for Pavarotti would be roughly a month. During that time he had to complete his study of a new role, Enzo, in *La Gioconda* with which he would be opening the San Francisco opera season in September; complete his study of Rossini's voice-destroying tenor role in *William Tell;* work on his autobiography; sit for a *Time* magazine cover story, listen to and judge aspiring singers, scheduled and unscheduled; drive to Modena for conferences about his business interests; and play host to large numbers of friends and relatives. This is the vacation.

An overriding project for Pavarotti during these seaside interludes is assessing and adjusting the characters of his three daughters, who are careening into teenage with their father absent most of the time. The weeks at Pesaro are Pavarotti's main chance to criticize and issue paternal edicts.

For this reason, the summer weeks at the Villa Giulia are less popular with the girls than they are with their father. Another reason his daughters are apathetic about the swimming pool, the beach, the escape from Modena's heat, is the enforced separation from school friends and beaus. Then, too, the many visitors who move in and out of the Villa Giulia each day Pavarotti is in residence are friends, associates, or admirers of their father. Pretty teenaged girls in Italy, as in America, are more accustomed to being at the center of things.

On a day in August 1979, Pavarotti, who likes to stay up late, rises around ten and has coffee. He wears sneakers, a white beanie-like sun hat, white bathing trunks, and an orange plastic windbreaker. The day is warm and sunny; a number of sailboats dot the bright seascape. He chats with his daughters, his father-in-law, Guido Veroni, a cheerful, friendly man who has had three strokes. Pavarotti's own parents have just left after a week's visit. Also staying in the house are his wife's sister, Loredana, her husband, son, and daughter.

Several temporary members of the household are career-related individuals who have traveled great distances to be with Pavarotti during his leisure period. One of these is an assistant conductor of the Metropolitan Opera, Gildo di Nunzio, who has been hired by London Records to coach Pavarotti in the *William Tell* score, which he will be traveling to England to record in late August, en route to Philadelphia. Di Nunzio and other such work-related guests are housed in a nearby hotel but are expected for meals at the Villa Giulia. Nothing is said about this unless the guests should not show up for a lunch or dinner; an empty place at the table is not well regarded in Pavarotti's Italy.

Someone is always at hand around the villa wherever Pavarotti alights—on the terrace, in the salon, by the pool, or on the covered veranda where his easel is set up. Here on this day he sits for twenty minutes dabbing bright colors on a painting in progress, a scene of a Venetian canal. Some friends from Modena who arrived earlier in the day look over his shoulder.

"What is that, Luciano? New York City?"

"Yes, that's it," another says. "A view of the New York subway."

"You morons don't know art when you see it!" Pavarotti says, never taking his eyes from his work, his white beanie low on his forehead.

Di Nunzio no longer tries to coax Pavarotti to the piano. His presence is silent entreaty. Suddenly Pavarotti says, "Gildo! *andiamo lavorare!*" and di Nunzio is at the piano in a flash playing the staccato lead-in to one of the three Rossini passages he and Pavarotti have decided needs work. Pavarotti sits on the arm of the stuffed chair near the piano so he can read the score over di Nunzio's shoulder. They go through each of the passages once, Pavarotti singing them, high C's and all, full voice. Pavarotti has difficulty with the last passage. They go over it four times.

Exactly six minutes after Pavarotti sat down to work, he announces, "Now I go for a swim."

Around eleven the *Time* photographer, Enrico Ferorelli, arrives and he puts Pavarotti to work, posing him first in the pool, then in a number of positions around the house, first alone, then with his three daughters. As lunch approaches, more and more people begin to fill the broad terrace, chatting in groups, sitting on a glider swing or at the outdoor dining table until the housekeeper and a young assistant start setting it for a meal. One of the arrivals is Pavarotti's close Pesaro friend, Cesare Castellani, who found the house for Pavarotti. Castellani takes his vacation from the Pesaro bank to coincide with Pavarotti's annual visits.

Not far from the dining table is a metal cooler, the kind that opens from the top, which used to be found at filling stations across the United States. Pavarotti keeps his cooler stocked with cold mineral water, beer, and soft drinks, particularly the sugar-free ones that he constantly drinks. From time to time, guests help themselves.

A visiting American was later asked how the days were spent at the Villa Giulia. He thought for a moment, then said, "Most of the time we just milled around waiting for the next meal."

The photographer has now gotten Pavarotti to change into an approximation of the Venetian Renaissance costume that he will wear in *La Gioconda*. On his head sits a gold-embroidered black toque. His hefty body is covered with a black caftan, sheer enough to evoke Frederick's of Hollywood. Now the photographer is using a metal sun reflector; the intense light gives the Villa Giulia terrace a movie-set look.

Gildo di Nunzio approaches the photo session at the edge

of the terrace. Pavarotti whistles at him the three bars of Rossini that had given them trouble at the piano. Di Nunzio sings the phrase back to Pavarotti, correcting the rhythm slightly while the photographer clicks away.

The photographer announces he has enough shots for the time being. They will continue after lunch. Pavarotti removes the toque but stays in the caftan. Delicious aromas are wafting from the kitchen, which also opens onto the terrace. Pavarotti wanders into the room and is greeted by the housekeeper.

"*Buon giorno, Signor Tenore*," she says heartily.

"*Buon giorno, Anna*," he replies. "*Cosa faciamo?*"

He dips a wooden spoon into a steaming pot and tastes. The housekeeper, Adua, and a young maid stop what they are doing and await his verdict.

"*Perfetto*," he says. "*Forse poco più pepe.*"

Smiling happily, the housekeeper shakes some pepper into the pot. Someone calls to Pavarotti to say a car with new guests has arrived. It is a young woman from Vicenza, an aspiring soprano, who had telephoned Pavarotti that morning from Pesaro, having found his number in the phone book, to say she had driven this distance for no other reason than to sing for him. Could she come up? He had told her to come ahead. Now she has arrived with her husband and two friends. Pavarotti greets them warmly and ushers them quickly to the piano. With one of her companions accompanying her, she launches herself into "*Tacea la notte placida*" from Verdi's *Il Trovatore*. The music is clearly beyond her thin soprano.

When she finishes, the others, who had drifted into the room to listen, look to Pavarotti for his comment.

"I cannot evaluate your voice, I am sorry," he says. "It is because you are not supporting it from the diaphragm, it is all coming from up here . . ." He motions to his throat. "You may have a wonderful voice, but you have not yet found the way to let it out."

The girl expresses her gratitude for his attention. They chat for a few minutes about singing, then Pavarotti excuses himself for lunch. The visitors shake hands with everyone in the house and on the terrace, then depart.

Finally the group, now totaling seventeen, is called to the table. Pavarotti, still dressed in the black caftan but minus the hat, sits at the head facing the sea; Adua is to his left; the others sit where they like, except for special guests whom Pavarotti usually summons to his right. A pattern develops among the regulars: the professional associates bunch toward Pavarotti's end of the table; the family and close friends retreat discreetly to the far end. The division may speak less of diffidence than of Pavarotti's ability to handle guests who do not speak Italian. Segregation, even self-imposed, would be out of place in the convivial atmosphere.

The housekeeper appears on the terrace carrying a large bowl of homemade gnocchi. Pavarotti, without ceremony, launches into a food-laden dish already at his place. It is a dietetic mélange of cold chicken and cooked vegetables. As the others help themselves to white and red wine from the bottles lining the table, Pavarotti pours a small quantity of Lambrusco into a tumbler, then fills it with mineral water.

"Wine is terribly fattening," he confides to his companion on the right. Others exclaim at the aroma of the gnocchi and finish conversations started before coming to the table. Clearly delighted to have so many friends stretched out before him, Pavarotti throws out his arms and sings in a conversational voice that could come from anyone, "*Ridi, Pagliaccio, sul tuo amore infranto* . . ." The melody is not Leoncavallo's; he is singing the *Pagliacci* words to the melody of Bizet's "Toreador Song."

The random conversations merge into the news that day that seven brands of whiskey are suspected of causing cancer. Everyone at the table—Italians and Americans—have suggestions about what the next carcinogen will be. Several agree it will be vitamin pills.

Everyone but Pavarotti digs into the cheese-laden gnocchi with gusto. Pavarotti passes the basket of bread to Gildo di Nunzio. "No thanks, Luciano," Gildo says, "I'm trying not to eat bread."

"Not eat bread!" Pavarotti explodes. "How can you taste anything?" He takes a large hunk and slams it on Gildo's plate. Pavarotti has none himself.

Pavarotti and Gildo di Nunzio talk about the phrase of Rossini's *William Tell* that they both felt was still not firm in Pavarotti's mind. Very lightly Pavarotti sings the phrase. One of the American guests says, "That's not right, Luciano. It goes like this." The guest sings the phrase, changing only the last note from the way Pavarotti had sung it.

"What cheek!" Pavarotti says, then appeals to the others. "He's not even a musician. My friend, you're singing it the way it ends the *first* time, but it is repeated *twice*."

Pavarotti hums the phrase to himself several times, then his attention is drawn by a discussion at the other end of the table about the killer whale movie, *Orca*. Does the word "orca" have any meaning in Italian? No one is sure. People submit possible definitions which are all cut off by Adua saying in her throaty contralto, "*Orca Madonna*," in a pun on the vulgar expletive.

Someone mentions that it rained the night before for a short while. Another says it never used to rain in Pesaro in the summer. One Modena friend says the changed weather patterns are the result of atomic bombs. Everyone laughs. "No, no. I'm serious," he says. "That's what the farmers say, and I think they are right. We never had rain in the summers until the late 1950s."

Pavarotti, finished with his own meal, is preoccupied with stealing gnocchi from his wife's plate.

Several of the women help clear the pasta dishes. A huge

platter adorned with lemon wedges and filled with veal cutlets fried in the Milanese style is brought out. With these is a large bowl of sliced red and yellow peppers stewed with onions. The conversation turns serious with a discussion of the breakdown of the Italian school system. The mild Cesare delivers a brief dissertation on the rapid deterioration of the quality of instruction.

"Young people today learn about one third of what they did twenty years ago," he says. "They come to the bank for jobs knowing *nothing* and expect three times what they expected before."

While Cesare speaks, Pavarotti turns to the guest on his right and says, *sotto voce*, "He is wonderful—of another generation."

An Italian guest says that much of the blame for the breakdown should be given to Herbert Marcuse, who taught nothing but rebellion and disrespect for authority. "It is one thing in an adult," he says, "but in younger people it is a disaster. What motive does a kid have to learn anything if he is taught that all his elders are misguided and corrupt? As they push down the age for defiance to younger and younger children it will soon be impossible to toilet-train them. They will say it is oppression, forcing them to use the bathroom."

Adua Pavarotti addresses the table: "I wish that when Herbert Marcuse was born someone had said, 'Go away. We don't need you here on earth.'"

From the other end of the table, her eldest daughter, Lorenza, says in a quiet voice that all can hear, "He was a great man."

Another discussion, less inflammatory, has broken out: the best way to make popcorn. The argument is being conducted in Italian so Pavarotti helpfully translates the gist for an American guest. "They are talking about how to cook Corn Flakes."

Addressing the table, Pavarotti describes the method he has developed after many experiments. Adua interrupts several

times, inserting points she feels are essential to successful pop-
ping. On the third such break-in, Pavarotti turns to Adua and
delivers the universal marital line, "Are you going to tell it or
am I?"

Someone asks Pavarotti if he has seen the review that day in
an Italian paper of a Salzburg *Magic Flute* in which James
Levine's conducting is panned. "You can't believe these Italian
critics," Pavarotti says. "They will say anything—particularly
if you have a big reputation."

Someone else points out that the reviews by the Milan critics for Pavarotti's *L'Elisir* at La Scala were ecstatic.

"This time, yes," Pavarotti replies, "but I would make a
mistake to count on it the next time, even if I sing the same as I
did in February. Levine conducted *Magic Flute* several years
ago and the same critics called it a great triumph for him."

After the main course is cleared there is a salad of escarole
and lettuce. This is followed with a large platter of eight
different cheeses and two bowls of fruit. No one at the table has
slowed. All dive into the new course as though they had not already eaten three others. For the first time since the meal's start,
Pavarotti partakes to a modest degree in what the others are
eating.

A phone that sits on a windowsill from the living room
rings. Pavarotti is told it is New York. He takes the phone from
the window and, standing at the far end of the lunch table, talks
across the Atlantic. "Herbert, my friend, how are you? Yes, everything is fine. We are doing the *Time* pictures today . . ."

With Pavarotti absent from the table, conversations, even
those that had not included him, drag to a close and the seventeen people seem momentarily de-energized, like a string of
Christmas tree lights that has lost its power source.

Pavarotti is silent as he listens to his manager from across
the Atlantic. "No," Pavarotti says firmly. "That is the program
I do for the concerts. The Bellini songs, the Tosti. They always

want me to spend the evening singing the showpiece arias. It is cheap. I'm doing the 'Nessun dorma' and 'Furtiva lagrima' as encores. It is enough. Tell them that is my program—take it or leave it."

Breslin apparently takes it, because Pavarotti changes abruptly back to his expansive good humor. "What are you doing, Herbert, my friend? Do you go to Long Island?" Pavarotti, whose English is clear but strongly accented, exaggerates the "g" sound in Long Island in parody of the native mispronunciation.

Pavarotti hangs up and returns to his place at the head of the table. Talk becomes animated again.

After the fruit and cheese is cleared, a dessert is produced, a tray of pastries—cream-filled *cornetti*, éclairs, almond cakes. This is followed by a tray of coffee cups, then Anna carrying a large espresso pot. A young girl follows her with a bowl filled with what looks like brown whipped cream.

It is a house specialty, Pavarotti tells a guest. When the first coffee bubbles up through the espresso pot, it is poured off into a bowl that contains generous amounts of sugar. The coffee, already filled with air, is whipped vigorously with the sugar until it becomes a smooth brown sauce that is then dolloped into each cup for a festive and super-rich coffee.

The pastries disappear with startling speed. Then a bottle of the sweet almond liqueur, Amaretto, is passed around the table to many takers.

Adua Pavarotti is telling an animated story to the group to her left. Turned slightly from her husband, she gesticulates with one hand while the other rests lightly on her glass of Amaretto. Not in the discussion, Pavarotti watches his wife's dormant hand like a cat watching a mouse hole, hoping for action.

As her story mounts, Adua's quiescent hand starts to move slightly as though yearning to assist the hand that was accompanying the narrative alone. As the story reaches its climax, the

Amaretto hand flies into the air and becomes a full participant in
the story's finale. The moment the hand is aloft, Pavarotti grabs
the glass of Amaretto and drains the remaining half inch of
liquid.

"She is Italian," he explains to someone who has watched
the game. "I knew she couldn't get through the story using only
one hand."

Pavarotti joins in a discussion about difficult tenors. He
leaps in with a story.

"Francis Robinson told me a wonderful thing that happened at a dinner party in Rome in the 1950s. Mrs. Leonard
Warren, the wife of the great baritone, was doing a monologue
on what terrible examples of humanity Italian tenors were—
how they were conceited, arrogant, rude, uncooperative . . .

"Di Stefano was at the table and interrupted her. 'Excuse
me,' Pippo said, 'but I don't think you should be saying these
things. After all, I am Sicilian.'

"Among the other guests listening to the exchange was
the legendary soprano Zinka Milanov. Without looking up from
her soup, she growled, '*Worse!*'"

After some more conversation, Pavarotti's three daughters ask
to be excused from the table. No one else makes any move to
leave. Pavarotti tells a joke in Italian.

"An old man is married to a young woman, a beautiful
young woman . . ."

"Are you going to tell us the story of *Don Pasquale?*" a
Modena friend asks.

". . . and the old man detests the woman and says she is
killing him. He asks a friend what is the best way to get rid of
her. The friend is a doctor. The friend tells the old man to make
love to her ten times a day for six months. That will kill her.
The six months are almost up when another friend visits the old
man and is shocked to see him looking so weak and decrepit.

The young wife, on the other hand, looks in the best of health. The friend remarks on how well the wife looks. The old man replies, 'She doesn't know it, but she's only got three days to live.'"

Two and a half hours after the lunch began, it is clearly finished. The guests, immobilized by enough food and wine for a Sicilian wedding, make no moves to leave the table. The housekeeper runs up to the table, *"Signor Tenore! Viene, subito!"*

She leads Pavarotti to the edge of the terrace and points skyward. The other guests follow, craning their necks upward. In the sky, over the beach, an airplane has disgorged itself of five parachutists, each parachute a different bright color. As the chutes float to the beach, the housekeeper crosses herself a number of times muttering, *"Che meraviglia!"*

Everyone is entranced as the red, blue, green, yellow and violet parachutes drift to the sand where a large crowd has gathered. Pavarotti's terrace is an ideal spot for watching the spectacle.

When the last parachute lands, the Villa Giulia lunch party disbands, some leaving for town, others going to their rooms, and a few remaining on the terrace with a book or newspaper. Pavarotti and his wife climb into the large hammock that hangs between two trees on the sea flank of the terrace. Adua Pavarotti nestles in her husband's huge arms. Within minutes, the couple is asleep.

LUCIANO PAVAROTTI

Questo e Quello

I wasn't at all sure I would like giving concerts. Vocally, it was much more work than singing an opera—and no one ever said that singing an opera was easy. You have no rest periods when others carry the evening, no one to console the audience if you are not in top form, no other element—sets, costumes, dancers, other singers—to divert them from your weaknesses. It is the ultimate test for the singer—the *mano a mano* of the vocal world.

One thing I particularly like about giving recitals and concerts is the immediate feedback you get. After each selection the audience tells you how you did. In an opera, the audience doesn't really give their final judgment until the end of the evening, and then the judgment can be strongly affected by other things. For instance, if they hate the production, it very likely will lessen the applause they show each singer, even if they had no special complaint with any singer. Maybe it is their way of punishing you for being in an ugly production.

In any case, in a concert, you have no doubts. They give you a running progress report all evening.

Of course, singing concerts around the globe is very lucrative and helps build the name, but I like it more for other reasons. I like visiting new places; singing concerts makes possible many more new places.

If, for example, I want to sing in South America, as I did for the first time in 1979, it is very difficult to arrange to go there in an opera production. I think they would invite me—they have many times—but it is such a risk to undertake an elaborate performance with people you don't know—new conductors, directors, singers. Even if you can agree on an opera they want and you want to sing, there are so many other variables. It is a major and complex undertaking and must be planned years in advance.

Compared to all this, a concert is relatively uncomplicated. It is quite possible with a full orchestra. With only a piano,

235

if I can take my own accompanist, John Wustman, then it is easy and requires little advance effort. All that is needed is a piano and a theater—oh, yes, and an audience.

After that first concert in Liberty, Missouri, in 1973, I relaxed quite a bit about this form of singing. My voice had no difficulty holding up and the audience was anything but bored with only one performer. There is a reverse side to the dangers of the one-man concert. If it succeeds, if the audience likes you, it succeeds in a way an opera never can. The experience becomes a far more intensely personal one for everyone, me and the audience. It comes down to this: bigger risks and bigger rewards.

It was with my second concert, in Dallas, that I took up the habit of carrying a large white handkerchief. I know it looks silly in some ways, like those old divas who used to carry a fichu. I use it, actually, to make myself look *less* silly. I went to a concert given by a colleague of mine and found myself horrified by the way my friend in every aria gesticulated wildly and pranced around. He looked like a crazy man. I decided I must do something to prevent myself from getting carried away like that.

By holding the white handkerchief, I keep myself more in one spot. If I were to start making large gestures, the handkerchief would fly all over the place and catch my attention like a warning flag. Then, too, I have gotten used to it now and it relaxes me. It is my security blanket while on the concert stage.

I suppose my first concert in New York was an important milestone in my entire career. It was in March 1973 at Carnegie Hall. At first we weren't sure that we would sell out the hall. However, even with the audience filling the stage, we had to turn away many people who wanted tickets. As I say many times, I am always nervous before singing, but this was worse. I

236

was facing the tough New York audience in venerable Carnegie Hall. And I was alone. There was no soprano to hide behind, no sets and costumes, no orchestra—just me and my accompanist.

The program was all Italian music—after all, I am an Italian singer—but I still managed to get quite a variety of music to make a concert program acceptable by the most traditional standards. I did songs of Tosti, Bellini, Rossini, and Respighi. For encores I did *"Torna a Surriento"* and *"La donna è mobile."*

I was not very far into the program before I realized the audience was completely with me. Once I have this feeling, I can relax a little. I am still working and concentrating very hard, I assure you, but I lose some of that sick nervousness that afflicts me before every performance. The concert was a big, big success—even with the critics. I had passed another exam.

With Carnegie Hall behind me, I began giving concerts more and more frequently. In the next months I sang my program, with a few variations, in Washington, Hollywood, Dallas, Minneapolis. I loved being able to reach all those people who probably could not travel to where I am singing an opera. Big as I am, I am a lot more portable than an operatic production.

At the time I sang that first concert in Carnegie Hall, I believed that was about as tough a test possible for my voice and my nerves. But early in 1978 we figured out a much tougher one—a recital from the stage of the Metropolitan Opera House that would be televised nationally at 4 P.M. on a Sunday afternoon.

This was surely the most nervous I ever was before doing anything. When you give a performance before a few thousand people, you are terrified of singing badly, but there are ways you can lessen the nervousness. If you should sing below top form, maybe only a few people in the audience would be hearing you for the first time and say, "This Pavarotti is not everything he is said to be." But it is only a few people. With luck, you can sing enough good performances later to put the disappointed ones in the minority.

But if you sing on national television and your voice cracks on a high C, you then have a terrible amount of statistics to overcome. My manager and others are always telling me how wonderful television is for the career, how quickly and efficiently it gets across to vast numbers of people the good news about Luciano Pavarotti. They don't always remember that on certain days the news may not be so good—and all that efficiency and mass-audience aspect of television can work just as strongly against you.

But *I* remember it. Sometimes I feel that I am the only one who realizes that things can go wrong. I don't think I am a type that worries too much. I am just realistic and know what can happen. As the moment approaches for this kind of appearance to begin, the worry and anxiety take over and pretty much crowd all other thoughts from my mind.

I remember that on the day of the live television concert from the stage of the Metropolitan, I sat in my dressing room in a cold sweat, every five minutes asking what time it was. One friend told me I was crazy to worry, that the audience out there loved me.

He didn't understand a very simple thing. "Maybe they do now," I replied, "but that doesn't mean they will still love me after this is over."

God was good to me that day. He let my voice work and he kept my nervousness from destroying me. The television audience was estimated at twelve million viewers. I was told that was some kind of record—the largest audience for a classical singer, I think. I know it was a record for me.

It took me three years to work up the program of songs that I generally sing. I wanted it to be a program of music that would please the critics, which means difficult music that displays different aspects of singing and interpretation. I also wanted it to be a program that would please the sophisticated audience, people who are bored to death with the most popular tenor music and want some less familiar dishes. At the same time, I didn't want a program that would lose the general public. I didn't want these people to sit there growing angrier and angrier that I wasn't singing *"Torna a Surriento."* For them I made sure that the music I picked, while satisfying the first two groups, would also have some melodies and musical values that could be enjoyed on first hearing by unsophisticated concertgoers.

It is still a marvelous experience for me to do a concert in a new city, one where I have not sung before. People go to such efforts to make me feel welcome and comfortable, and I must confess I love being spoiled in that way. The summer of 1979 when I sang in Tel Aviv is a good example of this sort of hospitality.

We were met at the airport with flowers and gifts for my wife and daughters. A limousine was placed at our disposal the entire time we were there. We were put up in Orchestra House, a residence maintained by the Israeli Philharmonic for visiting artists. It is a beautiful house, full of art and interesting artifacts and run by an excellent staff who obliged our smallest whims.

The house has a resident host and hostess, a Mr. and Mrs. Redlech. They are a charming couple; Mrs. Redlech has the added virtue of being a gourmet cook. So I was treated to gourmet meals three times a day. I was in heaven! Mrs. Redlech makes a chocolate cake, moist, with a creamy frosting, that is Zubin Mehta's favorite. I can see why. She makes it for him every time he is in town.

Our Israeli hosts made people available to take my wife and

daughters shopping or sightseeing while I rehearsed. And the orchestra's rehearsal hall is attached to Orchestra House, so I didn't have to move myself—only sing. The necessary interviews and press conferences were so well arranged that they were not chores at all, only pleasures.

For the first days when I arrive in such places, however, I see or experience little of all this. My mind is so concentrated on the concert, I often have little idea of where I am. I don't relax until after I have done my singing.

Audiences tend to be the same everywhere. They may have heard a lot about you and formed notions ahead of time, but it is still up to me to confirm the good things they may have heard. If I am in good form, they respond well, if I am in less good form, they respond less well. I never blame an audience if they are not enthusaistic. Herbert Breslin tells me this is rare for a tenor. The reason I don't is simple. I have never sung in a way that satisfied me and had an audience remain cold. If the audience senses I am not at my best—it certainly happens sometimes —I know it before they do.

Once the concert is over, I really enjoy being in new cities, new countries. I am fascinated by the little differences. For instance in Rio, if they say 8 P.M. they mean 8:30. In New York, 8 P.M. means 8:05. I notice this because I am a little crazy about punctuality. I am very good at getting places on the dot of the agreed time. I am very bad at waiting for the person who is late.

These differences between countries may seem inconsequential, but they can reveal a profound difference in philosophy. I love spending time with people of different religions, different politics, different approaches to life. I think a person in my profession has an obligation to sing for as many different people as he can; the size of the fee is by no means the deciding factor in accepting invitations. But in addition to wanting to reach as many people as possible, I love the stimulation of unfamiliar settings. I am looking forward very much, for example, to singing in China.

And now I am making a film. Several possibilities had been presented to me, but I was anxious to wait for a role that I was interested in doing. All right, I'll confess it. I wanted to play a romantic part, just as I do in opera. I am very romantic by nature and that is the quality I feel I can convey the most believably as an actor. Luckily for me the movies have come far in the past twenty years and acknowledge that romantic situations and concerns happen to more than just the young and beautiful.

The movie is titled *Yes, Giorgio* and is being produced by MGM. In it I play an Italian opera singer (so far, so good) who is performing in America and falls in love with a young woman who is his doctor. Maybe by the time this book is read, the film will have been laughed off the screen, but I could not resist trying. I have always loved movies, particularly American ones. I often amaze my American friends by knowing more about their old films than they do. Someone will say, "I loved Grace Kelly and Jimmy Stewart in *Dial M for Murder.*" And I will say, "It wasn't Jimmy Stewart; it was Ray Milland." They look at me as though they suspect I am not really Italian, only pretend to be.

In any case you can imagine what a thrill it is for me to be acting in a Hollywood film. As I've mentioned, I'm a great believer in taking chances. So far the chances I've taken have not gotten me in too much trouble. I feel I'm entitled to be a little reckless.

This whole business of being a star, even in a specialized field like opera, has advantages, of course, and it also has some disadvantages. Foremost among the advantages is the fact that you get paid a lot more for your efforts. This simple economic fact is important for reasons besides fast cars, estates in Italy, and old-age security for me and my family. It also means that I am not as tempted to sing too frequently and wear out my voice or exhaust myself. It also makes it easier to turn down offers that I suspect are wrong for me either vocally or dramatically.

High among the pluses of being well known is the happy fact that I get so many offers. This heightens the chances of receiving an interesting, offbeat proposal. Of course I get numerous requests to sing another Rodolfo or the Duke all over the world, but many managements are more imaginative and I am in the fortunate position of being able to consider exciting projects in various places. Some of the places are, in themselves, tempting.

I must confess I enjoy being known when I go out in public. I like people, I enjoy making contact with them. If they already feel they know me, it makes contact easier. Some celebrities have so impressive a manner, the public is too much in awe of them to approach them. Others, the public feels they know and they go right up to them as they would to a friend. I am happy to be in the latter group and I hope I remain there.

There are disadvantages, but not what you might think. For instance, well-wishers and admirers can take up a great deal of your time. Recently I was asked to sit in Sam Goody's Record Store in New York to autograph my albums. I was to come at 6:00 P.M. and stay a few hours. I was there till 1:00 A.M.—they kept the store open—and I had to autograph six thousand records. Of course, I am very happy that we sold six thousand records rather than six hundred, but other artists might feel there are more pleasant ways to spend seven hours. For me, there are not. So much of my life is my relationship with these people—the public that likes my singing—that for me it is a very special pleasure to see them face to face.

So what some well-known people consider nuisances and

impositions on their time, I consider one of the benefits of success.

There are two disadvantages to my life that stand out so far above the others that they seem like the only two. They are the long separations from my family and having to fly all the time. I've already mentioned how terribly I miss my family when I'm away from them. Also, I never seem to be able to get over my dislike of flying. Each time I land in a plane, I suffer. But there is nothing to do about it.

One bad aspect of success is minor, compared to the constant travel, but it is still most annoying. I've just begun to realize that a well-known person is often judged more harshly when he or she behaves in a less than nice way. If an ordinary person—and by that I mean one who is not famous—gets impatient or loses his temper, it is forgotten in the general rush of good and bad things that happen in the course of a day. But if a celebrity snaps at someone or gets mad, it gets talked about and will probably end up on the big score card next to that celebrity's name. One or two such incidents and the world will say, "Oh yes, he or she sings well, but he or she is a nasty person, very difficult, a prima donna . . ."

And so often the "bad" behavior results from a misunderstanding. I'm not saying I am always one hundred percent reasonable, but often I am more reasonable than I might appear to an outsider. For instance, I gave a concert at Brooklyn College not long ago. When I make a special appearance like this, especially in a part of the world I am not familiar with, my manager hires a limousine to pick me up at my hotel, drive me to the concert, then wait at the concert hall until it is time to take me back to the hotel.

The night of the Brooklyn concert was especially cold, well below freezing. I was very late coming out of the concert hall because I always try to sit on the stage after performances like this to sign programs for anyone who wants me to. On that night I think everyone in the audience wanted my autograph. Then, in another part of the theater, there was a reception for the officials of Brooklyn College and the people who put on the concert. I had to go there. After about two hours I finally got to my dressing room to change out of my tails—my concert uniform—and into street clothes.

The car was at the stage door when we came out, but the driver had not turned on the motor. The inside of the car was like a deep freezer. I had to sit there in that icy car waiting for the others—my secretary, my accompanist, two friends—to collect themselves, say goodbye to people, and get into the car. I was angry that the driver hadn't thought to warm up the car and I told him so. I didn't yell at him or anything like that but I told him rather sharply that he should have warmed the car. After all, he was being paid to do nothing for three hours.

It is a small thing to be sure. Later, when I thought about it, I'm certain it appeared to the driver that I had gotten angry over a ridiculously small thing. I am sure the driver never thought about how terrified we singers are of catching cold. He didn't know that I think of my voice as something separate from me, something that I have been given and that I am entrusted to protect. He just saw an irritable man playing the star.

I like very much what Barbra Streisand once said about being a star. I didn't hear this myself. It was on a talk show several years ago and someone quoted it to me. She was explaining to the host that people accused her of becoming a bitch since she became famous "It's not true," she said. "I was *always* a bitch."

I hope I am not a bitch, but I hope that, whatever I am, it is what I always was.

A great advantage of having a name is that it makes it possible to pay back some of your own good luck. A recent project of mine is the singing competition I have initiated with the Opera

I am very proud of my part in bringing some two hundred thousand people to Central Park to hear our 1980 Met concert version of *Rigoletto*. They began arriving at eleven in the morning. CREDIT: William Wright (*above*) I am never happier than when the audience and I both agree that I have sung well. CREDIT: Suzanne Faulkner Stevens (*below*)

Riccardo in Verdi's *Un Ballo in Maschera* is one of my favorite roles. This was the Metropolitan Opera's 1980 production. CREDIT: J. Heffernan

When it is possible, Adua joins me abroad. Here we are sightseeing on California's Monterey Peninsula in 1975. CREDIT: Robert Cahen (*above*) It is wonderful when all my family can join me for an engagement, as here on a flight with my youngest daughter, Giuliana, in 1973.
CREDIT: Robert Cahen (*below*)

When I bought this outfit for my daughter Lorenza, on a Canadian concert tour, I thought I should try it out first. (*above*) My good friend Burt Lancaster was an opera fan before we met. Now I've invaded his field.
CREDIT: Robert Cahen (*below*)

Danny Kaye is very knowledgeable about opera, but here in his Beverly Hills home (in 1973), we were talking about cooking. CREDIT: Robert Cahen (*above*) Beverly Sills accepts refreshment during our 1972 *Lucia* in San Francisco. CREDIT: Robert Cahen (*below*)

My career has changed Adua's life almost as much as mine. She holds up
well, as this 1979 photo shows. CREDIT: Robert Cahen (*above*) With Adua
and John Wustman at my 1979 *Gioconda* debut in San Francisco.
CREDIT: Robert Cahen (*below*)

I love greeting everyone backstage after a performance, but especially when it's someone as pretty and talented as Joan Baez. CREDIT: Robert Cahen

When I was asked to be Grand Marshal of the 1980 Columbus Day parade in New York City, it gave me an opportunity to indulge my new hobby: riding horses. CREDIT: Simon Robert Newey

Company of Philadelphia. I owe my start in opera to winning the Achille Peri competition in Reggio Emilia; it gives me great pleasure to help launch a similar competition in the United States.

Helping young singers is not always the heartwarming and gratifying experience it might seem on first look. In competitions such as this, people forget that in order to have winners, you must have losers; they forget that for every promising voice you hear, you hear twenty hopeless ones. It is very unpleasant telling people who have been studying voice for years that they should think of other careers. Some of my operatic colleagues have no stomach for this.

I can't say I like it much either, but the alternative is, for me, much worse: talented singers remaining undiscovered. That is why I undertook this competition with enthusiasm. We are assembling a very distinguished board of judges—Kurt Herbert Adler, Richard Bonynge, Phyllis Curtin, Max de Schauensee, Lorin Maazel, Nathaniel Merrill, Julius Rudel, Bidú Sayão, Francesco Siciliani, Dame Joan Sutherland, and Antonio Tonini. The president of the Philadelphia Opera Company, Dr. Francesco Leto, and the general manager, Margaret Anne Everitt, will also serve on this board.

Each of us will be responsible for nominating young singers from all over the world. There will be a maximum number of forty singers competing. The winners will then sing with me in a series of performances in Philadelphia. I am planning to invite, in the years to come, others of my singing colleagues to take part in such showcase performances.

One of the most difficult things for a young singer is to find an opportunity to work and perform with first-rank talent. With all respect to the many great vocal coaches, there is no better instruction than working before an audience alongside top artists.

245

Philadelphia has a very interesting operatic history. It saw the American premieres of many important operas: *Der Freischütz, I Puritani, Norma, Luisa Miller, Faust,* and *The Flying Dutchman.* As with opera in other American cities, Philadelphia has had a number of different companies over the years, but to me that is unimportant when viewed against a strong opera audience that remains constant in its love and support for opera. This new company is a merger of two earlier ones. It has already shown strength and adventurousness—both are wonderful signs for its future.

I want to insert a few words about something very dear to me: my painting. I now paint every chance I get and usually travel with a few paintings I am either still working on or can't bear to be parted from. It all started not long ago as somewhat of a joke. It may still be a joke but it is growing more and more important to me.

It started when I was singing *Tosca* in San Francisco in 1978. Because the part I play, Cavaradossi, is a painter, a fan sent me a gift of a box of acrylic paints. I thought: why pretend to paint on stage? Why not try a real painting? I did and I've been addicted to painting ever since. I set out like a madman. That first year I did thirty pictures, not all on stage.

Though the activity is new for me, the desire is not. Every since I can remember, my dream was to be a great painter. A friend said he thought it was because I worried about the impermanence of singing—that I do a good performance and it disappears in the rafters of the opera house.

That is not it. First of all, we have recordings to give a certain permanence to our voices. But he is right that there might be a connection. What appeals to me about making a painting is that you are making something completely new, something that has never existed before. Perhaps it is because opera is such a collaborative effort from the composer through the lighting designer of your production. When we sing an opera, we are merely reading and interpreting someone else's creation. I have worked so much of my life on the creative products of others that it is refreshing to try something that comes from no one but me. That, to my thinking, is the most creative thing anyone can do. To make something out of nothing. Something completely new, something completely of one's self.

Everyone makes fun of my painting—my family, my friends—but that doesn't bother me one little bit. I work on the pictures everywhere—at home, when I am traveling in hotel rooms. It is an activity that takes me out of this world.

When I finish a painting that I like, I feel very, very happy, even if I suspect it has no artistic merit. I don't pretend to be good, although I am getting better, so I can't promise how long I won't pretend anymore.

If I could become a great painter, I could stop singing. But only if I could be a great one, and that will never happen.

I am still crazy about athletics, but, of all the sports I used to play, it seems to have narrowed down to tennis. It is a wonderful game and it is a sport easy to set up at any time of the year in different cities where I don't know a large number of people. I have a lot of fun playing and I always feel much better physically after a game. I am a pretty good player, but I prefer playing with people who are a lot better than me. Unfortunately, this preference comes into conflict with another aspect of my personality: I hate to lose. Still, the desire for a good challenging game is stronger. I can give top-level players a pretty good game, but I have no illusions about being anything terrific myself. I just love fast, tough tennis. I prefer doubles, because in doubles you can laugh and kid around.

When I say kid around, I mean between shots. When the

ball is in motion I am as serious about what happens as I am about singing. In fact, I see a big similarity between playing tennis well and singing well. They both require total concentration —concentration on what is happening, what you are doing or what you should be doing . . . You can't do either well—play tennis or sing—if you let your mind wander for one little second to anything else. One thought about what you are going to drink after the game, or how the audience is reacting during a performance, and things can go off very quickly.

So I am quite serious while playing tennis, but between shots, I love to harass and worry my opponents. Then, I must do *something* to make up for their greater skill.

A recent interest of mine is riding horses. Since living on a farm outside Carpi during the war when I was a boy, I have always loved animals, but horses have now become special for me. Because the new house in Modena has so much land around it, I thought it would be nice to own horses for riding. When I was singing in Dublin in 1979, I asked to be shown some horses that I might purchase.

I said I wanted to see the strongest horse in Ireland and was taken to see a fourteen-year-old named Shaughran who had been one of the best hunters in the country. He was also huge, which may have been why I took to him right away.

Because of his great size, I felt my weight would be no great problem for him. It wasn't. He also turned out to be gentle and well bred. I decided to buy Shaughran and another horse I saw at the same time, a four-year-old gelding named Herbie who was an excellent jumper. I thought having horses to ride would be a wonderful thing for my whole family, but particularly for my teenaged daughters.

This presented a slight problem: my girls had never ridden. I learned of a famous riding school outside Dublin, the Iris

Kellett Riding School; I decided it would be a fine idea to send the girls for several weeks of this school so they could learn to ride.

At first the girls were not enthusiastic, but enthusiasm for new places and new experiences is not one of the strong points of teenaged Italian women. Still, I persuaded them to try and, of course, they loved it. Why is it some people can't learn that in order to enjoy life to the fullest, you must take chances and try new things? I believe there is a strong connection between being bored and being cautious.

Now my daughters love riding, they love horses. I was told that they even got up for the 7 A.M. mucking-out of the stables with a certain cheerfulness.

I've started riding more and more. I enjoy it and feel it is good exercise for me. When I was on the Met tour in 1980, I rode in Dallas and again in Boston. If the horse is willing to take me, I am eager to ride. (Someone asked me if I remembered the name of the horse I had ridden in Boston. "No," I replied, "but I'm sure the horse remembers my name.") I look forward to riding in Central Park when I am next in New York and taking riding lessons to learn to ride correctly. I want to do the right thing by Shaughran and Herbie, who have emigrated from Ireland and joined the Pavarotti family in Modena.

I had another adventure with a horse in London. I was taken to meet a famous horse who lived in the stables behind St. George's Hospital. His name was Sir Harold and he was the biggest horse in England—eighteen and a half hands. A complete giant. I was invited to ride him and I was delighted. Sir Harold was less delighted, I think. He looked at me as though I was a small thing of no consequence to his massive back.

As soon as I got him into Hyde Park, he took off at a gallop. I could feel that my saddle was not fastened securely and it started to slip. Somehow I stayed on and got him reigned in. It is not permitted to gallop in city parks, so I must have been quite a spectacle galloping along on that giant horse. If people recognized me they might have thought it was a publicity stunt for my recording of *William Tell*.

The new house I have bought outside Modena is something that is making me very happy. It is a big place that at one time had been an elaborate estate. It has a large main house, with stables nearby. There is also a chalet, a small whimsy for parties, with *trompe l'oeil* painted on the outside plaster to look like curtains draped over the windows.

We completely remodeled the big house. An unusual feature is the way we rebuilt the main staircase to come right down into the living room. The second floor has the bedroom for Adua and me and a bedroom for each of the girls. The third floor has a separate entrance and is an apartment for Adua's sister, Giovanna, and her husband and their four sons. Adua and Giovanna are very close; their mother died when they were quite young. All the time that Adua and I have been married, Giovanna has lived with us.

Over the stables, which are only a few yards from the main house, I am building a beautiful apartment for my parents. There will be a place for my sister, Gabriella, and her son, Lucca. We are all going to live on this place—*everybody*. I want to prove that families can stay together in this day.

Stretching away from the main house, on the side opposite the side you enter, is a long allée of poplars. They are tall and in two straight rows. I think they are very beautiful. On either side of this are fields. When I bought this property, the local government, which is Communist, made me sign over a large portion of this land to them. It now doesn't belong to me—or to them either. It is referred to as "Government's disposition." I can't build on it or use it, but neither can anyone else. The way it is now, the Government could put a park on it. I am trying to get them to designate it "private Government land." That would keep it empty forever.

I still have a good bit of land I *can* use that I plan to farm. When we get it producing, I think we could get this place eighty percent self-sufficient. My father was a baker, so he could make the bread for us. There is a Lambrusco-type wine that is produced here—a little light but good. Also, facilities for keeping livestock. Already growing are many plum and apricot trees with plenty of ground left over for cultivating all types of vegetables.

As I get older, I look forward to spending more and more time here and to doing some of the work on the place myself. I was a farmer when I was nine, so it is logical that I should end up that way.

Pavarotti as Teacher
and Boss

Since I hope to have a singing career, I would never have taken the job as Luciano's secretary if he hadn't offered to coach me vocally while I worked. I would probably have taken some job, but being Pavarotti's secretary is not "some job." It is three full-time jobs.

When he is traveling, which is most of the time, he needs a highly efficient secretary to help him get around, keep straight his appointments, get him to them on time, screen visitors, attend to them, and handle the fan mail. Luciano also needs a full-time valet and a full-time housekeeper. With his painting, the tons of mail, and the gifts that people send everyday, keeping his apartment and hotel rooms livable is a constant job.

These are just the major duties of his secretary. There are many more. Anyone taking on this job can forget having a life of his or her own. Much as I love being involved in the Pavarotti whirlwind, I would not give up my singing ambitions for it. His agreeing to consider me a vocal apprentice while I worked for him made it all possible.

He really is a fantastic teacher. Perhaps because he worked so long and hard on his own development, he has a natural bent toward passing on to others what he has learned. The thing that distinguishes him as a teacher more than anything else is how incredibly patient he is. As a boss he is not a patient man; he wants things done right away. But as a teacher, he is the opposite.

If you make a mistake he will make you do it over and over, ten, fifteen times—however many times it takes to get it right. Then when you get it right, he makes you do it another fifteen times, to make sure that it was not a lucky hit; that the correct way sticks in your mind; that it becomes automatic. And he is listening intently each time. Most people would find that unbearably boring, but not Luciano. He even remarked one time that he amazes himself with how patient he is as a teacher.

I think there is a clue to his whole personality in that paradox of his impatience about small, everyday things and his re-

255

markable patience about things he considers truly important—
like singing. Maybe that is why he's quick to get irritated by
little things; he's used up his patience on perfecting his own artistry and coaching other singers like me. (In fairness about the
anger over little things, I should add that it always evaporates as
fast as it comes.)

The basics of singing—which, for Luciano, are correct
breathing and support—are, he feels, pretty much under control
in my case. So he is concentrating more on other aspects of my
vocal technique. We spend a lot of time on phrasing and interpretation.

Luciano's method of teaching—whether it's phrasing or
shaping the sound or whatever—is to imitate what you are doing
wrong, then do it again the way he feels you should. He is a
very clever mimic and sometimes his versions of what you are
doing are so devastating, there's no danger you'll do it that way
again. You might not get it right, but you'll surely find another
way to do it wrong. As a teacher he is relentless. He won't let
up on you until you do it right.

So much of what I learn from him is simply picked up by
observation. For instance, I have been studying with Luciano
for many months and I am only just recently catching on to the
way he produces vowels. The reason this is so important is that
it is the secret of how he gets that beautiful legato, and it is the
key to his phrasing, I am convinced.

He has accomplished miracles with my singing. I can now
sing high notes that were previously for me just a dream. He's
added at least four notes to my upper scale. He had me learn
"Casta Diva" from Norma as a vocal exercise; it must be one of
the most difficult arias for the soprano. Bellini takes you up to
the highest part of the vocal range and just leaves you there,
twisting slowly in the wind.

Most sopranos wouldn't dream of trying "Casta Diva" till
they are well along in their careers. But Luciano is a great

believer in stretching yourself. "If you can get through '*Casta Diva*,'" he says to me, "Puccini's arias won't seem so difficult for you."

Luciano is very big on risk-taking. He's always done it in his own career, and he expects aspiring singers to do the same. An example of one kind of risk he takes and makes others take was having me sing with him in some of his concerts. He just sprang me on the audience during the encores. He's done this with other students of his, I know. It's sink or swim. He just pushes us out on the stage and hopes we can handle it— and that the audience can handle us. I even got some good mentions in the reviews.

I sometimes have to trick him into giving me a voice lesson. When there is a few minutes' lull in the daily routine, I'll ask him if he minds my vocalizing a bit. He always tells me to go ahead, then wanders off to his room to study a score or make phone calls or whatever. As soon as I start singing, he shoots out of his room and says, "No, no, Maddalena. That's not right. You're not giving yourself the correct support." Or whatever the mistake of the moment happens to be. He ends up giving me a full lesson. We almost never schedule a lesson—I "take" them in the true sense of the word. It rarely fails. We may not work on my singing every day, but his teacher's instincts are always present. For instance, one time we boarded a plane to fly to a concert and he noticed I was reading *The World According to Garp*.

"What is this?" he said. "What are you reading this sort of thing for? If you want to be an opera singer, you should be studying the score of *La Bohème*, not reading for pleasure."

At other times, a pop singer would come over the radio while we were working on fan mail or some other nonsinging task. Luciano would stop what he was doing and say, "Listen, Maddalena. Hear how that singer handles the *portamento*. She doesn't slide from note to note, but hits each one squarely."

I have never heard of a major vocal artist taking as much time out to listen to young singers and give them advice. Sometimes this is arranged through professionals—people connected with the concert or opera house where he is appearing ask him to do it—but sometimes the singers write him directly or find the name of his hotel and call him up. Or they come to the stage door. He almost always listens to them sing. And Luciano believes it is difficult to judge a voice in a normal room. He often goes to the added trouble of arranging to hear these young singers in a hall. If he refuses to hear them it's because something unavoidable prevents it—no time before his concert, he's rushing to make a plane—something like that.

It's amazing how much of his time he gives up to this, and it's amazing how many famous singers won't do it at all.

Since there has been so much publicity about Luciano, the secretarial part of my life has tripled. There is now enough fan mail each day—at least fifty or sixty letters—to keep a secretary busy full time. Especially since he wants each one answered. Anyone who wants an autographed picture is sent one; even that job is getting to be costly and time-consuming.

A lot of the letters are so touching, they must be answered individually. It's amazing how many people write telling how Luciano's singing lifted them from despair. Some of these letters imply that Luciano has saved their lives. You can't ignore this sort of confidence—or just send back a photograph and a form letter of thanks.

Then there are all the gifts. People go to such trouble to make him things—articles of clothing, drawings of Luciano, figurines, sculptured heads. He's received enough bent nails to build a crooked house. All of these items must be acknowledged. Luciano insists on it.

It amazes me the way fans send him things to eat. I know they do it out of affection, but it is incredibly thoughtless.

Doesn't everyone know he is struggling so hard to lose weight? Why do they send him cookies, candy—everything that is forbidden. I must hide these food gifts from him or eat them myself when no one's looking.

This has become one of the most difficult of my tasks: acting the diet ogress. When he has guests for lunch or dinner, he eats his diet food and serves the others normal meals. He always tries to steal a little of theirs—either at the table or in the kitchen. I must watch him constantly and tell him to stop when his hand goes foraging for food. He gets upset at the time, but he is really grateful and has told me he wants me to continue doing this. I don't mind because Luciano is much happier when he is sticking with his diet and knows he is losing weight.

Not only must I keep the refrigerator stocked with the diet dishes when he is settled in an apartment in New York or San Francisco, but also, on the short trips he often makes, I must carry plastic containers of his cooked diet food on the planes. Of course, Adua looks after this when he is at home. She and I have, on occasion, exchanged plastic containers in airports.

One of the most important tasks I have is making sure Luciano has everything he needs when singing a concert or recital. In the opera houses there are a number of people to look after him—dressers, makeup men, people to run last-minute errands. But for recitals, there is only me. He is always nervous before singing a concert or recital, so if an article from his white-tie-and-tails outfit is missing or not in the right condition, it can be a disaster. I've gotten so anxious about this, I usually bring two of each item—shirts and ties for example—in case something happens. God help you if you forget the suspenders.

I also must see to it that he finds the things he likes in the dressing room—mineral water and ice, perhaps some fruit. Usually managements see to this without asking; if they don't, I must dig up the items or request them or check ahead of time. I must also remember to bring along a hair dryer and plenty of Rolaids.

Luciano encourages me to attend rehearsals and will ask my opinion about his singing or performances. He has told me he thinks students are the best critics. He often seeks out the opinions of other young singers or students. It's his way, he says, of keeping in touch with young people. This is important to him.

He never wants to cut himself off from the everyday world, either. Stardom in any field has a tendency—it is more than a tendency really—to do this. There are any number of reasons why a famous singer is forced into a very narrow world of other artists, musicians, managers. Luciano hates the idea of sealing himself off from the rest of humanity. That is one of the reasons he spends so much time with his fans. And that is a reason why he makes such a point of listening to my opinions and those of other young people. Luciano doesn't forget what it is like or how he felt when he was a student.

MARIO BUZZOLINI

The Plane Crash

In September 1975 my wife and I were flying from Italy to New York. We had learned that Luciano Pavarotti would be on the plane with us and, since we are great fans, we asked the steward if he would pass along to Pavarotti our desire to pay our respects. Word came back that Pavarotti would be happy to meet us, but to stay in our seats. He would come to us. In a minute we saw the big man coming toward us down the aisle. Of course he had no idea what we looked like, so I stood up and waved.

We talked for several hours and became quite friendly. Several months later, my wife and I were returning to our hometown, Lugano, for Christmas. We were waiting for them to announce the boarding of our TWA flight, when who rushes up to the gate? Pavarotti. He had missed his Alitalia flight, so he had been switched to our plane. Like us, he was returning home for Christmas. He seemed delighted at the coincidence of finding us once again his traveling companions. Needless to say, we were thrilled.

We arranged with TWA to seat us together. Pavarotti always flies economy class. He likes to sit over the wing because he thinks it is the safest place. Also, he doesn't approve of the extravagance of first class.

We had a wonderful flight over the Atlantic. As the plane approached Milan, the pilot announced that the airport, Malpensa, was too heavily fogged in to attempt a landing. He would circle for a while in the hope that conditions would improve. After a time, the pilot told us over the loudspeaker that he was taking the plane down—not to land, he said, but to appraise the situation. We were all very scared. Luciano, who admits flying frightens him under the best conditions, was in a terrible state.

Our plane was a 707. I had been in the Swiss Air Force, so I knew a little about flying. I was next to the window and was surprised to see the pilot bringing the plane down at a 45° angle to the ground. As soon as the ground was visible, the pilot swerved the plane back up. Luciano almost died. Both he and my wife said they felt sick. Luciano put his head back against the seat and closed his eyes. He didn't want to talk.

The pilot's voice came over the intercom. If the weather did not clear soon, he was going to fly the plane to Genoa and land it there.

"Do it!" Luciano's voice called out.

Then the pilot announced he had changed his mind. He was going to try to land at Milan. I could see that, once again, the pilot was bringing the plane down at a very steep angle. Finally the plane touched the ground. Most of the passengers assumed we had arrived safely. People made noises of relief and there was even the beginning of applause from the back of the plane.

Through the window, however, I could see that we were speeding off the runway and into the grass. The instant that one wheel hit rough ground, the wing on that side, the right side, tipped down and broke off in the middle, sending one jet engine skyrocketing into the air. Almost immediately the next engine broke loose.

We were still moving at high speed when the broken stub of wing hit the ground. This caused the entire plane to pivot into the air. When it hit the ground again, the plane broke in two—literally. The part of the fuselage with the cockpit broke away right in front of where we were sitting. When the plane finally came to a stop, there was just this big gaping hole in front of us where the seats of first class had been.

Pandemonium broke out. People were screaming, struggling to get out of their seats. They rushed up from behind us to jump out through the hole. But Luciano and I could see that it was a long drop to the ground, and there was a lot of twisted, jagged metal that looked terribly dangerous. He and I both blocked the way and kept people from jumping.

Meanwhile someone was struggling to open the emergency door right next to our seats. He finally got it open. My wife and

Luciano were the first two out. The man who opened the door went next. We jumped onto the wing, what was left of it, and slid to the ground. It was like a sliding board, but a lot less comfortable. In fact, Luciano hurt himself on his way down. We all got to the ground safely and ran like crazy. We could smell the fuel. We thought at any second there would be an explosion.

Even when we were safely away from the plane, the ordeal was not over. The accident had happened at the far end of the runway. We were a great distance from the control tower and, because of the fog, out of sight of it. The tower had lost radio contact with the plane as well. They figured something had happened but they didn't know what—or where. The weather was below freezing. We all huddled out there at the end of the runway thinking that help would come at any minute. It didn't.

We found the pilot and co-pilot lying in the grass. They were moaning and seemed to be badly hurt. We did what we could to make them as comfortable as possible. Luciano was in his shirt sleeves and I could see he was freezing. He asked if I had anything he might put around him. I offered him the sweater I was wearing.

"Then *you* won't have anything," he said.

Making a joke of it, I offered him my handkerchief.

"I'll take it," he said.

It was a square of tan linen with my initials embroidered on it. I watched in surprise as he wrapped the piece of cloth around his throat and mouth.

We waited. A boy we had gotten to know on the plane, a Columbia University student, rushed by carrying a bottle of Southern Comfort. He told us he was setting out to find the terminal on foot. Luciano stopped him. "Then leave the bottle with us," he said.

We were out there a good half hour before anyone came to get us, but finally a jeep arrived—one jeep. Luciano and some others had herded all the children that had been on the plane into one group. Now Luciano loaded them onto the jeep, carrying some on his shoulders, hoisting others into the jeep. He went off with them.

Very shortly, enough buses and trucks arrived to take twice our number away from that spot. We were all deposited at the TWA offices. It was an incredible scene. Everyone was so happy to be alive, so excited, and whiskey and wine flowed freely.

Luciano was in a great state of excitement, almost frantic. He was running around getting people's names and home phone numbers; then he would phone the numbers to tell people not to worry if they heard about the crash on the news, their relatives were all right. Miraculously, no one was killed. Only the pilots and a few others were hurt but even they were not hurt too badly.

A friend had driven Luciano's Mercedes up from Modena to meet him. When they found each other, Luciano announced he was setting out immediately for the three-hour drive home. He said it would help him unwind. Before leaving, he looked for me to return my handkerchief. I told him to keep it as a souvenir.

"You know, my friend," Luciano said as he left, "we were fucking lucky."

GIUSEPPE DI STEFANO

A Fellow Tenor

I first heard Luciano sing in San Remo, in 1962, only one year after he made his debut. I knew right away he had a beautiful voice. I understand he later took over some *Bohème* performances for me at Covent Garden, but I wasn't aware of him then. It sounded to me as though he was singing too closed, that he could make an even more beautiful sound by opening up a bit, but tenors today think only about preserving their voices. It all comes down to money. And when they think too much about the voice, the interpretation suffers.

I try to sing the way Verdi told us to—to think only of the poetry, the words; the music should then come naturally. When most tenors sing, in their heads they see notes. I see words. Despite our different approach to singing, Luciano and I quickly became friends and we argued all the time about singing and interpretation. He told me that my way of singing would ruin my voice. Maybe it has, but I still sing all the time—every day—I don't listen to what they say about me. I just like to sing. I was teaching at a university in Mexico. They did an opera production and asked me what I thought. I said something to the effect that on some days it's better to stay in bed. I lost that job.

I think Luciano listens to advice. One time, I went backstage to see him after *L'Elisir*. He asked what I thought. I said, "Do you want the friendly, complimentary answer or do you want to know what I really thought?" He said he wanted the truth. He cleared his dressing room of all the other people and we talked for a long time. I said he should open his throat up more on certain notes. I said that if you keep it closed, it alters the notes and makes the technique obvious. Real technique shouldn't be heard. Once you close the throat, it is a cold shower on the whole effect. Luciano is very smart and he listens. I think he changed a little after that.

He thinks Gianni Raimondi was the best teacher. But I don't believe in teaching; that's why I've never done it. There's nothing to each. I study every night—I always have and still do. But no one else can teach you how to sing. We have a saying in this business: the student makes the teacher famous. The top teachers all have one famous artist—never two.

I worry about all this publicity for Luciano. It puts too much pressure on him. Caruso didn't have public relations. We are not cigarettes or Coca-Cola that can be advertised or marketed. It makes so many problems. I remember once I was singing in Rio and when I got there I saw the posters had my name as big as Gigli's. I went right to Gigli and said, "Maestro, I had nothing to do with this and I think it is wrong."

But the only person hurt by all the talk of number one tenor is Luciano, himself. It is very, very difficult to go out before an audience and sing. It is hard enough if you are just another distinguished opera singer, but if you are called "greater than Caruso," "the best tenor of the century," and all that, it puts an impossible burden on you. It is an impossible standard to live up to night after night. The public expects miracles.

We singers are only flesh and blood, we get frightened the same way everyone does. We are not made of steel. When we know the public is expecting too much it becomes unbearable. Look at Callas. I am convinced that Maria's troubles began when she started receiving ten thousand dollars a performance. That's when she started buckling under the pressure. I also think it was ambition that killed Maria. There is no limit, no possible satisfaction, when you want to be the number one artist, the number one woman. She wanted too much. And with Luciano, all this publicity is only the beginning.

I think maybe Luciano worries too much about his repertoire. Tenors should not be put into categories like boxers. We should all be able to sing *any* tenor role as long as we sing with our own voices, as long as we maintain our own natural color.

It's when a lyric tenor tries to sound like a dramatic tenor that he gets into trouble.

But I think Luciano will be all right. He's very realistic; he hasn't got his head up in the sky somewhere. I don't have to pay him compliments. He knows how highly I think of him.

LUCIANO PAVAROTTI

Conclusion

In the mid-1970s a terrible thing happened to me. I went into a depression. It was not severe but might as well have been, it was so unshakable. I am not sure what caused it. I had arrived at the top of my profession. I was singing in the principal opera houses of the world for the very top fees and singing the roles I wanted.

My family life was wonderful. As my professional and financial affairs grew, Adua became more and more an essential business partner as well as my wife. She had not bargained on this when she married me and she adapted brilliantly. My three daughters were growing up healthy, bright, and attractive.

With all this good fortune, I completely lost my zest for everything. I went through my singing assignments with no enthusiasm. The applause no longer worked like a hypodermic on my system. Everything had lost its point. This was incredible for me.

I am not a person of moods. I am a person of *one* mood: good. I can be impatient and short-tempered when matters concerning me are handled badly, but these outbursts always have a specific cause (whether I am right or wrong). When the problem is resolved, I return quickly to my normal state: happy, optimistic, and at peace with the world.

Now it was the reverse. Something might cheer me up for the moment—seeing an old friend, singing a particularly good performance, eating an exceptional meal—but as soon as the moment passed, I would sink back into my black mood.

I am sure the depression was related to my having succeeded as an opera singer. So many years had gone into the struggle. My whole being had grown accustomed to the climb, to the winning of one obstacle and looking immediately toward the next. Suddenly I saw that I had conquered all my goals. There were no more obstacles, only the chance of failure.

Friends often say to me when they see me suffering before a performance, "How can you be nervous? You are Pavarotti, the world-famous tenor!" They don't understand that the reputation can make it worse. Becoming famous, or, in some people's opinion, being number one in your field, doesn't turn you into a supernatural being. You are still a mortal man who can catch a sore throat, be out of form, or make a mistake. All the fame and talk of *number one* adds to the pressure but not to your excellence.

It wasn't the pressure that defeated me. If anything, that stimulated me more than depressed me. If at the beginning I hadn't learned to control my nerves, just as I had learned to control my breathing and diaphragm support, I would have given up my career long ago.

The problem, I'm sure, had something to do with having finally arrived and wondering what I had arrived at. There comes a point when you feel trapped by your voice. It is not a matter of wishing you were doing something else, only that, because of the voice, you cannot do anything else.

You must sing—another *Bohème*, another *Tosca*, another *L'Elisir*—on and on until you sing so badly no one wants to hear you anymore. Looking back on this strange thinking from my present happy viewpoint, I see how, if you are determined to be depressed, you can find aspects of even the happiest life to brood over.

I was also upset, I know, about my weight. I was very fat and I felt this was seriously hurting my career. I want to do everything I attempt as well as possible. I set high standards for myself; if I am going to try anything, I want to eventually excell at it or give it up. Perhaps this makes me a perfectionist; I certainly am very competitive.

I began to feel that in my profession as an opera performer, directors weren't bothering me about my acting. I sensed that they were paying little attention to my dramatic performances, either because they didn't think I could do it or they felt my weight would spoil whatever effects they attempted.

This hurt me very much. I know that I do not appear on

stage as every schoolgirl's dream of a romantic Rodolfo or Manrico, but I think a vigorous, well-thought-out characterization can go far toward overcoming my weight handicap. Now it seemed I was alone in this belief, and it greatly added to my depression.

Aside from what it was doing to my career, being fat depressed me very much. I didn't move—I don't mean on stage, although that was certainly true—but in my everyday life. Usually I am active. Not as much as when I was an adolescent, perhaps, but each day I try to exercise in some way and don't feel right if I don't. Now I had no energy and no desire to better myself for any purpose. In my profession I felt pushed aside, dismissed—and I disliked myself very much for growing so fat.

I did not see Luciano Pavarotti as I wanted to see him. I was so low, I thought that if I died the next day, I didn't much care.

I knew the problem was really serious when I returned home to Modena. Even seeing my family couldn't remove the feeling of emptiness, that everything was pointless. I suppose if this mood went on much longer I would have gone to a doctor.

They are making so many discoveries today about the chemical basis of certain types of depression. This is not to say that circumstances of your life can't start the bad feeling, only that when you are depressed, your body starts producing chemicals that keep you depressed. Something of this nature may have been happening to me. I am open-minded about medical remedies. At that time, however, I was so low, I didn't have the strength or the will to react, to do anything for myself.

Fortunately I never had to get into such experiments. Something very dramatic happened that completely cured my depression and has had me ever since feeling wonderful about everything.

On the twenty-second of December 1975, I was flying from New York to Milan in order to be home in Modena for Christmas. I always fly tourist class because I enjoy the kind of people I meet there more and because I think it is safer—tourist has the emergency exits and I try to get a seat beside one.

It was dark and quite foggy that night when the plane landed at the Milan airport. It was still going very fast, almost flying speed, as we hit the ground. I knew something was very wrong. Then it veered off the runway and broke in two pieces. It was horrible—people were screaming and fighting to get out of their seats. We got out but were all in shock and expected the plane to explode or burst into flames at any moment.

I was in a terrible state for hours afterward. A friend had driven my car up to Milan to meet me. No word of the accident reached my family at first. As soon as I found my friend, I got into my car and drove us to Modena. The fast drive down the autostrada helped calm my nerves.

When I arrived home, safe, with my family all around me, I realized what an idiot I had been in the past months. I saw how lucky I was; how much love I had, what a privilege it was to have a gift that made others happy. I also saw how good life was and how much there was about it that I enjoyed. I saw that I had allowed myself to drown in self-pity over things that didn't matter. I knew that all my talk about not caring whether I lived or died was just talk. I was nowhere near ready to die.

The shock of having come that close to death cured me completely of my disinterest in life. The cure was so thorough, I immediately set to work and study with the kind of energy and enthusiasm I had when I started vocal studies at nineteen. I threw myself into a diet that eventually got rid of eighty pounds.

The entire airplane crash experience was as though God had grabbed me by the neck and said, "You are so indifferent about life? Here, take a look at death and tell me how you like that!" If that was His plan, it worked.

Since that accident, I have been optimistic and happy, perhaps more so than ever. Because of the terrible things I saw during the war, because of that near-fatal illness as a boy, and then
the crash at the Milan airport, I think I know death. I also know
life—I know as well as anyone how precious and beautiful it is.

Even after losing eighty pounds, I am a long way from
looking as I would like. I will continue the battle, of course. For
one thing, it is much better for my health to lose the weight; I
have always been very concerned about my health. But I confess
I really do not care all that much about how I look. As long
as I am loved, that is the important thing.

I suppose it is too bad that we have to have a terrible calam-
ity jolt our lives, something as grim as a plane accident, illness,
or war, to make us appreciate the countless good things we otherwise take for granted. We humans have a terrible tendency to
stop feeling or seeing the positive things very soon after experiencing them. Not only do we stop appreciating them, we
stop seeing them altogether.

An example of what I mean is when you fly from nasty
winter weather into the warm sunshine. The first day or two,
you wander around marveling at the wonderful warmth, soak-
ing up the sun and thinking how lucky you are. But after a day
or two, you take the good weather for granted. It is your due,
your right. Then it gives you less and less pleasure until, so
quickly, you cease to notice it altogether. You start looking
around. What else do I lack? Something must be wrong. What
can I find to complain about?

It is a bad human trait and a common one. We see it so
much in young people today. I admire today's young people because they are bright, curious, aware of many things we were
ignorant of, but I see clearly how they go out of their way to
find problems, to find things to complain about, things to fight
against. They have all this energy and nothing on which to
focus their aggressions. I resent very much the philosophers and

political theorists who exploit this aspect of young people's lives. It is so easy to stir up the kids into a fury over one cause or another.

My belief is that complaining is common today because young people have never known real trouble. In Italy, today's young people have never experienced war. Few of them have ever known the kind of poverty that leaves you without enough to eat. Everything has been comfortable for them. They will not live in a truly philosophical way, I believe, until they know some disaster. A real disaster, not just too little money for a film or a record. It is sad—I wish no one a disaster—but it is necessary.

I see it in my family. My three daughters have never known a day of deprivation. They have always had a great deal of love and have always been given everything they wanted. They are really dear, marvelous girls, but they complain all the time. They don't want to go to San Francisco; they have *been* to San Francisco. They don't want to go to the beach house at Pesaro; their boyfriends are in Modena. They don't want to eat a lasagna their mother baked; it might make them fat.

I have a very good friend, Mazzoli, who was in a German prison camp for two years. He almost starved and weighed eighty-two pounds when he got out, almost a skeleton. Today he doesn't have all that much but he is one of the happiest men I know. He is happy to live without problems and does not go out looking for them.

My daughters are more symptomatic of what is happening in the world. They are adopting these elevated philosophies about the ills of mankind and are neglecting the relationships within their own family. Young people are so easily turned away from the things that should be the most important to them.

The more pampered young people are, the worse it gets. I

read an editorial recently in the Italian papers that said Italian boys should not be drafted into the Italian Army because of the terrible shock it might have on their system. Terrible shock! Can you imagine? We have people in Italy today who are against everything. They are not Communists, they are not Socialists, they are not Christian Democrats. They are simply *against*.

When I was young, I agreed with every philosopher I read. They were all right. Today, that readiness of youth to adopt whatever theories come along, as long as they are negative, is much more quickly translated into destructive action. I used to agree with *all* the theorists, then go out and play soccer. Today, they agree and go out and march in the streets—or worse.

Bad as I think the situation is today with the young, I still would not wish them a war. Even without the new horror of atomic weapons, war is too dreadful. But something must happen—the equivalent of my plane crash—to shock them into realizing that there is more to life than problems; every life has in it much to enjoy and be thankful for.

As is probably apparent from all I have said, I am not a political man. First, I believe that to hold strong political opinions you must be extremely well informed; I simply do not have time for such an educational program. Second, I am skeptical about political solutions to problems. I believe we should try to make the world more just, spread wealth more fairly, give everyone the same opportunities. So often, however, I see the same patterns repeated regardless of what political system is in power. The system may change, but men do not.

The situation in my country is so terrible today, it almost makes me ashamed to be Italian. Of course, being Italian means so many different things—a sense of history, a cultural inheritance, esthetic sensibilities—these and so many other things that make up what I am—these are very much part of what it means

281

to be an Italian. I am very proud of these things and would not want to be born any other way.

But in these days when you say to someone abroad that you are from Italy, they think of people shooting off kneecaps, businessmen being kidnapped, and a premier found dead in the trunk of a car in the middle of Rome. It is unbelievable. A destructive force has been set loose in my country. The grotesque violence is just the most dramatic symptom; it is far more widespread than the terrible acts that get in the newspapers. You see it in the cab driver who can think of ten reasons why he shouldn't take you from one part of Milan to another or the flash strikes that accomplish nothing but cause inconvenience for people not involved in the argument.

I know that injustices exist in Italy that must be corrected. And I offer no solutions to bring about the necessary changes. But this destructiveness I see spreading through my country like a lethal epidemic is not bringing us any closer to better social conditions, yet it threatens the economy's ability to function. I have no idea where it will end, but I confess to being quite pessimistic about the direction Italy is headed.

Perhaps a principal reason I am against politics is the experience I had during the war. Although I was only a child, I could see even then what politics could do to people. In one family I knew, a man killed his brother because one was a Fascist, the other a partisan. I won't say which killed the other, because it makes no difference to my point. Either could have killed the other; passions ran so high on both sides.

Doesn't that say something about political conviction, if it can make a man kill his brother? It certainly said something to me as a child. It made me see politics as a great black beast capable of unleashing the most violent anger and a sense of outrage capable of justifying any actions—even murder. This vision has stuck with me throughout the years; I see more clearly the violence than I see the causes that inspire it.

But enough about abstract matters. I can continue to philosophize without getting so far from the subject of this book.

One aspect of my personal philosophy sets me apart, I think, from many of my singing colleagues. I am speaking about my attitude toward the large number of people who are drawn to me as a result of my singing—opera enthusiasts, Italian enthusiasts, tennis enthusiasts, Pavarotti enthusiasts.

Friends who are experienced in this profession warn me that I am too open, too friendly—that I am too quick to trust people and assume they wish me well. I get this advice even more since I have become well known. They tell me, "You must be careful, Luciano, there are many people who want to take advantage of you, who want to make use of your friendship."

Maybe there are, but I cannot live my life like that—mistrusting everyone. I am not naïve. I know that I have friends who are friends mainly because I am a famous singer. That is not to say they don't like me. I think they do, but I know that when I lose my voice, they may not be friends anymore. I will call them and they will be busy. But I am philosophical about that. I don't mind. It is just the way things are.

Too often I have seen the other thing happen: a well-known person is taken advantage of by some unscrupulous person—maybe more than one—and they stop trusting *everyone*. I will not give up hundreds of good friends for one or two who try to screw me; I enjoy my friends too much. I need them too much.

I mentioned earlier how some people are generous enough to call me the number one tenor today. Of course, this pleases me in one sense. I have been given a gift. I have worked very hard to develop it the best way I can. To hear praise like that makes me think I have done my job, I have fulfilled my duty. But I really don't care about being number one or number two or number fifteen, as long as I have brought myself to where I was meant to be.

I am not falsely modest—there are too many like that in my profession—I think I am really modest. The voice is something separate from me. The voice was given to me. It would be wrong for me to congratulate myself for it. On the other hand, I would feel terrible if I ever heard someone say, "He had such a good voice, it is too bad he never developed and trained it and used it correctly."

So, when I hear "number one" I do not cry out in triumph over my colleagues. I never set out to be better than the twenty tenors who sang better than I did when I started. I never expected to be considered number one; I do not know now that I *am* number one. I am gratified only because that kind of praise makes me feel I have done what I intended to do, that I have done my duty toward God who gave me the voice and toward the public who enjoys it.

It is also a problem for me when people compare me to this or that great tenor of the past. I know they mean it as a compliment, but in a way it robs me of my individuality. When you feel that you have done something very well, done it in a special way, it is a little deflating to be told that it was "as good as so and so" or "sounded like so and so." I am I and he was he.

As for Caruso, there are no comparisons. With all due respect, I do not agree with Maestro von Karajan's remarkable comment that my voice is greater. To me, Caruso is rightly the tenor against whom all the rest of us are measured. I do not say this so much for his voice, which was indeed very beautiful and too distinctive for comparisons. He started as a baritone and always had the brown color of a deeper voice. I say this because, with his incredible phrasing and musical instincts, he came closer than any of us to the truth of the music he sang. There will never be another like him.

I don't know what Caruso's secret was and I don't want to

know. Everybody must find his own secret. Tenors who try to imitate Caruso usually lose their voices. It is all but impossible to sing the way someone else sang. And then, too, you cannot forget the personality. Even if you somehow matched the voice of another singer, it would not sound right for your personality. A voice expresses the composer's music, to be sure, but it also expresses the personality of the singer. To set out after another's voice is a profound mistake.

So while I am naturally flattered by comparisons with Caruso, they also worry me. I hope to achieve something special in my own way, not his. We are two different tenors.

For me, the proper person to compete against, to strive to go beyond, is myself. I feel that to be given a rare gift like a voice and not to develop it fully or use it in the best way possible—this is a great sin. I have so many little sins on my conscience, I will be happy if I am judged innocent of this big one.

As for retirement, I used to tell myself that when I no longer sang my best, when I heard deterioration in my voice, I would stop singing for good. I have changed my mind. This kind of talk is just ego. Doing anything well is wonderfully satisfying. I am very competitive and a little bit of a perfectionist. To feel that I am singing in an exceptional way is very gratifying to me. But that is not the only thing I enjoy about my singing. My satisfaction does not come from believing that each time I open my mouth I am beating out a number of other tenors. Singing by itself gives me enormous joy. So does the feeling that I am making music.

But that is not the only thing I enjoy about my singing. My satisfaction does not come from believing that each time I open my mouth I am beating out a number of other tenors. Singing by itself gives me enormous joy. So does the feeling that I am making music. But the greatest satisfaction comes from knowing that my singing makes many people happy. As long as

285

I feel that is true, even if to a lesser degree than today, then they will not be able to force me to stop.

My father is over seventy and still has a beautiful voice. Maybe God, who has given me so much, will give me that too.

APPENDIX

PAVAROTTI'S
FIRST PERFORMANCES
OF HIS ROLES

(AND SIGNIFICANT SUBSEQUENT PERFORMANCES)

Rodolfo in *La Bohème* (Puccini)	Reggio Emilia, April 28, 1961 (Covent Garden, 1963; La Scala, 1965; San Francisco, 1967; Metropolitan, 1968)
The Duke in *Rigoletto* (Verdi)	Carpi, 1961 (Palermo, 1962; Vienna, 1963; La Scala, 1965; Covent Garden, 1971)
Alfredo in *La Traviata* (Verdi)	Belgrade, 1961 (La Scala, 1965; Covent Garden, 1965; Metropolitan, 1970)
Edgardo in *Lucia di Lammermoor* (Donizetti)	Amsterdam, 1963 (Miami, 1965; San Francisco, 1968; Metropolitan, 1970; Chicago, 1975)
Pinkerton in *Madama Butterfly* (Puccini)	Reggio Calabria, 1963 (Palermo, 1963; Dublin, 1963)
Idamante in *Idomeneo* (Mozart)	Glyndebourne, 1964
Elvino in *La Sonnambula* (Bellini)	Covent Garden, 1965
Nemorino in *L'Elisir d'Amore* (Donizetti)	Australia, 1965 (San Francisco, 1969; La Scala, 1971; Metropolitan, 1974)
Tebaldo in *I Capuleti e i Montecchi* (Bellini)	La Scala, 1966

Tonio in *La Fille du Régiment* (Donizetti)	Covent Garden, 1966 (La Scala, 1968; Metropolitan, 1972)
Arturo in *I Puritani* (Bellini)	Catania, 1968 (Philadelphia, 1972; Metropolitan, 1976)
Oronte in *I Lombardi* (Verdi)	Rome, 1969
Des Grieux in *Manon* (Massenet)	La Scala, 1969
Riccardo in *Un Ballo in Maschera* (Verdi)	San Francisco, 1971 (La Scala, 1978; Metropolitan, 1979)
Fernando in *La Favorita* (Donizetti)	San Francisco, 1973 (Metropolitan, 1978)
Rodolfo in *Luisa Miller* (Verdi)	San Francisco, 1974 (La Scala, 1976; Covent Garden, 1978)
Manrico in *Il Trovatore* (Verdi)	San Francisco, 1975 (Metropolitan, 1976)
Italian Singer in *Der Rosenkavalier* (Strauss)	Metropolitan, 1976 (Hamburg, 1977)
Calaf in *Turandot* (Puccini)	San Francisco, 1977
Cavaradossi in *Tosca* (Puccini)	Chicago, 1976 (Covent Garden, 1977; Metropolitan, 1978)

Enzo in *La Gioconda* (Pon-   San Francisco, 1979
chielli)

RECORDED BUT NOT PERFORMED ON STAGE

Orombello in *Beatrice di Tenda* (Bellini)	London, 1966
Fritz in *L'Amico Fritz* (Mascagni)	London, 1968
MacDuff in *Macbeth* (Verdi)	London, 1971
Leicester in *Maria Stuarda* (Donizetti)	Bologna, 1974
Canio in *Pagliacci* (Leoncavallo)	London, 1976
Turiddu in *Cavalleria Rusticana* (Mascagni)	London, 1976
Arnoldo in *William Tell* (Rossini)	London, 1979
Faust in *Mefistofele* (Boito)	London, 1980

Discography

Almost all of Luciano Pavarotti's recordings are on London Records. The exceptions are an early recording of *L'Amico Fritz* on Angel and three recordings originally issued on the CIME Label that are to be re-released by London.

COMPLETE OPERAS AND CHORAL MUSIC

Bellini, *Beatrice di Tenda*. Luciano Pavarotti, Joan Sutherland, Josephine Veasey. London Symphony Orchestra, Richard Bonynge conducting. London, 1966.

Complete   3-LONDON OSA-1384

Bellini, *I Puritani.* Luciano Pavarotti, Joan Sutherland, Piero Cappuccilli, Nicolai Ghiaurov. London Symphony Orchestra, Richard Bonynge conducting. London, 1973.

Complete   3-LONDON OSA-13111

Bellini, *La Sonnambula.* Luciano Pavarotti, Joan Sutherland, Nicolai Ghiaurov. National Philharmonic Orchestra, Richard Bonynge conducting. London, 1980.

Complete   3-LONDON LDR-73004

Boito, *Mefistofele.* Luciano Pavarotti, Mirella Freni, Montserrat Caballé, Nicolai Ghiaurov. National Philharmonic Orchestra, Oliviero de Fabritiis conducting. London, 1980.

Complete   3-LONDON

Donizetti, *L'Elisir d'Amore.* Luciano Pavarotti, Joan Sutherland, Spiro Malas, Dominic Cossa. English Chamber Orchestra, Richard Bonynge conducting. London, 1970.

Complete   3-LONDON OSA-13101
Hgihlights   LONDON OS-26343

Donizetti, *La Favorita.* Luciano Pavarotti, Ileana Cotrubas, Fiorenza Cossotto, Gabriel Bacquier, Nicolai Ghiaurov. Orchestra of the Bologna Teatro Comunale, Richard Bonynge conducting. Bologna, 1974.

Complete   3-LONDON OSA-13113

Donizetti, *La Fille du Régiment*. Luciano Pavarotti, Joan Sutherland, Monica Sinclair, Spiro Malas. Orchestra of the Royal Opera House at Covent Garden, Richard Bonynge conducting. London, 1967.

Complete   2-LONDON OSA-1273
Highlights   LONDON OS-26204

Donizetti, *Lucia di Lammermoor*. Luciano Pavarotti, Joan Sutherland, Sherrill Milnes, Nicolai Ghiaurov. Orchestra of the Royal Opera House at Covent Garden, Richard Bonynge conducting. London, 1971.

Complete   3-LONDON OSA-13103
Highlights   LONDON OS-26332

Donizetti, *Maria Stuarda*. Luciano Pavarotti, Joan Sutherland, Huguette Tourangeau, James Morris, Roger Soyer. Orchestra of the Bologna Teatro Comunale, Richard Bonynge conducting. Bologna, 1974–75.

Complete   3-LONDON OSA-13117

Leoncavallo, *Pagliacci*. Luciano Pavarotti, Mirella Freni, Ingvar Wixell. National Philharmonic Orchestra, Giuseppe Patané conducting. London, 1976–77.

Complete   3-LONDON OSA-13125

Mascagni, *L'Amico Fritz*. Luciano Pavarotti, Mirella Freni, Vicente Sardinero. Orchestra of the Royal Opera House at

Covent Garden, Gianandrea Gavazzeni conducting. London, 1968.

Complete   2-ANGEL S-3737

Mascagni, *Cavalleria Rusticana*. Luciano Pavarotti, Julia Varady, Piero Cappuccilli. National Philharmonic Orchestra, Gianandrea Gavazzeni conducting. London, 1976–77.

Complete   3-LONDON OSA-13125

Ponchielli, *La Gioconda*. Luciano Pavarotti, Montserrat Caballé, Agnes Baltsa, Sherrill Milnes, Nicolai Ghiaurov. National Philharmonic Orchestra, Bruno Bartoletti conducting. London, 1980.

Complete   3-LONDON LDR-73005

Puccini, *La Bohème*. Luciano Pavarotti, Mirella Freni, Elizabeth Harwood, Rolando Panerai, Nicolai Ghiaurov, Gianni Maffeo. Berlin Philharmonic Orchestra, Herbert von Karajan conducting. Berlin, 1972.

Complete   2-LONDON OSA-1299
Highlights   LONDON OS-26399

Puccini, *Madama Butterfly*. Luciano Pavarotti, Mirella Freni,

Christa Ludwig, Robert Kerns. Vienna Philharmonic Orchestra, Herbert von Karajan conducting. Vienna, 1974.

Complete   3-LONDON OSA-13110
Highlights   LONDON OS-26455

Puccini, *Tosca*. Luciano Pavarotti, Mirella Freni, Sherrill
Milnes. National Philharmonic Orchestra, Nicola Rescigno
conducting. London, 1978.

Complete   2-LONDON OSA-12113

Puccini, *Turandot*. Luciano Pavarotti, Joan Sutherland, Montserrat Caballé, Nicolai Ghiaurov. London Philharmonic
Orchestra, Zubin Mehta conducting. London, 1972.

Complete   3-LONDON OSA-13108
Highlights   LONDON OS-26377

Rossini, *William Tell*. Luciano Pavarotti, Mirella Freni, Sherrill Milnes, Nicolai Ghiaurov. National Philharmonic Orchestra. Riccardo Chailly conducting. London, 1978–79.

Complete   4-LONDON OSA-1446

Rossini, *Petite Messe Solennelle*. Luciano Pavarotti, Mirella
Freni, Ruggero Raimondi, Lucia Valentini, Romano
Gandolfi conducting. Milan, 1976.

Complete   2-CIME C3S-134

Rossini, *Stabat Mater*. Luciano Pavarotti, Pilar Lorengar, Yvonne Minton, Hans Sotin. London Symphony Orchestra, István Kertész conducting. London, 1971.

Complete   LONDON OS-26250

Strauss, R., *Der Rosenkavalier*. Luciano Pavarotti, Régine Crespin, Helen Donath, Yvonne Minton, Manfred Jungwirth. Vienna Philharmonic Orchestra, Sir Georg Solti conducting. Vienna, 1969.

Complete   4-LONDON OSA-1435
Highlights   LONDON OS-26200

Verdi, *Un Ballo in Maschera*. Luciano Pavarotti, Renata Tebaldi, Regina Resnik, Helen Donath, Sherrill Milnes. Orchestra of the Accademia di Santa Cecilia, Bruno Bartoletti conducting. Rome, 1970.

Complete   3-LONDON OSA-1398
Highlights   LONDON OS-26278

Verdi, *Luisa Miller*. Luciano Pavarotti, Montserrat Caballé, Anna Reynolds, Sherrill Milnes, Bonaldo Giaiotti. National Philharmonic Orchestra, Peter Maag conducting. London, 1975.

Complete   3-LONDON OSA-13114

Verdi, *Macbeth*. Luciano Pavarotti, Elena Suliotis, Dietrich Fischer-Dieskau, Nicolai Ghiaurov, Riccardo Cassinelli.

London Philharmonic Orchestra, Lamberto Gardelli conducting. London, 1971.

Complete   3-LONDON 13102

Verdi, *Requiem*. Luciano Pavarotti, Joan Sutherland, Marilyn Horne, Martti Talvela. Vienna Philharmonic Orchestra, Sir Georg Solti conducting. Vienna, 1967.

Complete   2-LONDON OSA-1275

Verdi, *Rigoletto*. Luciano Pavarotti, Joan Sutherland, Huguette Tourangeau, Sherrill Milnes, Martti Talvela. London Symphony Orchestra, Richard Bonynge conducting. London, 1972.

Complete   3-LONDON OSA-13105
Highlights   LONDON OS-26401

Verdi, *La Traviata*. Luciano Pavarotti, Joan Sutherland, Matteo Manuguerra. National Philharmonic Orchestra, Richard Bonynge conducting. London, 1979.

Complete   3-LONDON LDR-73002

Verdi, *Il Trovatore*. Luciano Pavarotti, Joan Sutherland, Marilyn Horne, Ingvar Wixell, Nicolai Ghiaurov. National Philharmonic Orchestra, Richard Bonynge conducting. London, 1976.

Complete   3-LONDON OSA-13124

D I S C O G R A P H Y

VERDI AND DONIZETTI ARIAS
(Vienna, 1968)
Verdi: *Luisa Miller*, Quando le sere
al placido; *I Due Foscari*, Ah sì, ch'io senta
ancora . . . Dal più remoto esilio; *Un Ballo
in Maschera*, Ma se m'è forza perderti;
Macbeth, Ah, la paterna mano;
Donizetti: *Lucia di Lammermoor*, Fra poco
a me ricovero; *Il Duca d'Alba*, Inosservato
penetrava . . . Angelo casto e bel;
La Favorita, Spirto gentil; *Don Sebastiano*,
Deserto in terra
LONDON OS-26087

PRIMO TENORE
(Vienna and London, 1969–70)
Rossini, *William Tell*, Non mi lasciare . . . O muto asil;
Bellini, *I Puritani*, A te o cara;
Donizetti, *Don Pasquale*, Com' è gentil;
Boito, *Mefistofele*, Giunto sul passo estremo;
Verdi, *Il Trovatore*, Ah sì ben mio . . . Di quella pira;
Ponchielli, *La Gioconda*, Cielo e mar;
Puccini, *La Bohème*, Che gelida manina;
Cilèa, *L'Arlesiana*, Lamento di Federico;
Pietri, *Maristella*, Io conosco un giardino
LONDON OS-26192

KING OF THE HIGH C'S
(Anthology of earlier recordings)
Donizetti, *La Fille du Régiment*, Ah mes amis quel jour de fête . . . Pour mon âme;
Donizetti, *La Favorita*, Spirto gentil;
Verdi, *Il Trovatore*, Ah sì ben mio . . . Di quella pira;
Strauss, *Der Rosenkavalier*, Di rigori armato;
Rossini, *William Tell*, Non mi lasciare . . . O muto asil;
Bellini, *I Puritani*, A te o cara;
Puccini, *La Bohème*, Che gelida manina

LONDON OS-26373

THE WORLD'S FAVORITE TENOR ARIAS
(Anthology)
Leoncavallo, *Pagliacci*, Vesti la giubba;
von Flotow, *Martha*, M'apparì;
Bizet, *Carmen*, Flower Song,
Puccini, *La Bohème*, Che gelida manina;
Verdi, *Rigoletto*, La donna è mobile;
Gounod, *Faust*, Salut, demeure;
Puccini, *Tosca*, E lucevan le stelle;
Verdi, *Aïda*, Celeste Aïda;
Puccini, *Turandot*, Nessun dorma;
Verdi, *Il Trovatore*, Di quella pira

LONDON OS-26384

PAVAROTTI IN CONCERT
(Bologna, 1973)
Bononcini, Per la gloria d'adorarvi;
Handel, *Atalanta*, Care selve;
A. Scarlatti, *L'Honestà negli Amori*,
Già il sole dal Gange; Bellini, Ma

rendi pur contento, Dolente immagine
di fille mia, La Malinconia (Ninfa gentile),
Bella nice che d'amore, Vanne o rosa
fortunata; Tosti, La serenata, Luna
d'estate; Malia, Non t'amo più;
Respighi, Nevicata, Pioggia, Nebbie;
Rossini, La Danza

LONDON OS-26391

OPERATIC DUETS WITH JOAN SUTHERLAND
(Anthology)
Donizetti, *Lucia di Lammermoor*, Sulla tomba . . . Verranno a te;
Verdi, *Rigoletto*, È il sol dell'anima;
Donizetti, *L'Elisir d'Amore*, Chiedi all'aura lusinghiera;
Donizetti, *La Fille du Régiment*, Oh ciel . . . Depuis l'instant;
Bellini, *I Puritani*, Finì . . . Me lassa

LONDON OS-26437

SUTHERLAND PAVAROTTI (DUETS)
(London, 1976)
Verdi, *La Traviata*, Brindisi, Un dì felice, Parigi o cara;
Bellini, *La Sonnambula*, Prendi l'anel ti dono;
Donizetti, *Linda di Chamounix*, Da quel dì che t'incontrai;
Verdi, *Otello*, Già nella notte;
Verdi, *Aïda*, O terra addio

LONDON OS-26449

O HOLY NIGHT
(London, 1976)

300

Adam, O Holy Night; Stradella, Pietà Signore;
Franck, Panis Angelicus; Mercadante, Quinta
Parola; Schubert, Ave Maria; Yon, Gesù Bambino;
Bach/Gounod, Ave Maria; Schubert, Mille
Cherubini in Coro; Bizet, Agnus Dei;
Berlioz, Sanctus; Wade, Adeste Fideles

LONDON OS-26473

THE GREAT PAVAROTTI
(Anthology)

> Donizetti, *L'Elisir d'Amore*, Quanto è bella, quanto è cara, Una furtiva lagrima;
> Verdi, *Un Ballo in Maschera*, La rivedrà nell'estasi, Di' tu se fedele;
> Verdi, *Rigoletto*, Questa o quella, Parmi veder le lagrime;
> Verdi, *Macbeth*, Ah la paterna mano;
> Verdi, *Requiem*, Ingemisco;
> Rossini, *Stabat Mater*, Cujus animam;
> Donizetti, *Maria Stuarda*, Ah rimiro il bel sembiante;
> Donizetti, *La Fille du Régiment*, Pour me rapprocher de Marie;
> Puccini, *Turandot*, Non piangere Liù;
> Donizetti, *Lucia di Lammermoor*, Tu che a Dio spiegasti l'ali

LONDON OS-26510

HITS FROM LINCOLN CENTER
(Anthology)

> Donizetti, *L'Elisir d'Amore*, Una furtiva lagrima;
> Gluck, *Orfeo e Euridice*, Che farò senza Euridice;
> Rossini, La Danza; Beethoven, In questa

tomba oscura; Bellini, Vanne o rosa
fortunata, Vaga luna; Donizetti, Me
voglio fa' na casa;
Verdi, *Luisa Miller*, Quando le sere al placido;
Donizetti, *Lucia di Lammermoor*, Fra poco a me ricovero;
Tosti, 'A vucchella, Aprile;
Puccini, *Tosca*, E lucevan le stelle;
Leoncavallo, Mattinata;
Puccini, *Turandot*, Nessun dorma

LONDON OS-26577

BRAVO PAVAROTTI
(Anthology)
Donizetti, *Lucia di Lammermoor*, Sextet, Tu che a Dio;
Puccini, *La Bohème*, O Mimì, tu più non torni;
Strauss, *Der Rosenkavalier*, Di rigori armato;
Verdi, *Un Ballo in Maschera*, La rivedrà nell'estasi, È
   scherzo od è follia;
Donizetti, *La Fille du Régiment*, O mes amis, Pour me rap-
   procher de Marie;
Donizetti, *L'Elisir d'Amore*, Chiedi all'aura lusinghiera;
Verdi, *Luisa Miller*, Quando le sere al placido;
Verdi, *La Traviata*, Libiamo, Un dì felice;
Verdi, *Requiem*, Ingemisco;
Verdi, *Rigoletto*, Parmi veder le lagrime, La donna è mo-
   bile, Quartet;
Bellini, *I Puritani*, A te o cara;
Puccini, *Turandot*, Non piangere Liù;
Puccini, *Tosca*, E lucevan le stelle;
Verdi, *Il Trovatore*, Ai nostri monti;
Donizetti, *La Favorita*, Spirto gentil

2-LONDON PAV 2001

O SOLE MIO
(Bologna, 1977–London, 1979)
> Di Capua, O sole mio; Tosti, 'A vucchella;
> Cannio, O surdato 'nnammurato; Gambardella,
> O marenariello; Anon., Fenesta vascia;
> Tosti, Marechiare; De Curtis, Torna a
> Surriento; Pennino, Pecchè; D'Annibale,
> O Paese d' 'o sole; Tagliaferri, Piscatore
> 'e pusilleco; De Curtis, Tu, ca nun
> chiagne; Di Capua, Maria, Mari'; Denza,
> Funiculì, funiculà

LONDON OS-26560

PAVAROTTI'S GREATEST HITS
(Anthology)
> Puccini, *Turandot*, Nessun dorma;
> Donizetti, *La Fille du Régiment*, O mes amis . . . Pour
>   mon âme;
> Puccini, *Tosca*, Recondita armonia;
> Puccini, *La Bohème*, Che gelida manina;
> Strauss, *Der Rosenkavalier*, Di rigori armato;
> Leoncavallo, Mattinata;
> Rossini, La Danza;
> De Curtis, Torna a Surriento;
> Donizetti, *La Favorita*, Spirto gentil;
> Bizet, *Carmen*, Flower Song;
> Bellini, *I Puritani*, A te o cara;
> Verdi, *Il Trovatore*, Ah sì ben mio . . . Di quella pira;
> Verdi, *Rigoletto*, La donna è mobile;
> Franck, Panis Angelicus;
> Bellini, Vanne o rosa fortunata;
> Gounod, *Faust*, Salut, demeure;

303

Verdi, *Requiem*, Ingemisco;
Verdi, *Rigoletto*, Questa o quella;
Verdi, *Aïda*, Celeste Aïda;
Schubert, Ave Maria;
Leoncavallo, *Pagliacci*, Vesti la giubba;
Ponchielli, *La Gioconda*, Cielo e mar;
Donizetti, *L'Elisir d'Amore*, Una furtiva lagrima;
Puccini, *Tosca*, E lucevan le stelle;
Denza, Funiculì, funiculà

2–LONDON PAV 2003

LE GRANDI VOCI DELL'ARENA DI VERONA, Vol. 2
(Verona, 1977)
Donizetti, *L'Elisir d'Amore*, Una furtiva lagrima; Other
arias performed by Raina Kabaivanska,
Piero Cappuccilli, Katia Ricciarelli,
and Ruggero Raimondi

CIME ANC 25004

VERDI ARIAS
(Parma, 1976)
Verdi, *La Traviata*, Lunge da lei . . . De' miei bollenti
spiriti;
Verdi, *Macbeth*, Ah la paterna mano;
Verdi, *I Lombardi*, La mia letizia;
Verdi, *Otello*, Già nella notte
(with Katia Ricciarelli); other arias
performed by Katia Ricciarelli from
Aïda, *La Forza del Destino*, *Il Corsaro*,
and *Falstaff*

CIME ANC 25001

VERISMO ARIAS
(London, 1979)
    Giordano, *Fedora*, Amor ti vieta;
    Boito, *Mefistofele*, Dai campi, dai prati,
      Giunto sul passo estremo;
    Cilèa, *Adriana Lecouvreur*, La dolcissima
      effigie, L'Anima ho stanca;
    Mascagni, *Iris*, Apri la tua fenestra;
    Meyerbeer, *L'Africana*, O Paradiso;
    Massenet, *Werther*, Pourquoi me réveiller;
    Giordano, *Andrea Chenier*, Un dì all'azzurro
      spazio, Come un bel dì di maggio, Sì, fui
      soldato;
    Puccini, *La Fanciulla del West*,
      Ch'ella mi creda libero;
    Puccini, *Manon Lescaut*, Tra voi, belle,
      Donna non vidi mai, No! No! pazzo son!
                     LONDON LDR-10020

PRIVATE RECORDINGS

Private or "pirate" recordings occupy a gray area in the world of opera. While technically illegal and frowned upon by artists and major record companies who do not derive any revenues from their sale, they are nonetheless essential to the Pavarotti aficionado for whom one recording of, say, *Tosca* or *I Puritani* is not enough. In addition, one can find his interpretation of operas like Massenet's *Manon* or Verdi's *I Lombardi* that he has not yet recorded commercially and perhaps never will.

    Any attempt to develop a comprehensive discography of

private recordings is perilous inasmuch as new items periodically come on the market and old items disappear from the shelves and go out of print. Listed below are some of the principal private recordings that were available in New York at press time for this book:

Historical Recording Enterprises

Bellini, *I Puritani*. Luciano Pavarotti, Beverly Sills, Louis Quilico, Paul Plishka. 1972.

HRE 311-3

Puccini, *Tosca*. Luciano Pavarotti, Magda Olivero, Cornell MacNeil.

HRE 312-2

Concert Album. Puerto Rico, April 1978. With Mirella Freni and Kurt Herbert Adler conducting. Arias and duets from *La Forza del Destino, La Gioconda, Turandot, Un Ballo in Maschera, Aïda, La Bohème, L'Elisir d'Amore, Tosca, L'Amico Fritz*, and *La Traviata*. Also included is the St. Sulpice scene from *Manon* (La Scala, 1969) and Act 4 of *I Puritani* (Rome, 1970).

HRE 248-2

MRF Records

Bellini, *Bianca e Fernando*. Hayashi, Savastano, Fissore, Machi. Ferro conducting. Turin, 1976. Side 6 of this album contains Act 3 of *I Puritani* complete with Luciano Pavarotti, Mirella Freni, Sesto Bruscantini. Riccardo Muti conducting. Rome, 1970.

MRF-133

Bellini, *I Capuleti e i Montecchi*. Luciano Pavarotti, Renata Scotto, Giacomo Aragall. Claudio Abbado conducting. La Scala, 1969.

MRF-55

Verdi, *I Lombardi alla Prima Crociata*. Luciano Pavarotti, Renata Scotto, Ruggero Raimondi. Gianandrea Gavazzeni conducting. Rome, 1969.

MRF-48

In addition to the above, the following recordings distributed by the Unique Opera Records Co. are available for listening on tape at the Rodgers and Hammerstein Archives of Recorded Sound, New York Public Library at Lincoln Center, New York City:

Donizetti, *La Favorita*. Luciano Pavarotti, Maria Luisa Nave, Renato Bruson, Bonaldo Giaiotti. Carlo Felice Cillario conducting. 1975.

UORC-294

Massenet, *Manon*. Luciano Pavarotti, Mirella Freni, Rolando Panerai. Peter Maag conducting.

UORC-215

Puccini, *Tosca*. Luciano Pavarotti, Carol Neblett, Cornell Mac-Neil, Italo Tajo. Jesús López-Cobos conducting.

UORC-348

Verdi, *Luisa Miller*. Luciano Pavarotti, Katia Ricciarelli, Giorgio Tozzi. Jesús López-Cobos conducting.

UORC-239

Concert Album. Arias and songs. Bononcini, Per la gloria d'adorarvi; Pergolesi, Tre giorni son che Nina; Scarlatti, Già il sole dal Gange; Rossini, La Promessa; Bellini, Vaga luna; Donizetti, Me voglio fa' na casa; Verdi, De' miei bollenti spiriti, O mio rimorso (from *La Traviata*); Respighi, Nevicata, Pioggia, Nebbie; Verdi, La mia letizia (from *I Lombardi*); Tosti, 'A vucchella, L'ultima canzone, L'alba separa dalla luce l'ombra; Donizetti, Una furtiva lagrima; Puccini, Nessun dorma. 1976.

UORC-313

Also available at Lincoln Center is an album entitled *Golden Age of Opera*, EJS 518, in which Pavarotti performs arias from *Rigoletto*, *I Puritani*, and Rossini's *Stabat Mater*, along with selections by other artists, including Franco Corelli, Alfredo Kraus, and Nicolai Gedda.

Index

INDEX

I N D E X